D0997575

ETHICS AND
EGULATION

REFERENCE

We work with leading authors to develop the
strongest educational materials in business and media studies,
bringing cutting-edge thinking and best learning
practice to a global market.

Under a range of well-known imprints, including
Longman, we craft high quality print and
electronic publications which help readers to
understand and apply their content, whether
studying or at work.

To find out more about the complete range of our
publishing please visit us on the World Wide Web at:
www.pearsoneduc.com

# MEDIA ETHICS AND SELF-REGULATION

Chris Frost

*An imprint of* Pearson Education

Harlow, England · London · New York · Reading, Massachusetts · San Francisco
Toronto · Don Mills, Ontario · Sydney · Tokyo · Singapore · Hong Kong · Seoul
Taipei · Cape Town · Madrid · Mexico City · Amsterdam · Munich · Paris · Milan

**Pearson Education Limited**
Edinburgh Gate
Harlow
Essex CM20 2JE
England

and Associated Companies throughout the world

*Visit us on the World Wide Web at:*
*www.pearsoneduc.com*

First published in Great Britain in 2000

© Pearson Education Limited 2000

ISBN 0 582 30605 1

*British Library Cataloguing-in-Publication Data*
A CIP catalogue record for this book can be obtained from the British Library.

*Library of Congress Cataloging-in-Publication Data*
A catalog record for this book can be obtained from the Library of Congress.

10  9  8  7  6  5  4  3
05  04  03  02

Typeset in 10/13pt Palatino by 35
Produced by Pearson Education Asia Pte Ltd
Printed in Singapore

# Contents

Contents

# Abbreviations

| | |
|---|---|
| AP | Associated Press (a US news agency) |
| ASA | Advertising Standards Authority |
| BBC | British Broadcasting Corporation |
| BCC | Broadcasting Complaints Commission |
| BSC | Broadcasting Standards Commission |
| BSE | Bovine spongiform encephalopathy |
| CJD | Creutzfeldt-Jakob disease |
| GBNE | Guild of British Newspaper Editors |
| IBA | Independent Broadcasting Authority |
| IoJ | Institute of Journalists |
| IRN | Independent Radio News |
| ITA | Independent Television Authority |
| ITC | Independent Television Commission |
| ITN | Independent Television News |
| NPA | Newspaper Publishers' Association |
| NS | Newspaper Society |
| NUJ | National Union of Journalists |
| PA | Press Association (a news agency supplying national and international news to regional newspapers and broadcasting stations) |
| PC | Press Council |
| PCC | Press Complaints Commission |
| PPA | Periodical Publishers' Association |
| Pressbof | Press Standards Board of Finance |
| QC | Queen's Counsel |
| SDNS | Scottish Daily Newspaper Society |
| SNPA | Scottish Newspaper Publishers' Association |
| RA | Radio Authority |
| TMAP | Teenage Magazine Advisory Panel |

# Acknowledgements

I would like to thank my wife Vanessa and my children Emma, Julia and Alice for putting up with me whilst I wrote the book. Look, it really is finished now, OK? My thanks also to Mike Nally for his help and unfailing support.

I would also like to thank the helpful people at the NUJ, the PCC, the BSC, the ITC and the Radio Authority, and to thank all those who have given me permission to reproduce material from their publications.

# Introduction

•••••••••••••••••••••••••••••••••••••••••••••••••••••••••••••••••••••••••••

This book intends to plumb the depths of the professional morality of journalists. Not, I hope, in the way that journalists are often accused of plumbing the depths, but in a wide-reaching and thoughtful way that, whilst unlikely to find any answers, will at least illuminate some of the problems and allow us to navigate around them. Writing about journalism ethics is the sort of martyristic foolishness which probably only the bold or the pompous should or would attempt. I had hoped I was neither, but on re-reading the manuscript that seems unlikely. US political columnist David Broder once wrote: 'It is difficult to write about "journalism ethics" without sounding like a jerk' (Broder, 1983: op-ed page). After years of studying journalism ethics and 27 years' experience as a newspaper journalist (the last eight of those as a journalism lecturer) I think I have all the proof he needs. But it's too late. I've signed the contract and have a legal and moral obligation to finish the job, complete with all the pomposity and jerkishness that writing about morals can dredge up.

The idea of this book first came to me because I was having great difficulty finding suitable texts to recommend to my students. A number of 'How to . . .' journalism books contained a little advice about ethics but most were of the breezing-through style which mirrored ethics teaching on most journalism courses until very recently. Only with the advent of degree courses in journalism have institutions had the time and the opportunity to teach journalistic ethics in a way that really gets to grips with the issues. The early 1990s saw an increase in the number of books that looked at ethics more seriously, but most of those were from academics more interested in the sociological issues and the way the media influences society than the everyday problems of working journalists. There are a large number of books written by Americans for Americans. In the US, journalism has been an area for serious study and informed and educated practice for some consider-able time. But the differences of approach there, particularly the implications of the first amendment to the constitution and the power this gives to the media, means that interesting and important though many of these books are, they are of limited value to British journalists and journalism students. Lambeth's *Committed Journalism* (1992), Klaidman and Beauchamp's *The Virtuous Journalist* (1987), Meyer's *Ethical Journalism* (1987) and *Media Ethics* by Christians et al. (1998) are all books that I found instructive to read and am happy to recommend. However, the differences in culture and background between the US and the UK means that their perspective tends to waver in and out of focus, leaving the reader faintly confused. Too much is taken for granted. The American journalist's ethical roots are firmly bedded in the first amendment and no further manuring is required. Of course many a cynic will say the British journalist already has his or her ethical roots firmly bedded in manure and that it will require the ethical equivalent of dynamite to move many of them away from the 'don't let the facts get in the way of a good story' style of journalistic morality.

There is a difficult balance to be struck when writing a book of this sort. I hope it will be read by practitioners, both students and professionals, who want to gain a clearer insight into their work as well as academics seeking to discover why a body of intelligent people who often claim to be driven by pure and noble motives seem to fail both so often and so publicly. To achieve this aim I cannot produce a mere handbook on good and bad journalistic practice filled with bullet-pared truisms. This would be of no more help to the practitioner than a copy of the Press Complaints Commission (PCC) Code of Practice and would be rightly discarded by academics. Yet how many practitioners will be prepared to devote the time necessary to wade through tens of thousands of words justifying or attacking some subtle point of moral philosophy as it applies to journalism? I hope that quite a few will because any move towards a more ethically-based journalism must be driven by journalists if is to be sustained. For too long, too many journalists in the UK have tended to shrug their shoulders and assume morals are for someone else and then wonder why there are calls for legislation on such issues as payments to witnesses and privacy. The events surrounding the death of Diana, Princess of Wales, in August 1997 raised public awareness and concern about the way the press can intrude into the private lives of public figures to an unprecedented level and calls for legislation became even stronger and more widely supported. Clearly, in the light of such widespread public interest and concern, journalists cannot ignore or remain indifferent to the ethical aspects of their profession. The industry has been lucky. Since the Princess's death there have been few major invasions of privacy and so few opportunities for the press to be attacked for its conduct. But the willingness of such figures as the Prince of Wales and Tony Blair to complain to the PCC about invasions of their children's privacy shows that the pressure on the media has stepped up a gear or two.

We have two stark choices in the UK. Either we will have to have legislation to deal with the excesses of the media, particularly the tabloid press, or journalists will have to get their act together and start to behave responsibly. Journalists can only do this if they are educated to consider the issues raised by their work. All too often the general consensus seems to be that ethical issues are a once-in-a-blue-moon problem – crises that pop up from time to time requiring considerable thought before a decision is arrived at. This, of course, is not the case. Ethical problems are dealt with almost on a minute-by-minute basis in journalism. They happen so regularly that many of the decisions are part of the natural working pattern and require no particular conscious thought process. If we make an ethical decision not to steal, we do not need to remake that decision every time we encounter something that is not nailed down. This does not apply to someone who has not taken such a decision. For the habitual thief, the only decisions (which must be taken on every occasion) are not ethical but entirely practical: Is the item worth stealing? Is the physical effort required worth it? Am I likely to be caught? Many journalists seem to go through the same logistics-only processes in their work. Shall I invent this part of the story? Is the mental and physical effort required worth it? Am I likely to be caught? Only the punishments for those caught out seem markedly different. Time in prison for the thief, a slap on the wrist from the PCC and possibly disciplinary action by the editor for the journalist. Only by making the moral decision not to invent stories in the first place can the journalist avoid mental turmoil of this sort during the writing of every story.

Of course journalists are often under pressure, or at the very least perceived pressure, from others, such as editors, to stretch ethical elasticity to its limits and sometimes beyond. There have been suggestions that journalists should have the PCC's Code of Practice written into their contracts of employment and the PCC has already asked proprietors to do this for editors. This idea does spark some questions. For instance, if a contract of employment contains the code and an editor instructs a journalist to breach the code, can the editor then sack the journalist for breaching it? What if the journalist refuses to follow the instruction? Can he or she be sacked for insubordination? How can journalists be expected to adhere to a code which they have not been involved in drawing up? The PCC Code of Practice is agreed by editors only and neither journalists nor their representatives are consulted about the process.

Many journalists and editors seem to believe that others can do the job of taking moral decisions for them; that they can continue to behave badly and avoid new legislation if they get the Public Relations right. Many editors and other commentators seem to believe that by having a PCC that is seen to work by government and public, there will be no need to bring in laws. But a self-regulatory system can only work if the editors want it to work. At the moment they do – but almost always for the wrong reasons. Many seem to want to be ethical only when it is marketable. Only when publication of unethical material will damage the profits does a newspaper normally refuse to publish. The Princess Diana video hoax, purporting to feature Princess Diana and James Hewitt in the midst of a sex romp and shot through the windows of a large suburban house, but which, in reality, featured actors, was used by the *Sun* newspaper because they knew it would skyrocket circulation. The hoax could have been easily exposed by journalists more concerned with the ethical debate about publication than the commercial debate about circulation. Few editors and proprietors seem keen to see ethical journalism if it interferes in any way with their position in the market and their ability to make profits. In a market-dominated culture that has dispensed with social responsibility I actually find it difficult to understand why anyone should be surprised that our newspapers give priority to profit over ethics, circulation over public responsibility. We can count on one hand the number of times over the past ten years that the press has restrained itself for unselfish motives.

Broadcasting has a better reputation, but even this is slowly being eroded as the market becomes the dominating factor. The public service broadcasting ideal and the need for high-quality commercial television is being diluted by the increase in channels on cable, satellite and now digital television. We are in the era of 'cheap is best' because it is all about profit. Ethics come a very poor second when the journalist is under constant pressure to get the story regardless. The fear of 'dumbing down' is now constant in TV and a rash of scandals over 'fake' guests on confessional programmes such as *Vanessa* or 'stunted' programmes such as Carlton's award-winning drugs exposé ('Inquiry ordered into faked TV programme' – *Guardian*, May 1998: 1) emphasises TV's desire to get viewing figure-boosting programmes without necessarily spending the time or the money to ensure rigorous standards. The Broadcasting Standards Commission in its 1997–98 review said about confessional TV: 'Some suspect that much of the confession and reaction is scripted and rehearsed and occasionally faked. At least one participant has claimed that he was encouraged to be outrageous in order to help the ratings' (BSC, *Annual Review*, 1998: 19). We also need to consider why it is acceptable to have legislative control of broadcasting ethics but not of print. What is it about newspapers that suggests self-regulation is good enough when we are told that only statutory regulation will do for broadcasting?

Journalistic ethics have never been a seriously regarded subject for study by practitioners and journalism academics in the UK (see Stephenson and Bromley, 1998: Chapter 10). A two-hour session on a wet weekday afternoon half-way through a one-year course was very much the standard teaching for would-be journalists until towards the end of the 1980s and early 1990s. Even now there are few one-year courses that do more than a couple of sessions. A letter from the NUJ's Ethics Council to scores of colleges teaching journalism offering guest speakers on the subject saw only a handful of responses. In a letter to journalism colleges in 1996, the late Sir David English, then Chairman of the PCC's Code of Practice committee, drew attention to a report from the National Council for the Training of Journalists about their National Certificate Examination in which they say that many trainees seemed unaware of the provisions of the PCC's Code of Practice. 'There was even a suggestion by trainees that the code could be disregarded if a better story was the result,' reprimanded Sir David in his letter. He pointed out that this was a matter of grave concern, and asked trainers to make clear to students what the Code of Practice had to say. But the people taking this exam were working journalists with about two years' experience on a newspaper in addition to their training course. These were, probably still are, practitioners who, one can only assume, picked up their attitude from other practitioners and trainers. This poor attitude and lack of concern for ethics is then put into an environment where the market rules. A story that will sell becomes the most important element, not the ethics of its gathering or publication. Unless a journalist's understanding of ethics and journalistic morality is firmly rooted, then he or she will have neither the educational background nor the inclination to stand up for what he or she believes is journalistically right against the pressures of profit and a threat to career development. Even with a strong ethic to support them, journalists will still, on occasion, go for the sensational or invasive story. I hope that after reading this book, they will at least think about it and know why they breached their ethics in the name of profit, career, malice or whatever and will be able to decide whether it was worth it.

## The structure of the book

This book is planned to try to lead the reader through the elements of journalistic morality in a way that I hope is helpful and interesting. Chapter 1 starts with a short appreciation of some of the classical philosophers from the early Greeks to modern day. I believe that whilst these philosophers may seem a long way from modern journalism, their thinking has something to say about the way journalists work and morality in general. It is very difficult to discuss journalism ethics without being aware of what journalists are trying to do and so Chapter 2 looks at what news is, how journalists identify it and why news is abstractly different from the event it is describing. It helps explain the temptation to sensationalise and shows why even the most ethical practice of journalism is unlikely to prevent that. The freedom of the press is probably one of the most abused clichés in the English language. Raised almost exclusively on occasions when there has been an abuse of that freedom, it is at the root of the journalist's need for ethics. Chapter 3 looks at the links between morality and a free press and how society often uses the law to enforce elements of morality. In the chapters that follow I look at a range of professional issues that help explain how society has developed Western-style journalistic ethics. In Chapter 4 the relationship between the press and the public is explored and in Chapter 5 I look at what makes a 'good journalist' and how and why definitions of this concept differ so greatly. This is followed by a discussion in Chapter 6 about codes of practice, how they work and why they are useful. The main reason for codes of practice is to give standards against which practitioners' behaviour can be measured and Chapter 6 also looks at how regulating agencies are formed and structured. Chapter 7 explains the main ethical issues facing journalists. It looks at what the various codes of practice have to say about the issues, government committee recommendations, the law, and also what working journalists have to say. In Chapter 8 we look at the ethical implications of deciding what to publish and the editing and presentation of material. Chapters 9 and 10 are about the way the media is regulated in Britain. There is a history of regulation in the UK, a discussion on how ethics interrelates with the law and how the Press Complaints Commission, the Broadcasting Standards Commission, the Radio Authority, BBC and National Union of Journalists operate. In the final Chapter I look to the future. I consider the problems raised by the growing opportunities for journalists to work across international borders, the use of new technology and of course the World Wide Web and the problems that may arise, and the implications for the future for ethics regulation.

I hope I have produced something that is readable, interesting and helpful. Throughout the text chapter outlines, exhibits, summaries and questions are used to highlight the major points. Case studies are used to show ethical concerns in the context of real-life situations and news stories and I have included a short glossary of terms used within the text. Most of all I hope this book will move the argument away from media regulation to media ethics in the realisation that no matter how much regulation you have it will change little until journalists and editors themselves are allowed to take ethics seriously.

# Chapter 1

## What are ethics?

**Chapter outline**

- This chapter looks at why the public's right to know is the foundation of the freedom of the press.
- It shows that this right to know is essential to the proper running of a true democracy.
- It discusses some of the theories propounded by some of the world's greatest thinkers on morality and how they relate to journalistic ethics.
- It considers the language used to talk about morality.

Ethics is defined by *The Concise Oxford English Dictionary* as 'the science of morals, treatise on this, moral principles or rules of conduct' (1964: 415). The word comes from the Greek *eethikos* meaning 'of or for morals'. Morals are described by the same dictionary as being concerned with '. . . the distinction between right and wrong'. This comes from the Latin *mos* (pl. *mores*) which means 'a measure or guiding rule of life; as determined not by the law but by men's will and pleasure' (Lewis and Short, 1900). Clifford G. Christians *et al.* define ethics as: 'The liberal arts discipline that appraises voluntary human conduct insofar as it can be judged right or wrong in reference to determinative principles' (1987: 7).

In practice ethics is a way of studying morality which allows decisions to be made when individuals face specific cases of moral dilemma. At their most praiseworthy, the journalist's tussles are going to be between the right of the public to know and some other moral tenet – perhaps the invasion of an individual's privacy – which would militate against publication. This right of the public to know springs from the theory of representative, democratic government. Mill tells us:

> There is no difficulty in showing that the ideally best form of government is that in which the sovereignty, or supreme controlling power in the last resort, is vested in the entire aggregate of the community; every citizen not only having a voice in the exercise of that ultimate sovereignty, but being, at least occasionally, called on to take an actual part in the government, by the personal discharge of some public function, local or general. (Mill, 1991: 245)

In his excellent essay supporting this view, Mill makes it clear that correct and detailed information about how the country is run is an important pre-requisite for any person involved in taking political decisions and this must surely apply, even if the decision taken is only how to vote every few years.

However, all too often the right to know is used as an excuse to pub-lish circulation-boosting journalism. Whether this is designed to appeal to readers' prurient natures or pander to their prejudices does not seem to matter as long as there is a profit to be made from increasing sales.

## Do journalists need professional morality?

If we lived in a locked room with access to no one else would we need to be moral? If no other entity existed and we were totally alone would our day-to-day existence contain any need to modify our behaviour with moral-ity? How could we steal? The only person offended by our violence, bad language and behaviour would be ourselves. All morality depends upon us interacting with other people or (some would say) with a deity. Without any-one else, entirely marooned, there would be no moral dilemmas to solve. Moral dilemmas are the penalty of our involvement with society; the price we pay for the benefits of living in close proximity with others. Being part of society means we need to adhere to rules that help that society work. An ordered society is one in which everyone knows, accepts and, ideally, adheres to the rules and also accepts the right of society to judge and pun-ish those who break those rules.

Some elements of unacceptable social behaviour are damaging enough to a society for the whole of that society to be concerned with their suppres-sion. If, for example, we were to allow murder or serious violence to be used as methods of solving disputes, the benefits of society would soon cease for many people and day-to-day living would become largely unbearable. 'Might is right' is fine when you are one of the mighty, but none of us are mighty all of the time. It is in all our interests to ensure that we all adhere to the rules and that those who don't are punished. Because of the poten-tial for breakdown, many societies formalise the rules under which that soci-ety exists. These become the laws of that particular society and allow it to lay down penalties for transgressors. The death penalty is the most extreme penalty society can impose for serious crimes whereas prison is generally seen as a milder form of punishment. However, there are a number of issues which are not so clearly 'wrong' but are more things one 'ought' to do rather than what one 'must' do. These issues do not directly threaten society as a whole but concern what is generally considered to be acceptable behaviour.

Although society is naturally concerned with actions that apply to the whole of society, there are a number of actions that can only be perpetrated by certain people in certain positions. Some of these actions are so important to society that they are legislated for. For instance, corruption of officials only involves a few people in powerful positions but the corruption may affect many other people. Consequently we enshrine such matters in our legal system. Other issues, medical confidentiality for instance, may affect individuals but do not directly damage society and consequently are not enshrined directly in law. This is where professional ethics become important. A doctor who reveals matters about a patient is deemed to have breached professional ethics; he or she has not broken the law. A journalist is in the same position. For example, if he or she takes advantage of a situation and does not deal fairly with those to whom he or she owes loyalty (e.g. revealing a source who wishes to remain anonymous), then it is unlikely that society will suffer directly but the individual might well suffer. There are a wide range of issues in which journalists are involved that are not subject to the law but must be considered from an ethical viewpoint.

The concept of an ethical journalist may seem to be a contradiction in terms. The phrase 'you shouldn't believe all you read in the papers' sums up the attitude of many people. However, if one were to define a *good* journalist as 'someone who gathers, in a morally justifiable way, topical, truthful, factually-based information of interest to the reader or viewer and then publishes it in a timely and accurate manner to a mass audience' many would accept this as a reasonable description. However, all too often journalism falls far short of this ideal. Nor is this necessarily a description that would be used by all journalists to describe excellence in the profession. The professional virtues of 'getting the story' – the ability to find an interesting story, research it and return it to the news centre by the deadline – is how many colleagues would describe a good journalist. How the news was gathered and sourced, together with the degree of accuracy, would seem to be secondary considerations in this definition of a 'good journalist'. 'Don't let the facts get in the way of a good story' is an instruction that has been heard in more than one newsroom.

The suggestion that journalists are perhaps more concerned about the story than how they get it, or whether it is truthful, highlights the pressures under which those in the profession work. Commercial pressures to provide the most interesting stories combine with tight deadlines to make journalists more single-minded than perhaps they should be. Essentially this is an argument of functionality. Is a good journalist one with high principles or one who brings his employer, within the deadline, stories that will boost circulation? The reader may say the former even though they add support to the latter every time they buy a newspaper or magazine. All too often a journalist can forget his or her loyalties to the reader in the rush to show loyalty to his or her employer.

## Classical theory

Why is it that we behave the way we do? Why do we feel guilty if we do something 'wrong'? Moral obligations can be explained by a number of different theories, some of them overlapping and some completely at odds with one another. Some of these theories can help journalists try to determine the morality of their professional actions. I will consider a few of the more important theories and their implications for journalism. There are many other leading philosophers whose work I have ignored as either being derivative or not so easy to apply directly to professional morality.

### Aristotle

Aristotle (d. 322 BC) was a Greek philosopher who believed that the function of human beings was to pursue happiness or Eudaimonia. 'Eudaimonia is often translated as happiness, but that can be misleading. It is sometimes translated as flourishing. Which although slightly akward, has more appropriate connotations' (Warburton, 1998: 18). To achieve happiness Aristotle said one should live moderately. His theory is known as the 'golden mean'. He argued that one should live neither to excess nor to frugality but live in moderation somewhere between the two. Aristotle's theory is extremely useful provided you can decide what is excess and frugality and where the mean lies. Bravery, he tells us, is a virtue that lies somewhere between the extremes of cowardice and rashness. When Aristotle talks about a mean, however, he is not talking about an average. To take the example of drinking, it is not to say that at one extreme is drinking far too much alcohol or at the other drinking none at all and taking an average of say four units of alcohol a night is the mean. Aristotle contended that the right mean may well vary from person to person. So there are people who say it is wrong to drink alcohol but it is also true that they could be seen as too self-satisfied and sanctimonious to be considered morally good. Nor are they acting in their own best interests as present health research shows that a drink every now and again is good for you. Refusing to drink a toast to peace or friendship in Western Europe because you do not believe in drinking alcohol could be perceived as being mean spirited. On the other hand, few people would see drinking fifteen units of alcohol every night of the week as acceptable. It is also bad for your health. Most would see a drink now and again as the 'golden mean'.

Aristotle also believed that one had to learn to be virtuous. Virtue was not something that was given to all automatically. It explained why children and animals had not achieved Eudaimonia.

> Virtue, then, being of two kinds, intellectual and moral, intellectual virtue in the main owes both its birth and its growth to teaching (for which reason it requires

experience and time), while moral virtue comes about as the result of habit.... From this it is also plain that none of the moral virtues arise in us by nature; for nothing that exists in nature can form a habit that is contrary to its nature. For instance, the stone which by nature moves downwards cannot be habituated to move upwards, not even if one tries to train it by throwing it up ten thousand times ... (Aristotle, 1980: 28)

A problem with Aristotle's theory about the mean, however, is that there are some virtues that seem to be absolutes. Truth, for instance, does not seem to be a virtue to be delivered in moderation. Either one is truthful or one is not. It is in its failure to address the issue of moral absolutes that Aristotle's theory is seen to be deficient.

## Religion

Jesus answered, 'The first is, "Hear, O Israel: the Lord our God, the Lord is one; you shall love the Lord your God with all your heart, and with all your soul, and with all your mind, and with all your strength." The second is this, "You shall love your neighbour as yourself." There is no other commandment greater than these.' (Mark 12:29–31)

Religion is the basis of much moral teaching in the world. The West has been mainly influenced by Judaeo-Christian ethics whereas much of the Arab and North African world has seen Islam as a strong and uncompromising influence. In India, Hinduism is a powerful religious and social system, which includes the use of the caste system as the basis of society.

Whilst theoretically, religious moral teaching requires a belief in God to underpin it, this seems in practice to be unimportant. In Britain, and indeed most Western countries, Christianity has become so entrenched within the culture that much moral teaching and thought comes from it without being based on active belief. Our basic structures of right and wrong, good and evil tend to be based on the Bible's teachings.

Whilst its use by Christians is understandable, many people in the West who claim not to believe in God also use this ethical system to underpin their moral values, if only because they have absorbed the established cultural moral underpinning without much thought as to its origins. Christians accept the entire teaching. However, those who do not believe in God seem to be able to accept the guidance on living a good life without the religious belief and to use it as an ethical system.

The main criticism of religion as an ethical system is the need for faith. What if God is not a loving and moral God? Using religion, we judge our moral code by our own interpretation of God (be that personal or cultural) and what he expects of us and not vice versa.

5

## Ethical egoism

Aristotle's view that people should behave so as to achieve happiness is challenged by some philosophers as being fundamentally flawed. To do what is right because it makes us happy is just self-interest, they claim. Supporting his maxim of a universal law, Kant (1993: 15) says that: 'To be truthful from duty is, however, quite different from being truthful from fear of disadvantageous consequences; in the first case the concept of the action itself contains a law for me, while in the second I must first look around elsewhere to see what the results for me might be connected with the action.' Kant believed it is motive that is important. The consequences of whether that be happiness or the absence of misery is not significant in making an act a good act.

Writing about the ideas of Plato, H.A. Prichard (1949: 110–11) goes further and proposes that what Socrates must have meant in 'introducing the subject of the Idea of good' was 'that in all action what we are striving to bring into existence is – not what is good but – what is really good for us, or for our own good'. He goes on to say: 'If we accept the idea we shall be involved in very awkward consequences. For we shall then be forced to allow (1) that there is really no such thing as a conscientious action or a benevolent or a malevolent action, and also (2) that there is really no difference in the motive between the acts of a so-called good man and those of a so-called bad man' (ibid.: 112).

Prichard does not think Kant's use of the categorical imperative gets us out of this difficulty: 'it should be noted that the summary attempt to elucidate the nature of moral obligation by the analogy of law . . . is only mischievous, because it represents our being morally bound to do some action as if it were our being commanded to do it' (ibid.: 95).

Ethical egoism suggests that all morality is in reality merely self-interest. If doing my duty either brings good consequences or simply makes me feel happier because I have done my duty, then surely my action is indistinguishable from self-interest?

## Utilitarianism

> Utility, or the Greatest Happiness Principle, holds that actions are right in proportion as they tend to promote happiness, wrong as they tend to produce the reverse of happiness. (John Stuart Mill, 1991: 137)

Utilitarianism is also widely accepted in the West as an ethical system. Jeremy Bentham (1748–1832) and John Stuart Mill (1806–73) are usually credited as being its most significant proponents. Utilitarianists believe that an action that produces an excess of beneficial effects over harmful ones must be the right one. Certainly this a system that has considerable appeal for journalists. It justifies, for example, ruining the life of a children's home superintendent by exposing him as a child abuser on the basis that it has saved children of the future from a good deal of misery.

One problem with utilitarianism is that it depends on who makes the decision. For instance, one could justify the killing of a homeless down-and-out who has no family in order that his organs could be donated to several desperately ill patients on the basis that four people could live with consequent benefits to their families for the loss of only one life. But this depends on each unit of happiness being the same, something Friedrich Nietzsche (1844–1900) condemned ruthlessly. He believed that some people were more important than others. Writing about the English utilitarians in less than complimentary terms, he said:

> Not one of all these ponderous herd animals . . . wants to know or scent that the 'general welfare' is not an ideal, or a goal, or a concept that can be grasped at all, but only an emetic – that what is right for one cannot by any means therefore be right for another, that the demand for one morality for all is detrimental to precisely the higher men, in short there exists an order of rank between man and man, consequently also between morality and morality. (Nietzsche, 1973: 139)

Not only can one argue that one person is more important than another but that actions have different perceived values. For instance, money given to a beggar has more significance when that money comes from a poor student than from a millionaire. Utilitarianism also does not require any measurement of the motive of the action. Provided the consequence is an increase in the sum of happiness, an evil act can be justified.

## Kant: the categorical imperative

> To be truthful from duty, however, is an entirely different thing from being truthful out of fear of untoward consequences, for in the former case the concept of the action itself contains a law for me, while in the latter I must first look about to see what results for me may be connected with it. (Immanuel Kant, 1990: 19)

The German Immanuel Kant (1724–1804) is a highly significant figure in modern philosophy. He helped to develop the concept of duty ethics. Kant believed that a moral act was one that denied self and followed only obligation. If I have promised to meet someone tonight then I am morally obliged to do that regardless of my inclinations. If, however, I have made no such promise, then I am free to follow my inclinations. But whatever I do would be merely a matter of taste and not a moral act.

Kant went on to develop the theory of universalisability, often called the 'categorical imperative'. This determines that: '[I] ought never to act in such a way that I could not also will that my maxim should be a universal law' (Kant, 1990: 18). Categorical imperatives are different from hypothetical imperatives. Hypothetical imperatives are concerned only with prudential action, or those actions that it would be sensible (but not necessarily moral) to take. If you were about to be run over by a car, then a hypothetical imperative would be: 'To avoid being run over, run fast to your left.' This would be a prudent action and has no moral component. On the other hand, it is a duty to maintain one's life and so there will be a categorical imperative to that effect. Categorical imperatives enjoin action completely without qualification, they deal solely in absolute duties.

Kant's theory allows the development of a set of universal laws for journalists with a matching set of licences that can be applied in many varied circumstances. This is the basis for codes of conduct. Kant also believed that one would have to examine the motives of a person to see whether their behaviour was good or bad. Their intentions are more important than the act itself. If they acted solely from a sense of duty and not out of self-interest, then their action could well be morally justifiable no matter what the consequences. If a journalist were to report something that was not true, despite thorough checking (perhaps he or she had been lied to), then the journalist could not be blamed for the consequences, even if these were damaging. He or she would have been behaving morally in printing the truth as he or she had determined it to be.

However, Kant's formulation does not handle conflicts of interest well. For example, if a journalist were asked by police to suppress the story of a kidnap in order to protect the victim's life, how could the journalist not publish when it should be a categorical imperative to publish known information, yet to protect someone's life when such protection is required must surely also be a categorical imperative? Since much of the ethical debate within the media is balancing the right to publish against some other right, such as a person's right to privacy, Kant is not always that helpful.

Kant believed that every person had equal value and the same right to have their view taken into consideration. He thought that the end did not justify the means. Only by acting from duty could one be said to be acting morally and the consequence was not something that could always be foreseen. This makes his views useful when drawing up codes of conduct.

## Ross

The philosopher Sir William David Ross (1877–1971) took the view that we all have duties of fidelity. In other words, we are bound by our own words or acts. If we sign a contract, we are duty-bound not to break it. If we make a promise we are bound to keep it. He also believed in the concept of reparation. If you do 'wrong' you are duty-bound to undo the wrong and make good the damage as far as possible. This duty extends to gratitude. If someone performs a good act for you, you are under an obligation to return the favour at some point. Ross believes that this duty of gratitude can extend to friends, relatives, employers and employees.

Ross's ideas have a direct application to journalism as it can be said that journalists have a duty of gratitude to readers, advertisers, employers and so on. We will use this view of duty a lot throughout this book, although I will refer to it more often as a duty of loyalty as I think this better describes the relationship. I might be grateful that you are reading this book, but I do not see that that entails me in any duty. But my loyalty, induced by that duty of gratitude, will mean that I will produce the most accurate, informative book that I can.

Ross also talks about other duties:

- *Beneficence* – our duty to improve the lot of others.
- *Justice* – we all have a duty to see that people get what they deserve, whether this is pleasure or punishment.
- *Self-improvement* – we have a duty to try to improve our own condition of virtue, intelligence or happiness.
- *Non-injury* – our duty not to hurt others or allow them to be hurt if we can prevent it.

Ross chaired the first Royal Commission into the press in 1947.

## The language of morals

The former [objectivists] lay stress on the fixed principles that are handed down by the father, the latter [subjectivists] on the new decisions which have to be made by the son. (R.M. Hare, 1995: 77)

Much of the ethical debate over the last century has revolved around the analysis of the language of morals and what the words 'good', 'bad', 'ought', 'right', 'wrong' and so on mean. A number of theories have been developed by philosophers such as G.E. Moore, A.J. Ayers and R.M. Hare which attempt to shed some light in the area of value words and our use of them. Most of these theories are essentially theories about theories and as such require much supportive argument. However, Table 1.1 summarises the main ideas. To put some of the theories in Table 1.1 into context, let us look at a dilemma and how the various theories would address it. I promise a friend that I will meet her in town at six o'clock. Is it acceptable to break my promise in order to rescue someone from a burning building, thus making me late for my appointment? A motivist might say 'yes' as my motive for breaking my promise would be to save a life or 'no' if my duty was to keep my promise. Consequentialists believe that only the

## Table 1.1 The language of morals

| | |
|---|---|
| Naturalism | If a moral judgement can be reduced to some other branch of science, then ethics must be naturalistic. In other words, if I do something 'good' in order to please someone else, then that is a matter of psychology rather than ethics. |
| Non-naturalism | If ethics is a true branch of science by itself with its own laws, if the world contains moral elements in the same way it has physical elements, then ethics must be non-natural. Followers of religion see morality in this way: morals are not a branch of science, but the divine will of God. These people are non-naturalists. |
| Emotivism | Emotivists claim that all ethics are about how people feel, not in the sense of feeling right or wrong, or indeed any real evaluative phrase at all. Emotivists believe it is impossible to verify moral judgements scientifically. |
| Subjectivism | A subjective theory of morals is one in which ethical judgements are neither true nor false or if those judgements are true or false they are always individualistically applicable to the psychology of the person who utters them. If I believe that it is wrong to steal, but you believe it is all right, then we are both right although I may well disapprove of your actions. All we can argue about is how we feel about the act, not the moral questions of the act itself. Your right to believe your beliefs would be as valid as mine because there are no provable precepts, only individual psychology. This takes on an important role when comparing international sets of ethics, particularly in journalism. |
| Objectivism | An objective theory is one that is not subjectivistic. It allows holders to say that there can be a set of guiding principles which will hold true for all, and we can then debate the rights and wrongs of an issue and not just how we feel about it. |
| Motivism | Motivists believe that only the motive for an action needs to be considered when looking at whether it was a moral act. Even if the act leads to disastrous consequences, if the motive was pure, then the action was a moral one. Kant believed that it was immoral to tell a lie to hide a friend from a mad axe-murderer even if the consequence was that the friend was later found and killed. |
| Consequentialism | Consequentialists are little concerned about motivation. Provided the act has good consequences, it is moral. The end justifies the means. |
| Deontologism | Deontologists believe that the very words themselves carry an obligation. They believe that neither the motive nor the consequences are of significance, only the nature of the act itself. If you promise to do something, then the obligation contained in the word 'promise' leads to a duty to fulfil the act no matter what the circumstances. This has particular reference when we look at the punishment of crime. Do we punish the motive, the consequence or the act? We punish the act, but use the motive and consequence as mitigating factors. It is against the law to steal, but stealing a few items of food from a major supermarket to feed one's hungry children would not be punished as severely as stealing thousands of pounds from gullible investors (one would hope!). |

consequence of the act is significant. Therefore, a consequentialist might say 'no' as the consequence of braving the flames would be to break my promise or 'yes' as the consequence is to save a life. A deontologist believes that the act of promising to do something performs an act which by its very nature obliges one to carry it out regardless of the consequences. I have promised to meet my friend at six o'clock; if I do not do so I am breaking my promise (no matter what the excuse) and that is not acceptable. From this viewpoint a journalist would automatically be acting immorally if he or she did not gather truthful information and disseminate it to the public because by the nature of the act, that is what journalists should be obliged to do. Clearly deontologists need to be careful with their promises!

## What is a right? Why do people have them?

The importance of laws and ethical matters to society has already been discussed but another issue that is often talked about is that of rights. 'I know my rights,' we say. Yet do we have rights? The United Nations Declaration of Human Rights and its European equivalent suggest we do. *The Concise Oxford English Dictionary* describes rights as 'being entitled to privilege or immunity, thing one is entitled to' (1964: 1075).

However, rights are not things we have automatically and in many areas of the world breaches of human rights are commonplace. Human rights in this country are ours by agreement – a pact we have with the authorities of the country in which we live. In many countries that right is underscored by a constitution or a 'bill of rights' which lays down the rights or special privileges citizens can claim whilst listing the responsibilities that follow from them. Following the passing of the Human Rights Act (1998) in the UK, we too have such rights guaranteed by law. By living in a democracy, however structured, a complex structure of rights and obligations is built up. For instance, we have a right to be considered innocent until proven guilty, if we should happen to face accusations in a court of law, because the law grants us that right. In exchange, we are obliged to live in peaceful co-existence with our neighbours under the law. If our neighbour annoys us, we don't punch him on the nose, we take him to court. There are a number of other rights that we have which all have consequent duties that we are obliged to fulfil to ensure that others have their rights.

## Summary

- There are many issues that are not enshrined in law but are subject to professional ethics because of the detrimental effects they could have on individuals. For instance, a doctor revealing matters about a patient may not be breaking the law but would be breaching the ethics of his or her profession.

- Journalists have to consider the public right to know, rights of privacy, the wishes of their employer and their responsibility to the reader when working on a story.

- Some ethical theories can help journalists understand the morality of their actions.

- Living in a democracy involves accepting a complex structure of rights and obligations, and acknowledging and supporting the rights of other people.

## Questions

1 A journalist is asked by the police to suppress a story about a kidnap in order to protect the victim. Explain what he or she should do according to the theories of Kant, Aristotle and Ross.

2 If open access to information is important in a true democracy, is there anything that should be kept secret by government?

3 How can we balance the right to information against the right to privacy?

# Chapter 2

·········································································································

# News: towards a definition

**Chapter outline**

- This chapter discusses the practical difficulties involved in turning newsworthy events into news.
- It explains the difference between news as an observed phenomenon and a product to be selected for coverage and inclusion by news executives.
- It looks at some of the more common theories used to explain why news is selected.
- It shows how the need to satisfy the information requirement of readers often drives sensationalist and inaccurate reporting.

Newspapers are full of information: reviews, listings, features, profiles, forthcoming events, sports, advertisements and news. Readers expect this information to be truthful and accurate, yet often it isn't. Why is this?

In order to understand what we mean by truth and accuracy and to have some insight into the temptations that lead journalists, on occasion, to distort and twist the truth we need to know what it is that makes something newsworthy and therefore attracts the journalist's attention in the first place. What is it about a newsworthy event that makes it stand out from all the other elements of information that someone, somewhere, would like a journalist to use in his or her newspapers or news bulletins. Until we know what a newsworthy event is, it is very difficult to understand the problems, both practical and ethical, facing the journalist who wishes to report newsworthy events.

## Practical problems

There is a difference between a newsworthy event and news. A newsworthy event will not necessarily become news, just as news is often about an event that is not, in itself, newsworthy. By definition, an event that is recorded in a newspaper or a broadcast news bulletin is news, regardless of whether it is about a newsworthy event. The very fact of its transmission means that it is news. However, not all newsworthy events make it on to the news.

One of the problems with evaluating news decision-making is that news is analogue rather than digital. We cannot say 'this is news and this is not' for each event we come across as a particular event's newsworthiness varies depending on the circumstances surrounding it and the target audience group. Whether an event is used as news may also depend on other criteria, such as the space available in a paper or bulletin or the number of other good stories about. There are many factors that influence the choice of good news stories. Threshold criteria must exist to separate events that make it into newspapers or broadcasts from those that do not. Some of the threshold criteria for news are the circumstances surrounding the medium (see Exhibit 2.1).

## Exhibit 2.1 Threshold criteria for news

**Space:** A newspaper with only a few pages will have a higher threshold than one with a lot of space to fill. The less space available, the more newsworthy the event must be to make it into the newspaper. Broadcasting regularly has a higher threshold than newspapers because it has less space.

**Logistics:** Several observers have identified the physical difficulties of putting a news report together as an important criterion in its selection. Paul Rock explains in a chapter called 'News as Eternal Recurrence' that:

> . . . in place of the random search [for news], news gathering takes routine forms. . . . Journalists position themselves so that they have access to institutions which generate a useful volume of reportable activity at useful intervals. Some of these institutions do of course make themselves visible by means of dramatisation, or through press releases and press agents. Others are known regularly to produce consequential events. The courts, sports grounds and parliament mechanically manufacture news which is effortlessly assimilated by the press. (in Cohen and Young, 1973: 64)

News is more likely to be reported from places where reporters are already working. An editor cannot afford to have reporters sitting around twiddling their thumbs waiting for unpredictable events. It is more likely, therefore, that a report from a criminal court will be used than a newsworthy event from a source that cannot be predicted, even if the unpredictable event is more newsworthy as measured by other objective criteria.

**Time:** Time plays an important part in any news-gathering operation both in terms of getting the story and in terms of when the event became newsworthy. An event must be topical within the period of publication. No newspaper wants to carry a story that has happened earlier than the publication of the previous edition. A radio or TV bulletin prefers to update the news given on the last bulletin.

Philip Schlesinger, in *Putting Reality Together: BBC News* (1978), supports the above ideas by identifying time constraints and logistics as reasons why journalists alter the threshold requirement for a newsworthy event to become news.

## What do other people think is news?

We have identified some of the criteria that affect the choice of news stories and these were mainly to do with the medium that the stories are to appear in. However, there are other factors that distinguish the events that become news from those that do not.

One of the first groups in the UK to define 'news' was the Royal Commission on the Press of 1947–49 (the Ross Commission). It said:

> There are, however, certain elements common to all conceptions of news. To be news an event must first be interesting to the public, and the public for this purpose means for each paper the people who read that paper, and others like them. Second, and equally important, it must be new, and newness is measured in newspaper offices in terms of minutes. (1949: 103)

The Commission went on to list items of interest identified in a questionnaire as follows: sport; news about people; news about strange or amusing adventures; tragedies; accidents; crimes; 'news whose sentiment or excitement brings some colour into life' (1949: 104). In the 1960s, Alastair Hetherington, editor of the *Guardian* newspaper, drew up a list of news priorities for new staff which contained the seven factors outlined in Exhibit 2.2. Although Hetherington's list is of some use for media decision-making, it is not as helpful as it could be for understanding news. It is merely the distillation of his considerable experience and professional skill.

**Exhibit 2.2 Alastair Hetherington's news priorities**

- **Significance**: social, economic, political.
- **Drama**: excitement, entertainment.
- **Surprise**: unpredictability, newness.
- **Personalities**: royalty, showbusiness.
- **Sex**: scandal, crime.
- **Numbers**: scale of the event.
- **Proximity**: the geographical closeness of the event.

There are many other ideas about what news is: 'When a dog bites a man, that is not news, because it happens so often. But if a man bites a dog, that is news' (John B. Bogart, City editor, *New York Sun*, 1873–90); 'News is People'; 'News is what they talk about down at the local pub'; 'News is something someone wants to keep secret'. While all descriptions like these have an element of truth and wit, they are not much help in sorting news from the rest of information. After all, what if, for instance, the dog carries a strange new disease that is transmittable to man by biting and has only been recognised by medical science that week? The unusual element in the story means this certainly would be news.

So what about academics? Have they done any better? Johan Galtung and Mari Ruge were amongst the first academics to try to explain news. Their work is substantial and influential. It underpins the thinking of John Hartley in *Understanding News* (1982) and is used by John Venables in *What is News?* (1993). Galtung and Ruge originally published their research in the *Journal of International Peace Research* in 1965. It was a study of the presentation of the Congo, Cuba and Cyprus crises in four foreign newspapers, looking at the structure of foreign news. An extract entitled 'Structuring and Selecting News' was published in *The Manufacture of News. Deviance, Social Problems and the Mass Media*, edited by Stanley Cohen and Jock Young (1973). Galtung and Ruge saw news broken down into two categories: general news value and news values of particular importance to Western media (see Exhibit 2.3).

Useful though Galtung and Ruge's criteria are, they share many of the problems of Hetherington's list. He identifies news from experience; they identify news from observation. Both identify a series of criteria that helps explain the types of news story used, but they do not explain why they were chosen in the first place by the news selectors, nor do they explain why readers buy the eventual product. Nor do Galtung and Ruge analyse very deeply the reasons why some of these criteria are important. They also fail the logic test when we look at elements such as negativity. They attempt to show that 'bad' news is 'good' news. Although their arguments for this are sound, we need to be careful of identifying negativity with news.

In a way Galtung and Ruge are right in that a lot of news is bad news. However, as a major component of our need for news is to enable us to deal with threats, it is hardly surprising that a large portion of news will be about threats, either direct (e.g. a hurricane warning) or indirect (e.g. more violence on the streets). John Venables comes to the conclusion that 'change' and 'security concerns' are 'the fundamental factors which motivate attentiveness in an audience' (1993: 34). Although some changes are good, they all have threatening implications. Learning to deal with change requires intelligence and planning. He goes on to describe the importance of change: 'Without change, information cannot be interpreted as news. Change is important because it involves uncertainty, which in turn generates attention and concern' (ibid.).

All the observers, academics and practitioners discussed (except Venables) fall into the same trap. They categorise what is news but there is little consideration of what we mean by newsworthiness. There are many journalists who have developed their sense of what is newsworthy, their 'nose

## Exhibit 2.3 Galtung and Ruge's news criteria

The list of general news values relies on logical categorisation:

**Frequency**. The timespan of an event affects how it is used. If an event takes much longer to unfold than can be handled by the publication frequency of the media concerned, then it is 'marked' by the issuing of reports or sub-events.

**Threshold**. The size of a story. John Hartley explains this: 'There is a threshold below which an event will not be reported at all (the threshold intensity varies in intensity between, for instance, local and national news)' (1982: 76).

**Unambiguity**. Clear-cut events that require little explanation are more likely to be used as news.

**Meaningfulness**. An event which coincides with the cultural assumptions of the journalist or the target audience is more likely to be used. (There is a tie in with *unambiguity* here – a meaningful event is less likely to be ambiguous.) This is a similar criterion to Hetherington's *significance* (Exhibit 2.2).

**Consonance**. Something that accords with the media's preconceptions is more likely to be reported. It also works the other way around: an event is more likely to be reported in accordance with the preconceptions of the reporter.

**Unexpectedness**. Also appears on Hetherington's list as *surprise* (Exhibit 2.2).

**Continuity**. If an event is already making news, then it is likely it will continue to make the news.

**Composition**. An event might make the news even though it is not in itself that newsworthy, merely to balance the media presentation. In other words, a weak foreign story might be added to a radio bulletin merely to balance the home and away elements of the bulletin.

There are a further four news values of particular importance to Western media:

**Elite nations**. They believe there is a bias in Western media towards reporting events in the first world. This is also hinted at by Hetherington in *proximity* (Exhibit 2.2), but is not quite the same thing.

**Elite persons**. The activities of those perceived as important are of more interest than the activities of people considered less socially significant. Hetherington talks about *personalities* (Exhibit 2.2).

**Personalisation**. Events being presented as the actions of a particular person, e.g. 'Blair backs Clinton on Gulf', to invent an example.

**Negativity**. The view that bad news is 'good' news. Only news that is negative is used in the media. A complaint supported by Martyn Lewis, the television news reader, who campaigned for a good news channel.

for news', by copying the reactions of more experienced colleagues. We can hardly be surprised if a new reporter decides that something is newsworthy if it makes the news editor happy or excited. Unfortunately this empirical approach has the same drawbacks as all observational views on news-gathering. Observation alone is never enough by itself to deal with new circumstances. What happens when a new news editor takes over in the office and seems to work by different criteria? Are there really different criteria or has the inexperienced journalist merely misunderstood them? Journalists need to test their hypotheses about news criteria under a number of different circumstances if they are to become more efficient at news selection.

The Royal Commission used the word 'new' to indicate that the news item is recent. Since this can easily be confused with the word 'news', I will use 'topical' to indicate newness in the rest of this chapter. But remember, newness to a monthly magazine will not be the same as newness from a daily newspaper, which will have a different view of newness from a radio bulletin with an hourly schedule. Some events continue over a long period and so remain topical. Wars, for instance, remain topical despite their extended life-cycle. All events are sub-sets of other events. The Second World War was a sub-set in the flow of European political history. The retreat of the British Army from Dunkirk was a sub-set of the Second World War. We could no doubt find sub-sets of Dunkirk. Each of these would be handled in different ways by publications with different publication frequencies. A magazine that only publishes every ten years, assuming there were such a thing, may headline the Second World War as: 'European clash leads to global war: Allies triumph.' Weekly papers of the period looked at the retreat from Dunkirk in its totality, whilst radio bulletins and daily papers of the time broke that episode into sub-sets.

Almost everyone, academic and practitioner alike, agrees that there has to be a new or topical element for an item of information to be news. There is also widespread agreement that news needs to interest the public. In modern terminology, the public are generally known as the target group and what the Ross Commission called 'the people who read that paper and others like them' would now be described as the target readership. This is a sub-section of the general population that can be clearly identified, whether they actually read that publication or not. The *Daily Mail*, which has a clear view of its target readership, aims at women, aged 25–50, who are, or aspire to be, middle to upper middle class with a traditional view about life and therefore a propensity to see their purpose as family carers, even if this is manifested in a career which will provide financial security for the family. The difficulties arrive when we start to consider precisely what it is that is of interest to the target group. We can easily draw up a list of items that interest different target groups: sex, war, crime, health and so on, but this is still based on observation. We need to move beyond pure observation and start to look at what makes for newsworthiness.

## Sensationalism

Despite my concerns about our view of newsworthiness being based purely on observation, we now have an idea about what is newsworthy – what will sell a newspaper or broadcast to people seeking information. Following on from that, we need to consider why it seems that many journalists cannot bring information of an event to the consumer accurately and devoid of sensation.

There is little sensationalism in ordinary stories of the sort that usually fill our newspapers and the stories are generally accurate (within the limits that can be explained by tight deadlines and the explanation of topicality as a major criterion of the news judgement). If the information is easy to obtain, is detailed and the sources are credible, then there is little chance of the story becoming sensational. Journalists can supply all the information the consumer requires without stepping outside the wealth of accurate information easily available to them. However, with a big story things are different. Big changes, or matters that give people considerable anxiety about their security, raise the desire for information. People will take as much information as news outlets can give them. A big story will bring a heightened desire for news and the information requirement of the average consumer can soar. Additional consumers can also be drawn in. People who ordinarily do not buy newspapers suddenly start doing so in order to find out more.

If formal news sources are unable to provide enough information to satisfy consumers, then there is no way newspapers involved in a vicious circulation war are going to let that stop them making the most of their ability to capture consumers. People are prepared to pay for information whether the paper has it or not. Newspapers will carry stories from dubious, informal sources, knowing that the information is not well sourced, in order to provide enough copy for the consumer. This happens less often in broadcasting as the fixed timing of news bulletins reduces the opportunity to use additional material. However, a story such as the bombing of Kosovo or the death of Diana, Princess of Wales, can change even that. Bulletins were extended to cover the NATO attacks on Serbia while the Princess's death and funeral received massive coverage from newspapers and broadcasters, even when there was nothing more to add. Similar treatment followed the murder of TV personality Jill Dando with several special programmes as tributes to her and extended news bulletins. Early reports told of her being stabbed to death. Only later did reports accurately report the murder as a shooting.

## Case study 2.1 The funeral of Diana, Princess of Wales

The death of Diana, Princess of Wales, in August 1997 shocked the world and her funeral received massive coverage from both newspapers and broadcasters. The coverage continued even when there seemed to be nothing more to add.

The funeral took place on Saturday 6 September and broadcasters felt obliged to broadcast all afternoon, long after the funeral had ended, forcing them to show repeats of selected items from the funeral, footage of the funeral cortege on the motorway, and interminable interviews with various pundits. None of this added any new information, yet broadcasters felt it necessary to carry on and viewers felt obliged to stay with the coverage.

On the following Monday the newspapers were full of pictures and reports of the funeral, despite the massive live viewing figures on the Saturday and extensive coverage by the Sunday papers. It seemed that people were willing to take as much information as they could get about such an important story.

Some newspapers that are covering big stories and are unable to supply enough information to satisfy the reader find that additional information can be built on the top of a relatively spurious incident. The whole story is driven by sensation and built on rumour. Figure 2.1 illustrates how the unfulfilled information requirement of readers is satisfied by sensation, rumour and fiction. It is impossible to give true measurements to make the graph completely accurate, but it shows how the system works. When the interest level of the target group of readers exceeds the available news, then a risk area

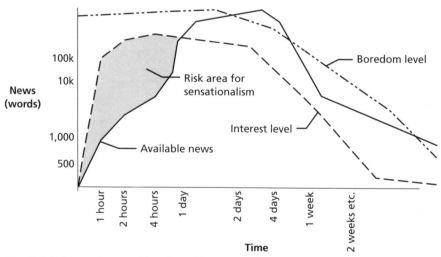

**Fig. 2.1 Information tracking in a big story of major interest to the target group**

for sensationalism is created and filled with stories that are designed to appeal to the target group's appetite for information about that particular subject. Examples of such sensationalist reporting can be found in the coverage of the death of the Princess of Wales. Stories of the car's speedometer being stuck at 120 mph were used in several papers (see, for example, the *Daily Mirror's* front page of 2 September 1997; it was not the only paper with this angle).

With a relatively un-newsworthy story the information available far outstrips the interest level of the target group (Figure 2.2). In this case, the only decision for an editor is what information to leave out of the story to ensure that the information offered to the reader matches closely the information required. There is no risk area for sensationalism with this type of story.

Because even a tightly targeted consumer group will not all want exactly the same information in a story, some information overload is needed to ensure the editor has fulfilled all the consumers' requirements. This is why the information requirement and boredom threshold (the point at which virtually all consumers have moved on to read something else) are some distance apart in Figures 2.1 and 2.2. The need for information overload may mean providing up to 100 per cent more information than one person requires to cover the personal variations between consumers.

From an ethical point of view, the major trouble area is where the interest level and the boredom threshold exceed the news available. Consumers seek more information and rather than risk them moving to another paper, a journalist can be tempted into trying to fill the gap (shaded in the Figure 2.1). As explained, this is the area in which sensationalism lives, and it

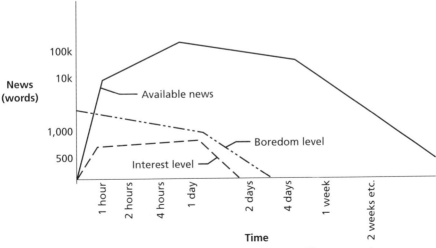

**Fig. 2.2 Information tracking on a story of minor significance to the target group**

is the place where the clash between journalism as a social service and the news media as a commercial enterprise is at its most vivid.

## Summary

- There are practical difficulties involved in turning newsworthy events into news, including the space available, logistics and time constraints.
- Practitioners and academics have tried to explain what it is that makes a particular piece of information a product that is selected for coverage and inclusion by news executives.
- There is widespread agreement that there must be a topical element for an item of information to be news and the information must be of interest to the target group.
- When the information requirement of the target group exceeds the available news, this creates a risk area for sensationalism.

## Questions

1 Look at some of today's newspapers. Try to imagine for each story on the front page the reasons why the news editor chose that story for the front page and compare the criteria with those identified by Galtung and Ruge (Exhibit 2.3). Can you identify any stories that have been used because the newspaper has already invested time and resources in them, rather than because they are newsworthy?

2 Read the stories again. Do they provide enough information for your needs? Can you recall times when the newspapers did not give enough information about particular stories to satisfy your needs?

3 Try to find the same story covered by two different newspapers and consider the differences in approach. Can you identify the differences between people-based coverage and issue-based coverage of the story? What are the advantages and disadvantages of both and which do you prefer?

# Chapter 3

# Media morality

### Chapter outline

- This chapter looks at how the freedom of the press to inform is often confused with the freedom of the press to make profit.

- It considers the close link between morality and the law and how society often uses the law to enforce elements of morality.

- It looks at the difference between truth and accuracy and why it is important that journalists and consumers do not confuse the two.

- It explores taste and decency and some of the criteria used to help decision-making in this difficult area.

There are a number of moral issues that are relevant to all forms of media and underline some of the justifiable fears that many people have about the media as commercial institutions. Although this chapter looks at these issues from the point of view of journalism and the journalist, it is worth remembering that they affect the whole of society and they are not just the preserve of editors and journalists.

## Press freedom

Much has been written about the freedom of the press and its 'duty' to inform the public. This duty is often expressed in terms of the public's right to know in a democratic society if, for instance, someone elected to a position of authority and trust is betraying that trust by accepting bribes. However, in practice, this duty to inform is often used not only to justify publication of information relevant to that person's public office (the taking of bribes), but also details of their private life (e.g. a sexual liaison) which have no direct relevance to the carrying out of their public responsibilities and only serve to satisfy the public's prurient curiosity and boost circulation or viewing figures. It is this central dilemma of press freedom that we will examine in the following chapter.

# The free press and democratic society

In many parts of the world and throughout most of Europe it is generally accepted that some form of democratic representation is the best form of government. If democracy is to work well and we are to exercise our right to vote responsibly, then we need to be reasonably well informed so that we are able to use our vote wisely and involve ourselves in the political debates of our times.

> It is by political discussion that the manual labourer, whose employment is a routine, and whose way of life brings him in contact with no variety of impressions, circumstances, or ideas, is taught that remote causes and events which take place far off, have a most sensible effect even on his personal interests; and it is from political discussion, and collective political action, that one whose daily occupations concentrate his interests in a small circle around himself, learns to feel for and with his fellow-citizens, and becomes consciously a member of a great community. (Mill, 1991: 328)

It is here that the media has its most important role – keeping the public informed and facilitating political debate.

But we would be fooling ourselves if we believed that democracy worked this way everywhere in the Western world. All too often it seems that people are too busy, too lazy, too cynical or too preoccupied to make the effort required to be well enough informed to reach a reasoned decision on voting choices. People often vote the way their parents did, or the way they did last time, or because of their emotive perception of the party for which they 'should' be voting. However, a concern that the system doesn't really work as it should is no reason not to continue working for the ideal, and this pursuit requires the continuing flow of information about what our political masters are up to in our name. It is for this reason that it is generally accepted in most Western countries that part of the media's remit is to inform and that part of that informing role will involve them in a close scrutiny of the motives and actions of people in positions of power and trust. A 1994 survey by the *Times/Mirror* Center for the People and the Press (1994), conducted in eight European countries and America, showed that despite sweeping criticisms that newspapers in Britain were inaccurate, biased and intrusive, 64 per cent of the public still felt that the news media kept politicians honest. It is worth noting that the survey highlighted a significant split between the credibility rating of television and newspapers in the UK (see Table 3.1), a split that was not so obvious in other countries surveyed. Measuring whether the media had a 'good influence' on society (see Table 3.2), whilst most countries put newspapers and television within ten percentage points of each other, British television was favoured by 66 per cent of respondents (one of the higher marks) whilst British newspapers gained

**Table 3.1 Credibility ratings**

| Country | Television | Newspapers | The Church | Politicians |
|---|---|---|---|---|
| Canada | 81 | 71 | 47 | 53 |
| France | 74 | 68 | 35 | 41 |
| Germany | 90 | 84 | 40 | 40 |
| Italy | 67 | 63 | 52 | 38 |
| Spain | 64 | 60 | 40 | 27 |
| United Kingdom | 85 | 53 | 44 | 26 |
| United States | 73 | 68 | 60 | 49 |

Source: The Times/Mirror Center for the People and the Press (now the Pew Center), (1994).

**Table 3.2 Media have a good influence on society**

| Country | Television | Newspapers | Entertainment | The Church |
|---|---|---|---|---|
| Canada | 71 | 73 | 36 | 61 |
| France | 55 | 59 | 39 | 39 |
| Germany | 49 | 47 | 18 | 24 |
| Italy | 50 | 37 | 26 | 45 |
| Spain | 64 | 71 | 33 | 48 |
| United Kingdom | 66 | 38 | 34 | 41 |
| United States | 71 | 74 | 25 | 73 |

Source: The Times/Mirror Center for the People and the Press (1994).

only 38 per cent support, coming virtually bottom with only one point more than Italy.

Political systems that do not require or allow the participation of all citizens through the ballot box do not need a free media. In such a system a free media is a potential voice of dissent that is likely to cause disruption in society. Nor is it likely to be of use to the citizens themselves unless they are seeking to change the government and introduce democracy:

> But political discussions fly over the heads of those who have no votes, and are not endeavouring to acquire them. Their position, in comparison with the electors, is that of the audience in a court of justice, compared with the twelve men in the jury-box. It is not their suffrages that are asked, it is not their opinion that is sought to be influenced. (Mill, 1991: 329)

But we should appreciate that even governments who face the ballot box on a regular basis will do the best they can to control the information voters have access to whilst trying to appear as though they support a free press and greater access to information. For instance, former Attorney General Sir Nicholas Lyell was quick to condemn a Freedom of Information Act as too inflexible to be useful following renewed calls for such legislation in February 1996 (Newsnight, BBC2, 17 February 1996). The Scott report, published the day before, had revealed that the government, having turned a blind eye to the export of weapon manufacturing systems to Iraq by a company called Matrix Churchill, had then tried to cover this up by getting ministers to sign gagging orders – public immunity certificates – preventing evidence of ministerial involvement being made known when Matrix Churchill directors were tried for illegally exporting weapon systems to Iraq!

A report on the affair, written by Sir Richard Scott after a long investigation, brought biting attacks on the government. Robin Cook, then shadow Foreign Secretary, led the attack by the Opposition.

'It was the secrecy that made this scandal possible,' the shadow Foreign Secretary said. 'The five volumes of the Scott report provide the firmest foundation yet of the case for a Freedom of Information Act.'

'And there were never better witnesses for a Freedom of Information Act than the long parade of officials and ministers queuing to explain to Sir Richard Scott that the public interest was best served by not letting the public know what they were deciding.' Mr Cook said the International Atomic Energy Agency found 30 Matrix Churchill lathes in Iraqi nuclear plants after the Gulf War. 'Faced with that evidence, how dare ministers claim they did not arm Saddam Hussein?' (*Independent*, 17 February 1996)

Yet despite promising a Freedom of Information Act, it was almost two years before a Labour government introduced a draft bill in June 1999. Ironically this was six months after a private member's bill was introduced into the House of Lords by Lord Lucas, a shadow Home Office spokesman. His speech emphasised the importance of free information, but did not seem to be concerned with the same worries of inflexibility affecting Sir Nicholas Lyell. The government's draft bill was met with almost universal condemnation as being weak and ineffective, particularly in the area of crime and health and safety.

In countries where the media is strictly controlled, only 'good' news about the government can be disseminated. It also means that few, if any, of the ethical problems facing journalists in a free media arise. If a journalist is limited in the sources he or she can use, is instructed by the authorities about what to write and how to write it, and how it should be used, the debate is not about ethics but about definitions. Indeed, it is debatable whether that person can be considered to be a journalist at all. Without media freedom the journalist's reason to behave in a way which may bring about direct moral conflict no longer exists. If the journalist's role is confined purely to that of entertainer or propagandist, the only criteria by which they can be judged are whether they get their work in on time and fulfil the brief provided by their political masters. Questions about matters such as invading privacy and obtaining information through straightforward means no longer apply; there is no public interest defence to obtaining information in this way and therefore no excuse to do so. There is not even an obligation to be truthful if part of a journalist's job is to distort the facts to present the government in a good light.

From this discussion it is clear that only if democratic decision-making genuinely exists does a fully free media also need to exist as a reliable source of information, comment and analysis. Journalists only need to behave in a way which might be morally debatable (e.g. intrude, breach people's privacy) if they have a justification and surely the only justification to publish such material is the citizen's right to know; the public interest.

According to the 1977 Royal Commission on the Press, freedom of the press is: 'that degree of freedom from restraint which is essential to enable proprietors, editors and journalists to advance the public interest'. However, it went on to say: 'Freedom of the Press carries different meanings to different people' (1977: 8). Thus when we talk about a free media we are not necessarily talking about the media's right to publish anything they like, but that people, including journalists, should have the right to spread information and ideas which can be justified morally in order to support the public's right to know. In other words, information published in the public interest, not merely information to sate the public's curiosity or desire to be entertained. This means that any pressure brought to bear on a person and his or her right to hold and disseminate ideas and information (whether from government agencies, proprietors, threats or bribes from outside agencies, including advertisers' pressure) damages the citizen's ability to have access to as wide a range of views on a subject as he or she desires.

On analysis it would seem that there is almost nowhere in the world that has a truly free media. In capitalist societies, proprietors and advertisers have a strong role in controlling what is published or broadcast and the line the journalist takes whilst covering stories. Societies which are controlled by totalitarian governments, or which face strong social control from organised religion or other sources, are also constrained in a way which militates against a free press, and even in democratic societies governments will try to control the information that is disseminated about them. It is these differing social pressures and expectations which account for the diversity of ethical views found amongst journalists around the globe.

## Morality and a free press

Following the news reflects and reaffirms our membership in a community of shared interests. (Joshua Halberstam, quoted in Cohen, 1992: 19)

Being part of a community brings responsibilities, yet only with enough information to form meaningful views can people make sensible, well-informed decisions about those responsibilities and so play their part in the community. As the journalist's prime objective is the discovery, disclosure and analysis of the information on which others will base their views, the decisions affecting a journalist's choices about what material to publish or broadcast should have as strong a moral component as the methods used to gather that material. But often the moral decisions are not about which news to use but are decisions about whether the text concerned is news at all.

Journalists have to make choices all the time about what to put in or leave out of stories, what stories to use in newspapers or broadcasts, which stories to cover and which ones to ignore. In Britain journalists often look at the commercial aspect of a story. They ask themselves whether a story is going to sell papers and if the story is what people want. It would be impossible for people to read every story written on a particular day, even if we, as journalists, could put our hands on our hearts and swear that we have been universal in our coverage. Consumers rely on journalists to give them the kind of information they want and we measure our success at doing this by sales. However, sales are not the only measure of success for most media. Total income, which includes income from advertising, is the most important yardstick of media success. The exceptions to this rule are the BBC and pay-per-view channels. These organisations are of course very different in that the first is a public service broadcaster and the second is a purely commercial concern. However, both are able to justify their coverage on the basis of consumer needs alone, although whether this is entirely the basis is of course open to question.

A journalist needs to determine right from the start of any story the reason why he or she is covering it. If the reasons for covering it are morally, not just commercially, viable, or if the moral reasons for using the story outweigh the moral arguments against, then we should publish. However, we also need to look at this in another way: are we *not* covering a particular story because it is morally, or merely commercially, unjustifiable?

## Morality and society

Most societies in the world feel strongly about some area of media ethics and ensure appropriate behaviour by legislating in that area. It is perfectly legitimate for societies to reach a consensus about what is acceptable for the media to publish or, more usually, not publish. Nearly all societies, for instance, prevent the publication of defence information that could put at risk the nation's security. In some societies, privacy is very important and so the law covers privacy, whereas in others the presumption of innocence is paramount and there the law will cover that and perhaps make no mention of privacy.

The emphasis that societies place on matters such as privacy and the way they deal with them differs greatly. For example, in France, the law covers a wide range of issues that are dealt with by other countries in their press codes of ethical conduct. It is no surprise therefore that France, with its tough constitution and laws, has a limited code of journalistic conduct whilst Sweden, which has practically no legislation in the area of ethical media activity, has a strong code and regulatory media council that is taken very seriously by practitioners.

Where there is strong law in a country for one area of journalistic morality, it often happens that the journalists in that country cease to see that area as a moral problem at all, except in very general terms. For instance, in Britain, journalists are restricted in what they report on criminal proceedings by a number of statutes. The 1981 Contempt of Courts Act lays down that once someone has been arrested, or a warrant has been issued for their arrest, nothing may be published or broadcast which 'creates a substantial risk that the course of justice in particular legal proceedings will be seriously impeded or prejudiced' providing the proceedings are 'active'. This is called strict liability contempt because there is no need to prove that there was any intention to prejudge a trial, only that there was a substantial, serious risk to an active proceedings. Should there be evidence that the matter was published intentionally to prejudice proceedings, then the older common law definition of contempt of court could still be used.

Once a matter comes to a trial the media can report provided it is a fair and accurate report of public legal proceedings published contemporaneously and in good faith. In addition, the court can make orders to hear evidence in private in certain circumstances and it is also, under section 8 of the 1981 Act, a contempt to 'obtain, disclose or solicit any particular statements made, opinions expressed, arguments advanced or votes cast by members of a jury in the course of their deliberations in any legal proceedings'. This means that British journalists tend to think of the issue of covering court cases in terms of the law rather than morality. Whereas a US journalist might take an ethical decision when considering whether to interview a jury member on the O.J. Simpson trial or talk to a witness before a trial, a British journalist would not even consider interviewing a juror on the Rosemary West trial as he or she would know this could be illegal and therefore pointless.

If a journalist is obliged by law to do, or not do, a certain action, then there can be no feeling of moral obligation. In practice this seems to have the effect of eventually eroding a person's consideration of the underlying moral principle that applies in that particular area. Doubtless the same would be true for journalists if the laws of contempt of court were removed. Present loopholes in the law are used at every opportunity for a story regardless of the ethical considerations, so, if the laws were removed, journalists would certainly have a field day with court coverage.

## Morality and commerce

Another important factor in the ethical debate is market forces. Most Western journalists work in a market place to some degree or another. Even if their newspapers or broadcasts are being consumed by a captive audience (public service broadcasters, for instance, or journalists working for fixed circulation publications), they still end up working to performance criteria which have audience approval as a major component. This inevitably puts pressure on the journalist to follow market-driven journalism rather than adhering to an ethical value system. Journalists will then often deceive themselves that they are doing the right thing by publishing a story which by any other standard would be considered unethical. Essentially this is an issue of loyalty. To whom does the journalist owe loyalty? Is it the employer, the consumer, the advertiser, the law, or some other authority?

The drive to improve circulation or viewing figures can tempt a journalist to use a story that morally-driven caution might have persuaded him or her not to have used. This shows loyalty to the employer; a chance for the company to boost profits by improving circulation or viewing figures and self-serving ambition. A journalist who is loyal to an employer and helps to boost profits is bound to be a more marketable talent. For the same reason, many journalists will allow themselves to back away from a story out of loyalty to the company or an advertiser or both. They may refuse to cover a story relating to a major advertiser, or potential advertiser, even though they feel that morally their readers should be told about the advertiser's questionable practices.

## Morality and truth

The quality of information offered to consumers is inevitably as variable as the sources from which it comes. A major part of a journalist's work in gathering material for publication or broadcast from a news source is to determine how reliable this information is. The journalist must then take a decision. If the information is known by the journalist to be totally accurate, then there is no problem. If, for instance, a journalist actually saw a politician smash his car into a wall, then that is an accurate fact that can be reported. But, when information comes from another source that is not so reliable, and which cannot be confirmed from sources that are any more reliable, the journalist has to make an assessment about whether to pass this information on to the consumer. Should he or she report claims that the young woman seen fleeing from the politician's car was a prostitute? Should the report mention that the politician had allegedly been drinking at a party shortly before the accident?

John Hartley makes the point that 'The way news "maps" the world and produces our sense of its reality depends very largely on the nature of the various signs it uses' (1982: 15). It is important, therefore, that the journalist carefully handles information from an untrustworthy or unreliable news source if the consumer is not to be inadvertently misled. In this sense unreliable means news sources which provide inaccurate or misleading information, information which is biased, or which present comment and propaganda as fact. Unfortunately, virtually all news sources, by their very nature, provide information that is distorted, either because of pressure of time or resources or because of a deliberate desire to deceive. Politicians will always want to suggest that their ideas are right or that their opponents are wrong. Does this mean they tell lies? It depends on the individual. No politician tells the whole truth all of the time whilst it is difficult to imagine someone (politician or not) who could lie the whole of the time. If consumers are to be able to tell which politicians are lying at any given time, they need to be able to test the information they are fed by the journalist to analyse critically the words of the politician.

Journalists have to take the middle ground when dealing with people. They should be sceptical about everyone, seeing them as neither good nor bad but merely human. This does not mean that a journalist has no duty to follow up information that shows a person to be lying. Quite the reverse. It means listening and watching carefully, picking up on the small signs that can help show someone has something to hide, and listening for inconsistencies and refusing to believe at face value what they are told. People do not tend to lie outright. It is too easy to be found out. Rather they use sentence forms that can have several meanings. They evade the questions. They twist and turn in the hope that the journalist will not notice. For instance, the question 'Did you take a bribe for £100,000' might elicit the response '£100,000? Of course not, my dear fellow. Would I still be sitting around London with that kind of holiday money in my bank account?' This straightforward denial of the charge stands up to little sceptical scrutiny. Assuming the speaker is telling the absolute truth, and we have no way of checking that, the only things we know for sure are that the speaker is in London and that any bribe he received was not for £100,000. We can assume that any bribe taken was for less, otherwise he would, by his own admission, be on holiday. Clearly, we need to ask further questions.

## Truth and accuracy

Sources of information are often not as accurate or as certain as we might like. A police chief dealing with a major incident may issue information to journalists which has not been checked and therefore could be inaccurate.

Because he or she wants to show the media that he or she is doing a good job the information is released before it is ready. Those in authority learn very quickly that the nature of news means that a story is soon forgotten, taking false or misleading statements with it into oblivion. Everybody in the news wants to show themselves in a good light and so are likely to distort the story in some way, even if unconsciously. Again the journalist must use his or her judgement to try to spot the leaps of faith by the source of information and put them in the right context.

Tom Koch, in *News as Myth* (1990), gives the example of a Hawaiian judge (Shintaku) who brought in a verdict which was unpopular with the authorities. He was later rushed to hospital with injuries gained in mysterious circumstances. It suited the authorities to ascribe these to an attempt at suicide even though the evidence for this was skimpy. Press reporting at the time seemed to support this conclusion by reporting only what the authorities said:

> ... Reportage of the Shintaku case was based on the generally accepted journalistic assumption that attributed fact is sufficient. Editorial judgement is for the op-ed page while reporters need not and should not judge the statements of those they are sent to cover. For Samuel Johnson, however, it was precisely here that the hack showed his or her skill, probing on the basis of prior experience the limits of a single event's description. ... The issue these cases raise is the efficacy of an institutionalised set of journalistic practices which presumably guarantees veracity but ultimately leads ... to the reportage of incomplete, misleading, 'false truths'. (Koch, 1990: 9)

Although the need to be aware about the accuracy of information has been stressed, we should not assume that all outlets claiming to issue news actually do so or that their customers are unhappy about the poor quality of information supplied. Consumers are often willing to be told stories that are amazing, funny, surprising and just plain entertaining, even if they don't always believe them to be true. There are many publications around the world that carry such stories. *The People* of 6 October 1996 carried the story: 'Elvis is alive' on its front page. The *Weekly World News*, published in the US but with an international circulation, is always full of unbelievable tales such as 'Couple with 8-inch tongues marry!' – complete with pictures (*Weekly World News*, 14 June 1994: 1). Furthermore, consider urban myths. These are stories that are usually spread by word of mouth, although they sometimes make it into the media. The Internet has fed their popularity and they are now spreading further and faster than ever. The events are usually described by the teller as happening to a friend, although if pressed they will usually admit to it being the friend of a friend, often several times removed. Urban myths are almost impossible to trace back to their origins and seem to be complete fabrications, yet people enjoy hearing them, hence their popularity on the World Wide Web.

If a media outlet is just aiming to entertain readers in this way then it does not need to provide accurate information because that is not what its market wants. People buy it to be entertained, not for accurate information. Most people, however, buy into information systems because they want high-grade information, not just entertainment, and any media outlet that claims to be an information provider and wishes to maintain its market would do well to justify the veracity of its sources. Any product that does not supply what its market requires, in this case accurate information, is soon going to go out of business. This does not mean the media never deals in inaccurate information. One of the prevailing dilemmas for the journalist is whether to publish stories of the 'Rumours have been denied . . .' sort. Publishing such a story gives it credence, but often the rumour is already widely known and believed and so requires the record being set straight.

Very often consumers need and want to know about information that cannot be verified as truthful. Much political reporting is of this sort. If, for example, one politician says that poor teaching is responsible for our children being ill-educated, whilst another says it is a lack of resources and a third says our children are actually the best educated in the world, it would not be surprising if a journalist reported this story as a row between politicians, only briefly mentioning their points of view. The only thing we can be certain is true is the row. The rest lies in the field of opinion, usually based on untested facts and one-sided statistics. It would be foolish, and indeed dangerous, for journalists to pretend that they can provide enough accurate information for the consumer to come to a firm conclusion. It is important, however, that we know that a debate about education has been started. The Secretary of State for Education then becomes involved in the debate, making a 30-minute speech on how the latest teaching methods are responsible for the failure of the education system in the UK. No journalist is going to be able to track down in detail all the theories and see whether the literature bears out the Education Secretary's view, but journalists can look at the obvious inconsistencies in the speech and use them as the basis of the story. In other words, a good story would be about the new methods of education, why the Secretary of State has allowed them to be used for so many years and now, ignoring the advice of the experts, is using them to excuse the poor state of education. Whilst it would be accurate to report just the Secretary of State's speech, it would not be entirely truthful to report that and only that. A journalist has a duty to set such a report in context for the consumer.

Accuracy is a word that causes more confusion in journalism than anything else. People expect the media to be accurate so that they can reassure themselves that their model of the universe, formed in part by the information the media feeds them, is accurate. Yet a considerable measure of that universal model will be formed from information that is not accurate or even truthful. Each person's model of the universe will be built around presumptions, assumptions and information that is either wrong or is at least unproved. Whilst consumers seek accuracy, there are other criteria which are just as important. There is no point in a reporter being absolutely accurate six months after the event because this would entail sacrificing timeliness to accuracy. The journalist must do all he or she can to minimise mistakes, distortions and untruthfulness but he or she must also be aware that time is an important component of this type of information-gathering (see Exhibit 3.1).

**Exhibit 3.1 Time and accuracy**

I learn, from a radio report, that the road I usually take to drive home from work is blocked because, police have reported, a lorry has shed its load. I am naturally interested in this news and listen closely to gather all the information that I can. I learn that the load is unlikely to be cleared for several hours and therefore the road will remain blocked. On the basis of this information I might decide to take a different route home or, if this were not possible or considered inadvisable, I might decide to stay where I am and work late. Either way, it would not worry me if I later learned that in fact the road was blocked because a car had broken down (unless of course the updated information meant that the road was cleared much faster than would have been the case if the original story had been correct, so invalidating my decision process). Since my purpose in having the information is to use it as the basis for a decision to take a detour before being caught in the traffic jam, it does not matter much that the reason for blockage is not fully accurate.

Because of the way we treat information, not only do we occasionally accept inaccurate information, we actually need it. Making mistakes can be an important part of news reporting. Whilst news media should aim to produce truthful information, it is as important that they get the information out quickly. Accurate information too late is of little value in news terms. For example, a journalist covering a train crash is told by the police chief that there are 60 people dead but the ambulance chief says 58, whilst the hospital says the number is 59. What should the journalist report? That a number of people were killed, or should he or she choose one of the numbers and try to confirm which is right later on? Of course it might be weeks before the final death toll was determined. Most consumers I suspect would prefer to know the approximate number rather than wonder what range 'a number of deaths' came into.

If we look at information-gathering from a Kantian viewpoint (see Chapter 1), the problem arises of how to draw up a universal law. It is clear from the above discussion that it would not be helpful or usefully attainable to propose that *all* information passed on by journalists should be accurate. The National Union of Journalists' Code of Conduct asks a journalist to 'strive to ensure material is accurate', but this leaves a problem: how hard should the journalist strive? If we exchange accuracy for truthfulness, we eradicate these problems. 'A journalist should always report truthfully' allows the journalist to report potentially inaccurate or untruthful information providing he or she ensures that the consumer is able to make a judgement about how reliable the information is. If the journalist has taken every care to ensure that the information is as truthful as possible and is properly sourced so that the reader is able to decide how far they trust the information, the journalist has surely dealt with the consumer fairly, even if the consumer's hope of completely accurate information has not been fulfilled. Furthermore, the journalist ought not to stop at only providing information from sources which are in themselves accurate, but he or she should also seek to put that information in the context of the wider truth. One can be accurate just by making a couple of telephone calls, but finding and presenting the truth often takes a lot more effort.

Readers expect that the information they are being fed is properly sourced, so journalists have a moral obligation, if they are unable to guarantee accuracy of information (although they do have an obligation to do their best to ensure accuracy), to at least ensure the reader or viewer is made aware of the source of any story and therefore the part it plays in the truth of the story. The process of belief/non-belief of the source (and therefore the information) lies with the consumer. It is the journalist's job to give them the information they need to make a rational decision, not to take that decision for the consumer. Accuracy can be seen as a market commodity. Any media claiming to sell information should ensure that it is accurate so that its customers return for more. But truth is a deeper ethical commitment which goes beyond the strict commercial contract between supplier and consumer. A good newspaper executive will want to ensure accuracy in order to continue selling papers; a good journalist will want to tell the truth in order to do what's right by the consumer.

## Truth and objectivity

Objectivity is another value that, it seems, is highly prized and desired by consumers and journalists. Consumers often complain that journalists are not impartial or objective, whilst many journalists are convinced not only that they should be objective, but that they are objective. As there are a number of words that are often used interchangeably in relation to objectivity, Exhibit 3.2 provides definitions of these terms.

## Exhibit 3.2 Impartiality and objectivity

**Bias or slant**. *The Concise Oxford English Dictionary* (1964) describes bias as prejudice. Its origin is from the game of bowls where the lop-sided construction of the ball gives bias – a twist in the path it follows. Bias, as used in this book, means the deliberate slanting of a story to favour one side of the argument rather than another on the grounds of the personal choice of the writer.

**Balance**. The idea that the journalist can and should present equally two sides of an argument.

**Comment**. An explanatory remark or criticism. 'Comment' in journalistic terms can range from the expert opinion of a correspondent to the unwarranted insertion of unsupported views.

**Objectivity**. In journalistic terms this means that the journalist should not let his or her subjective feelings or views intrude into a report. That which is objective cannot and should not contain that which is subjective.

**Neutral or impartial**. Taking neither side. This does not exclude subjectivity but necessitates that the journalist stands aloof from any decision-making.

**Prejudice**. A preconceived opinion. This differs from bias in that bias may slant a story without there being a preconceived idea. Prejudice is more likely to determine what information is gathered for a story while bias is more likely to determine how it is written and used.

**Fairness**. The idea that the journalist gives all sides of the argument a fair hearing.

Objective truth and journalistic impartiality may, at face value, seem to be suitable ideals and may also seem to be one and the same thing. However, it can be argued that not only are they different, and not especially desirable, but also they are probably completely unattainable. When we talk about objective truth, we should be aware that several concepts are involved:

- There is such a thing as objective truth in the abstract.
- The truth is capable of being reported objectively in a theoretical sense.
- The truth is capable of being reported objectively in a practical sense.
- What consumers actually want is objective truth in any case.

Many philosophers have argued about whether there is such a thing as objective truth. By using intuition or pragmatism alone we can usually arrive at some accepted idea of objective truth. 'There are words in English printed on this page' is a statement that is unlikely to cause a reaction more significant than a cautious nod of the head. There seems little cause for argument. There is a page, there are words; those who read English will recognise those words and that their use is consistent with English grammar and usage. The words now stand for themselves and your ability to understand what the words appear to represent is an objective truth.

However, it can be argued that this alone is an argument for there being no objective truth. My involvement in the message and the processes involved in your understanding of it means that the message contained in the words is entirely subjective. The truth of the existence of the message, assuming there to be one, has changed by being understood by you. But this is to ignore the physical evidence of the page and the print that can also be seen by others, even if they interpret the same message in a different way. In other words, the issue is whether there is any objectiveness in my meaning of the words, your understanding of the words or only in the imprint of the words themselves on the page.

We can say pragmatically, and with evidence, that the page exists. We can prove to other people that the page exists by showing it to them. However, that is the last objective truth we can show them. You cannot prove that the meaning you take from this page and these words is the same as the understanding I intended to give them or the same as the understanding someone else has. I hope that those understandings will be very similar, otherwise I have failed in my task as a communicator of ideas, but I would be foolish to think that I would have been able to transfer exact and identical understandings of a complex issue through anything I could write. I can only help present a perspective that would allow you to come to a closer understanding of how I view what is happening.

## Truth and impartiality

Judith Stamper, the former BBC news presenter and now a lecturer in television journalism, gave a lecture entitled 'Holding up the Mirror' to a media ethics conference in Leeds in September 1996. In it she claimed that the good journalist should hold up a mirror to the world to allow the viewer to see things as they really are. But it can be argued that this advice has two flaws. First, none of us see things in mirrors as they really are. We view ourselves according to our own prejudices. For instance, some will see a gorgeous creature smiling back, whilst those with lower self-esteem may see a less appealing reflection. Secondly, Stamper also makes the assumption that the reporter adds no distortions or unconscious changes to the image in the mirror. This is unlikely. Journalists may not deliberately remove a wart or minimise the grey hair, as some painters may, but they may concentrate on one feature more than another, or they may deliberately choose to minimise a feature which might otherwise add unnecessary confusion.

In his book, which sprang from the Leeds conference, Matthew Kierans criticises the view that objectivity is not possible, saying it has become 'increasingly fashionable, within cultural, media and even journalistic circles, to dismiss claims concerning objectivity' (Kierans, 1998: 23). He goes on to argue for impartiality, concatenating it with objectivity.

> Good journalism aims at discovering and promoting the audience's understanding of an event via truth-promoting methods. This is indeed why impartiality is important. For a journalist must aim to be impartial in his considered judgements as to the appropriate assessment of particular events, agents' intentions, why they came about and their actual or potential significance. A failure of impartiality in journalism is a failure to respect one of the methods required in order to fulfil the goal of good journalism: getting to the truth of the matter. (Kierans, 1998: 34)

He talks about objectivity in news reporting almost as an alternative word for impartiality. But the two are very different. Certainly a journalist who aims at the truth, and most commentators are agreed that that is what should be happening, would need to be impartial. But I hope such a journalist would not be so deluded as to assume that that means they would, or even could, be objective.

Hartley used Lewis's map analogy to explain his ideas about the interpretation of truth and meaning: 'A map organises, selects and renders coherent the in-numerable sense impressions we might experience on the ground. It does not depict the land. . . . Clearly a map is an abstraction from reality . . .' (Hartley, 1982: 15). A totally objective map would be so large as to cover the country it purported to map, inserting every feature to be found in the real thing and so becoming indistinguishable from the real thing. In order to use it as a map, it must reduce the detail and thus interpretation is needed. A road map of the UK may well be entirely truthful and useful to road users, but it would be of little value to someone walking in the Lake District where roads are sparse. The truth in any map is subjective because it is based on a decision-making process rationally reached by the map-maker to provide a useful map for a certain section of map users.

Like the map-maker, the journalist is never in the position of being able to present the whole picture. If a journalist is covering a plane crash, how much detail would he or she need to know about plane manufacture, safety testing procedures, production of aviation fuel, airport procedures, the private lives of passengers and crew members, the method of training pilots, and so on? The journalist has to draw a line somewhere or no copy would ever be filed. The instant a journalist decides that he or she has enough information to file a story, objectivity is out of the window; the editing process has begun and subjectivity is in. But that should not mean that impartiality goes out of the window as well, for that would mean the journalist abandoning the search for truth. There is a world of difference between looking for the truth and expecting to find it. Looking for the truth requires impartiality, reporting requires acknowledging you have failed to find it.

With newspapers and broadcast stations perpetually short of space, with time pressing on the reporter and the importance of getting the story as quickly as possible, there are a range of physical and practical problems which will prevent objective reporting. Reporters have to decide to whom they will speak and editors have to select what to publish in order to make deadlines and produce newspapers and news programmes.

Theodore L. Glasser offers some insight into the practical problems of objectivity. He believes that:

> Objectivity in journalism is biased in favour of the status quo; . . . against independent thinking; it emasculates the intellect by treating it as a disinterested spectator. Finally objective reporting is biased against the very idea of responsibility; the day's news is viewed as something journalists are compelled to report, not something they are responsible for creating. . . . Objectivity in journalism effectively erodes the very foundation on which rests a responsible Press. (Glasser, 1992: 176)

But it is Martin Bell who puts the case for the highly experienced practising journalist:

> I am no longer sure about the notion of objectivity, which seems to me to be something of an illusion and a shibboleth. When I have reported from the war zones, or anywhere else, I have done so with all the fairness and impartiality I could muster, and a scrupulous attention to the facts, but using my eyes and ears and mind and accumulated experience, which are surely the very essence of the subjective. (Bell, 1998: 16)

We also need to ask ourselves whether objectivity is what the consumer wants (see page 30). I am confident that the consumer wants the media to have made selections both in what stories are used and how they are used. Taking the above into account, it seems clear that anyone seeking practical objectivity in reporting has four areas of concern:

1 The pursuit of objectivity is biased in favour of the status quo.
2 The pursuit of objective reporting is biased against independent thinking.
3 The pursuit of objective reporting is biased against responsible reporting.
4 Objective reporting by its very nature is almost impossible and is in any case undesirable.

Let us look at why this is the case. First, the pursuit of objectivity is biased in favour of the status quo, such as the courts and public authorities, because that is where reporters inevitably tend to go when seeking stories (see 'logistics' in Exhibit 2.1). However, if we only give the views of the court and parliament, for instance, as being the objective truth, we only represent society from one point of view. It is a common failing of much reporting that only establishment or elitist sources are used.

Secondly, often this very limitation on the use of sources is seen as somehow being objective. The very act of attempting to be impartial leads some journalists to limit independent thinking for fear that using unusual sources or contacts would be seen as abandoning impartiality. How can a journalist use creative intellect to advance a story, make unusual connections or talk to different people to widen their readers' view of a topic and still remain objective? Surely this is just an admission that there is a wider story and that no one could ever get to cover it all. But the reporter who strives to be impartial and pursue the evidence of truth wherever it is to be found whilst understanding this does open the box to total and objective truth is bound to provide a wider truth. Martin Bell, perhaps one of the most successful and certainly best-respected journalists of his generation, says:

> . . . it is my experience that the campaigners and crusaders tend to find what they are looking for, ignoring inconvenient evidence to the contrary and the unstructured complexity of what is actually out there. Rather I have found it useful to do the opposite and seek out the unfavoured spokesmen of unpopular causes, whether the Afrikaners of South Africa, the loyalist paramilitaries in Northern Ireland, or the Serbs in Bosnia; they will often hold the key to a conflict and its possible resolution. (Bell, 1998: 16)

Thirdly, if a journalist is able to say 'it's not my fault, I have to report this story because my obligation is to provide impartial or objective reports', it can give a misleading impression to the consumer. It is quite common for a statement made by a person or group to be used as the basis for a story, despite the reporter knowing or suspecting that the information is misleading or even untrue. Many journalists do not want to risk destroying a good story by discrediting the statement, but use it on the grounds that it is a fact that the words were said, even if they are untrue.

Finally, trying to be objective is undesirable in that it tends to lull the reporter into writing only about what is immediately observable, using traditional and well-tested sources which are themselves supposed to be objective. When reporting a council meeting, for instance, one might think that by taking the argument for the motion, together with an argument against and the officer's briefing speech, and adding to it the outcome of the vote, this would result in a rounded impartial report. But of course this may not be the case. What if one of the speakers was mistaken, lying or simply speaking about the wrong agenda item? What if the officer's briefing was misleading because he or she was incompetent or corrupt? The article might well be objective about the debate, but it would be woefully inaccurate and misleading about the issue. It might also miss two or three much better stories that might have emerged if the reporter had been more concerned with presenting a full picture to the reader than an objective one.

There is also the view that objectivity is not even that desirable. Martin Bell talks of the journalism of attachment. This is not, he says, the same as campaigning or crusading journalism:

> By this I mean a journalism that cares as well as knows; that is aware of its responsibilities; that will not stand neutrally between good and evil, right and wrong, the victim and the oppressor. This is not to back one side or faction or people against another. It is to make the point that we in the press, and especially in television, which is its most powerful division, do not stand apart from the world. We are part of it. We exercise a certain influence, and we know that. The influence may be for better or for worse and we have to know that too. (Bell, 1998: 16)

Bearing in mind the duty to the reader to present truthful information, then, a journalist should endeavour to be fair (and therefore impartial in the sense of not taking sides) in his or her reporting, presenting to the reader a fair representation of what has happened, who said what, putting it into context and, where possible, a context of what is true, what is reliable and what is not. For instance, if a group called Smokers for Health existed and issued a press release saying that latest research, paid for by the group and carried out in their own laboratories, shows smoking not only to be safe, but positively beneficial to health, then objective reporting might require the publishing of this amazing revelation. A reporter determined to be fair and to present truthful information to the reader might dig a bit deeper, carry the same story but with additional information. He or she would add that Smokers for Health is funded by a cigarette manufacturer and carried out its research in an impoverished part of the world, paying its 'guinea-pigs' with resources such as food and water that were unavailable to the rest of the local population, and then leave the reader to decide why the survival rate for smokers was better.

## Balance and impartiality

While considering impartiality and objectivity we need to consider balance. Is this the same as impartiality (see Exhibit 3.2)? Journalists and the public often assume this to mean balance between the political parties, whether this is as simple as providing 30 seconds' coverage to each party, 100 words to all sides, or a little more sophisticated in terms of balancing over a period of time, an election campaign for instance. We must not forget, of course, that the Representation of the People Act 1983 places limits on broadcasters in that they must gain candidates' consent to broadcast and candidates retain 'copy approval' over what is broadcast about them. The Broadcasting

Act (1996) also requires broadcasters to be impartial on political programmes and in both these cases, some sort of arithmetical balance is what is required. That is, over the period of an election, each candidate in a particular constituency (local or national) should receive about the same amount of air time.

For the most part balance is difficult to achieve. This is the notion that both (or more) sides should have equal time and equal space to put their arguments. This balance, or fairness, is fine when two sides of the political divide are explaining their policies and the defects of their opponents' policies. But are we really suggesting in an article or report on child abuse that for every social worker or police officer talking about the problem we would have a child abuser extolling its virtues? If a journalist is reporting on a story that focuses on good and evil, should both sides get an equal share of neutral reporting? As we have seen, Martin Bell, now the MP for Tatton, believes not. Searching for the truth would certainly involve a good journalist talking to paedophiles or organisations supporting paedophiles, if such exist. Only by discovering the views of those so deeply concerned with the problem can we start to understand it. But I don't think anyone would suggest that the paedophiles' views should be put to balance the views of those who condemn paedophilia – only to help explain them.

Balance is not a juggling act between establishment sources. Whilst all the mainstream political parties are debating an issue from one point of view, is it either sensible or impartial only to cover those views? If all the major parties are in debate about which members of the royal family should be paid from the civil list, is impartiality about giving the different parties' views or is it about covering the view that no one should get anything from the civil list? Clearly, journalists need a wider concept than impartiality or neutrality in order to be fair to the consumers and to all those involved in the argument. Fairness, honesty and justice are required because these are the only concepts that allow journalists to look up to higher ideals than something as drab and unhelpful as objectivity. Objectivity, even impartiality maybe, requires diffidence, dispassion, an ability to step outside the society in which we live. Even if this were possible for a journalist, would anyone be interested in listening to or reading his or her reports?

## Morality and the consumer

Sometimes journalists will consider the consumer only when making 'moral' judgements. The argument is often put forward that a particular item has been published because the consumer wants to read it and therefore it must be accepted that it is morally right to publish. The reader has bought the edition of the paper or magazine and, because of the direct link between consumer and circulation, there is the proof that the newspaper was right to publish the item. However, the journalist or publisher is then upset when the decision to publish is attacked as immoral and tries to blame the reader for acting immorally by buying the product: if the consumer had not wanted this article, he or she should not have bought the publication.

This argument was raised in connection with the press coverage of the relationship between Diana, Princess of Wales and her friend Dodi Al Fayed, and the backlash against the press that followed their deaths. Max Hastings, the editor of the *London Evening Standard*, put forward the argument that editorial judgement was driven solely by market considerations. As news and photographs of the princess raised circulation figures, newspapers were right to publish them and would only cease when the public no longer wanted them. The late Sir David English, then chairman of the PCC Code of Practice Committee, considered that the public reaction against the press at that time was a warning: 'Public opinion . . . was telling us loud and clear that we needed to look to our laurels' (PCC, 1997: 15). The consumer cannot be blamed for buying a publication that contains material that is unethical for the following reasons:

- The consumer may be entirely unaware that the publication contains unethical material.
- Even when a consumer is aware that a publication contains material which is at the centre of moral controversy, he or she cannot be expected to make an ethical judgement until they have seen the article or pictures in question.
- A journalist uses the material knowing that many will be unable to resist buying something over which there has been so much fuss – if only to find out what everyone is talking about.
- The moral judgement about whether to use the material is the journalist's alone and is not a decision that can or should be shared with the consumer. The consumer's moral judgement that they ought not to be reading that story cannot encompass the moral judgement about printing the material in the first place.

As the case of the Princess of Wales illustrates, debates about morality often centre around the area of invasion of privacy. Journalists no longer debate whether it would be morally right to use this story or that image, but look merely at the commercial implications, as the view expressed by Max Hastings highlights. The question raised concerns whether more people will buy the paper than will be put off if a particular story or picture is published.

## Taste and decency

The whole topic of taste and decency is fraught with controversy. This is an area of censorship which, in a free society, sends up warning signals quicker than anything else. If an image or text is not used because it would offend a section of the public, where does this principle end? If it is permissible for editors and producers to decide against using this image or that quote, why is it wrong for governments to do the same thing? Judith Andre has some help here: ' "No one else has the right to decide what I can read" may work against governmental censorship; it will not work in areas where others are already and necessarily deciding among competitors for limited space' (1992: 78).

Anyone can set up their own publication and make their own decisions about what is or is not published in it – in theory at least, although there are laws to cover what may or may not be published in the area of decency and good taste in the UK. The Obscene Publications Acts 1959 and 1964, Race Relations Act 1976, Broadcasting Acts 1990 and 1996, Public Order Act 1986 and blasphemous libel as covered in the Law of Libel Amendment Act 1888 are just some of the laws which limit what may be published or broadcast in an attempt to avoid causing offence. Sexually explicit pictures and text are frequently edited in Britain because they are likely to offend. Pictures of death and violence are also handled with care for fear of upsetting consumers. However, people can be just as offended by the ideas some politicians put forward, so should these ideas also be edited to protect people? If not, why should there be protection from emotional offence but not intellectual offence?

Issues of taste and decency can be put under a number of headings: obscenity, sedition, blasphemy, violence, bad language, sex, explicit pictorial or video images (e.g. death), bigotry, nudity. In all the above areas, decision-making is tough for journalists, and indeed for many others in the arts and media. Is it right to use an image or an idea that would cause offence to consumers or audience? The Viewers and Listeners Association, a group led throughout the 1970s and 1980s by the vociferous Mrs Mary Whitehouse, believed that no images, pictorial or textual, that might offend their very traditional sensibilities should be used. They wanted to see tougher laws brought into force to allow government to censor such images. Their opponents take the ethical standpoint that all censorship is wrong and that all people should have full access to all information. Many pro-censorship moralists use religion as their ethic and the traditional view of family life inherent in the ethos of many religions explains their viewpoint.

Inevitably, there is another group of people who see things differently. They take a causalist approach and tend to be for or against censorship depending on whether they believe that images of a sexually explicit or violent nature are likely to corrupt and cause more crime or violence or the break-up of the family. They do not believe that using such images is either right or wrong. Only the pragmatic effect should be considered. According to Rajeev Dhavan and Christie Davies (1978) the intention of the journalist is irrelevant to causalists. They are only concerned with whether the article is likely to cause a bad affect. On the other hand, moralists are concerned with the author's intention because this could have a direct effect on whether the image is presented for morally sound reasons.

Whilst a moralist standpoint that there should be a law ruling out all images that are likely to offend is debatable, the vast majority of people in Britain tend to believe that there can be arguments made for using explicit images on occasion. This makes it almost impossible to work out a code of conduct for the use of nudity, describing or showing sexual practice, violence and death. The British Broadcasting Standards Council said in its Code of Practice:

> The words 'taste and decency' which provide the third area of its remit were broadly interpreted by the council in the first edition of the code. The past few years have deepened the council's understanding of them. It has, for example, considered a number of particular questions: the treatment in broadcasting of the survivors of disasters and their relations, the portrayal of disabled people; and the influence of racial, religious and gender stereotypes. (BSC, 1994: 8)

What might be acceptable on late-night television, if handled sensitively, might not be considered at all acceptable in the early evening. A pin-up nude picture of the sort carried by the *Sun* newspaper is considered by many Britons to be acceptable in a family newspaper, but carrying the same picture on a television commercial at 7pm would provoke outrage – and not just from the moralist minority. Furthermore, material that can be published without comment in the West would spark storms of protest in a Muslim country.

One way of measuring whether the consumer is happy is by sales figures, therefore many journalists start to equate the two together. Higher sales figures show the consumer is satisfied; therefore the decision to print, or not to print, was right both ethically and financially. Under the circumstances, journalists will often cease considering such problems as ethical tests and take each image, both pictorial and descriptive, on its merits, weighing it against the possible reaction of the consumer and any regulatory authority. Is the consumer going to feel better informed because of this image, offensive though it may be, or are they going to stop buying the newspaper? Is the regulatory authority likely to take action against the newspaper, or can they be persuaded that this story or image is part of an important truth-telling exercise? Whilst hardly anyone wants journalism to be a bland consideration of only those things with which we feel comfortable, this pragmatic approach to the use of image and text that might offend is fraught with difficulty. Whilst mainstream media outlets might well be taking sensible and balanced decisions, smaller circulation newspapers and magazines may not, as the following case study illustrates.

### Case study 3.1 Taste and decency

The *Sport* and *Sunday Sport* newspapers constantly use photographs of naked or semi-naked women in a way that many find offensive. Of course regular readers of these papers do not, and indeed they buy them precisely because they include such photographs. Therefore, if one considers providing such material to be their duty to the consumer and proprietor, journalists working on the *Sport* and *Sunday Sport* are ethically pure.

In contrast, compare the reaction to the women's magazine *Company* which ran a feature in 1995 about the pornography industry in the suburbs (*Company*, January 1995). This reasonably well-written, certainly unsalacious, article about suburban housewives who acted in pornographic videos for fun and profit was illustrated with explicit stills from the videos, with faces blanked out. It would have been possible to use photographs which showed the set-up just as well without being explicit but presumably the decision was taken to use pictures which would send the circulation soaring. The reaction was mixed. Sales soared but the main retailers, newsagents John Menzies and W.H. Smith, refused to stock the magazine that month.

What we have to recognise is that morality in any society is controlled by the whole society and not just sections within it. The *Sport* is well outside the norm that is acceptable to society as a whole and, whilst it is probably acceptable to allow some small deviation from the norm to specialist reader groups, the *Sport* probably falls too far outside this definition to be considered morally acceptable for its decision-making about the type of stories and pictures it uses. However, it is not just this area of the publication market that has problems. During the Gulf War, the *Observer* (3 March 1991: 9) used a picture (taken by Kenneth Jarecke) of a dead soldier in the turret of his burned-out tank. As an image it was upsetting and offensive, but it said much about the horror and brutality of war. There was much discussion before the picture was used. Only a broadsheet decided that its audience could handle the complex mixed messages contained in the image. No tabloid took the risk of upsetting a readership that was considered by them to be intellectually unable to deal with the image. The tank commander was Iraqi. It is unlikely that even the broadsheets would have risked using an image as offensive as the charred corpse of a British officer. According to John Taylor, no US paper used the picture either: 'The newspaper pushed an accusatory photograph of a burned man in its readers' faces. Yet forcing viewers to look at such a horrific picture, closing the gap between a distant action and its effect, is not enough to ensure its moral meaning' (Taylor, 1999: 182).

The teenage girl magazine market also came under fire in 1996 when Peter Luff MP proposed a private members' Bill (which attempted to limit what he saw as unnecessary sexual material appearing in magazines aimed at teenagers and young girls).

It led to the setting up of the Teenage Magazine Advisory Panel by the Periodical Publishers Association. This has issued guidelines for magazines to follow. The TMAP has not advertised itself widely and is seen by at least one researcher as ineffective: 'I have yet to meet a teacher or parent or journalist who has heard of it, even though it has now been in existence for almost three years' (McKay, 1999: 23).

So far I have tended to concentrate on the 'sex and violence' angle but bigotry, in the form of racism, sexism and blasphemy, can also cause offence and needs to be considered in the same way. It is important to remember that it is bigotry we should be concerned about and not the presentation of views that are opposed to our own and on which we may feel strongly. John Stuart Mill wrote about challenging true received opinion:

> Unless it is suffered to be, and actually is, vigorously and earnestly contested, it will, by most of those who receive it, be held in the manner of a prejudice, with little comprehension or feeling for its rational grounds. And not only this, but . . . the meaning of the doctrine itself will be in danger of being lost or enfeebled, and deprived of its vital effect on the character and conduct. (Mill, 1991: 59)

The BBC faces the problem of taste and decency more than most. As a public broadcaster it has to take the broadest possible view of its consumers and is therefore more likely to offend than almost any other medium. This is not because the BBC is careless or unthinking, but because more people are likely to be watching who will find they are offended by something. The BBC is required in the agreement associated with its charter not to broadcast programmes which 'include anything which offends against good taste or decency or is likely to encourage or incite to crime or lead to disorder, or be offensive to public feeling' (http://www.bbc.co.uk/info/bbccharter/agree_01.htm). The BBC says it seeks to apply this requirement to all its broadcasting, whether to a domestic or international audience.

> Taste and decency raise sensitive and complex issues of programme policy for the BBC. We broadcast to a much more fragmented society than in the past; one that has divided views on what constitutes good taste. People of different ages and convictions may have sharply differing expectations. Research suggests that while people have become more relaxed in recent years about the portrayal of sex and sexual humour they remain concerned about the depiction of violence. The use of language also divides the audience. Parents with children in the home are likely to be particularly concerned about what appears on the air. This applies especially when families are watching television before the Watershed. Many people expect to be given clear signals about what to expect, especially when new series or formats appear. These views deserve respect. (*BBC Producer Guidelines*, 1996: 05.htm)

The BBC goes on to say that while they must remain in touch with audiences, there are occasions when it is justified to run contrary to general expectations and challenge assumptions: 'The basic pillars of decency rest on telling the truth about the human experience, including its darker side, but we do not set out to demean or brutalise through word or deed, or to celebrate cruelty' (*BBC Producer Guidelines*, 1996: 05.htm).

Newspaper codes in Britain don't mention taste and decency. It is left entirely to the discretion of the newspaper or magazine. The Press Council used to entertain complaints about bad taste and found against the newspapers in question on several occasions. Importantly, nearly all of the complaints appear to be cases where the journalists involved had not thought through the full details and consequences of the material they were writing.

## Summary

- In most Western countries it is generally accepted that the press has a duty to inform the public of things about which it has a right to know.

- Journalists need to ensure that they report truthfully and minimise mistakes, but also that they do not sacrifice timeliness for accuracy.

- Many people think that journalists should aim for impartiality and objectivity. However, there are complex theoretical and practical problems involved and it has been argued that objectivity is impossible and undesirable.

- Journalists should consider the moral aspects of the stories and images they use. However, ethical considerations and the pressure to follow market-driven journalism and increase circulation often lead to a conflict of loyalty.

## Questions

1 The law is society's way of trying to enforce morality. Can you find examples of laws which enforce matters that British society no longer views as moral issues?

2 Find a newspaper story which you know quite well. Do you think the story is truthful and accurate? Under what circumstances will consumers accept inaccurate information?

3 Why might it be unfair to blame the consumer for buying a publication that contains material that is considered immoral?

# Chapter 4

## The press and the public

### Chapter outline

- This chapter looks at why it is important that the media has the same rights as individual citizens in the UK and how the freedom to publish is based on the right to free speech.
- It considers some of the reasons for putting constraints on the gathering of information by journalists.
- It outlines the problems surrounding the publishing of information.
- It looks at the difference between the quality of information provided by a journalist and that provided by general sources.

The rights to freedom of speech and access to certain information apply equally to the media as they do to private citizens. The press in the UK has always resisted attempts to make them different, partly because if the media were to have special privileges it might also be expected to have special obligations. However, this is not the case throughout the world and in some European countries journalists have special rights and special rights of access to information unavailable to the general public. In Belgium, for instance, journalists have special travel rights and cut-price telephone calls. In Portugal, journalists have special rights of access to government sources of information and a legal right not to be coerced into acting against their consciences, whilst in both Portugal and Italy, journalists cannot work for the media without being registered and obtaining a press card. France, Britain, Luxembourg and the Netherlands all have national identity card schemes in co-operation with the police. These are voluntary and you can operate as a journalist without them, but they do make working in dramatic situations such as demonstrations, riots and disasters much easier. The need for a free press in a free society was discussed in Chapter 3, but now we need to look a little closer at how this free press is intertwined with media ethics.

A free press is a privilege which needs to be handled with considerable care. People's reputations, possibly even their lives, could be at stake when journalists are probing into areas which, without the justification of the public interest, would normally be left alone. In such instances professional morality becomes crucially important. Without the concepts of freedom of speech and the protection of democracy a journalist would find it almost impossible to justify underhand methods of gathering information such as those involved in the *Guardian* 'cod' fax episode.

### Case study 4.1 Professional morality and the public interest

It would be naïve to suggest that every covert investigation carried out by a journalist could be completely justified by freedom of speech and the public interest. However, some stories of major public interest can only be exposed by using deceit or trickery. Long focal lenses and bugging devices, false identities and theft have all been used in order to obtain stories.

The *Guardian* newspaper, intent on showing that Jonathan Aitken, a Conservative MP, was corrupt, was trying to prove that Mr Aitken had stayed at the Ritz Hotel in Paris at the expense of Mr Mohammed Al-Fayed, the hotel's owner. Mr Al-Fayed, also the owner of Harrods, was co-operating with the newspaper and Mr Peter Preston, Editor in Chief of the *Guardian*, had no wish to reveal that he was the source of the information and had therefore breached client confidentiality. Instead, the *Guardian* sent a fax to the hotel on House of Commons notepaper, purporting to be from Mr Aitken asking about the bill.

Was the story worth the deceit? Peter Preston didn't think so later on when he apologised to the Commons Privileges Committee for sending the 'cod fax', saying it was a 'stupid and discourteous thing to have done'. 'The committee concluded that Mr Preston and the *Guardian* were "guilty of unwise and improper conduct"' (*Independent*, 25 January 1996).

Freedom of speech is an absolute; either you have it or you don't. If freedom of speech is removed in even the smallest part, it is removed almost in its entirety. Of course if I were to damage someone's reputation, then it is only reasonable that that person should be able to lay suit against me for damages. When we move into the area of publication, where a person's freedom of speech can reach a wide audience, other safeguards are felt to be required by society to limit what can be said to that wider audience. But otherwise, the free press is an extension of freedom of speech.

There are four main areas of a journalist's work in which professional morality is particularly important. They are:

- The limits that are placed on what information is gathered.
- The limits that are placed on how that information is gathered.
- The limits that are placed on what information is published.
- Guaranteeing the quality of the information that is published.

## Limiting what information journalists can gather

It is confusing and concerning that many people in Britain, and indeed in several other countries, appear to support freedom of speech and a free press whilst supporting censorship on specific matters. In a *Times/Mirror* Center (now the Pew Center) for the People and the Press survey taken in 1994 a worryingly low 52 per cent of Britons said they supported a free press (the lowest of all the countries surveyed). Yet 71 per cent of respondents in Britain favoured censorship to discourage terrorism, an even higher figure than those who would welcome censorship to restrict portrayals of explicit sex (72 per cent). Many might say this is because of the high levels of terrorism in this country, yet both Spain and Italy, which face similar problems, had much lower numbers of respondents calling for censorship (62 per cent and 42 per cent, respectively). (See Table 4.1 and Fig. 4.1)

The 1987–95 British broadcast ban, which prevented the broadcast of the voices of certain politicians, particularly those from Sinn Fein, the political wing of the Irish Republican Army (IRA), was a relatively thin edge of an

**Table 4.1 Support for censorship to discourage terrorism or displays of explicit sex**

| Country | Terrorism | Explicit sex |
| --- | --- | --- |
| Canada | 68 | 65 |
| France | 82 | 67 |
| Germany | 61 | 67 |
| Italy | 42 | 43 |
| Spain | 62 | 49 |
| United Kingdom | 71 | 72 |
| United States | 60 | 59 |

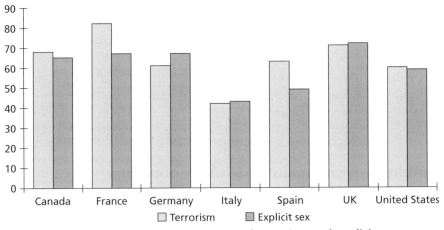

**Fig. 4.1 Support for censorship of reports of terrorism and explicit sex**

extremely dangerous wedge. Although there were many who believed that removing the 'oxygen of publicity' would stifle the IRA and therefore reduce the violence, there is no evidence that this was the case, indeed it defies logic. Violence is often the last resort of those who are otherwise unheard. Censoring the views and opinions of those who believe they have legitimate grievances or complaints is an almost guaranteed way of ensuring that they start using more direct and often violent methods. Extrapolating the broadcasting ban argument, it is a dangerously small step to move from accepting the principle that there are certain people in society who do not have the right to speak and be heard, to gagging anyone whose opinions are not welcome by the ruling group. To suggest otherwise is to live in ignorance of, or indifference to, the evidence presented by scores of tyrannical governments around the world who have imprisoned journalists, political opponents and others who have voiced opinions that were not welcome.

So, despite a worrying lack of support for free speech and a free press in Britain, they are essential to the free style of democracy that we all seem to favour, whether by choice or apathy, and, because of this, the journalist needs to take care that he or she does not step over the invisible mark that divides responsible reporting from licence to allow editorial choice to become censorship.

Should there be any limits set on the information journalists gather? The government certainly thinks there should and a number of laws are in place preventing journalists from researching stories involving some issues. The Official Secrets Act 1989 is one of these. The Act makes it an offence for a journalist to enquire into any government business that could be deemed sensitive without the approval of a minister of state. Of course, this is not the only law that governs what information journalists may gather. There are various Acts limiting the information a reporter may gather on crime. The Contempt of Court Act 1981, Sexual Offences (Amendment) Act 1976, Criminal Justice and Public Order Act 1994, Criminal Justice Act 1991, Criminal Evidence and Youth Justice Act 1999 and others all limit what information can be either gathered or published.

Inevitably, there are also ethical issues to be considered when gathering information and these can place limits on a reporter. They are mainly concerned with issues of privacy and intrusion. For instance, exactly how much information should a journalist be entitled to gather about an individual?

## Limiting how journalists gather information

There must also be limits to the way journalists obtain their information. For example, paying criminals for their stories is seen as unacceptable by the public in most countries. Society takes the view that criminals should not profit from their crimes and so the idea of a newspaper or broadcast station paying a criminal for his or her story is one that upsets many people. Intruding into private places, harassing people and deceit are also methods of obtaining information which are usually seen as unacceptable unless they are 'in the public interest', as the *Guardian* investigation into politicians taking free hospitality illustrates (see Case study 4.1 on p. 50).

## Limiting what information journalists can publish

There must be some limits on the information published by news sources in even the most free of societies. Protecting the honour of citizens, preventing excessive invasions of privacy and intrusion, protecting the innocence of those facing court proceedings are all rights protected under the UN Declaration of Human Rights, clause 12 and, if only for this reason, citizens expect state support for their rights. Most countries have laws of defamation and some, like France, have privacy laws. There have been defamation laws in Britain since the reign of King Alfred, who used to have the tongues of slanderers cut out. Countries which do not have laws about issues such as privacy (Germany, the UK and Sweden) usually have codes of conduct in these areas.

Many individuals and public figures have complained about excessive press intrusion into matters they feel should remain entirely private and, as Case study 4.2 shows, some have even called for tougher laws to protect their privacy.

### Case study 4.2 Privacy and press freedom

Earl Spencer, brother of the late Princess of Wales, began a campaign for tougher privacy laws after what he considered was intrusive press reporting about his marriage and the illness of Countess Spencer, his former wife.

In 1995 the *News of the World* published a front-page article saying that Countess Spencer was in a clinic. A photograph showed the Countess walking in the grounds of a clinic where she was receiving treatment for eating disorders and alcoholism. At the time a number of other tabloid newspapers also carried reports about the couple's marital problems.

The earl complained to the Press Complaints Commission, which later upheld his complaint and condemned the newspapers involved for their intrusive reporting. He then took his campaign for a tougher privacy law to the European Commission of Human Rights in Strasbourg. But the Commission rejected his attempt to take the British government to court, ruling that there were insufficient grounds for starting a case in the court over the government's alleged failure to protect the earl and countess under the European Convention on Human Rights. The Commission accepted the government's argument that British law provided adequate remedies to protect privacy and that the press code of conduct, monitored by the PCC, offered adequate safeguards to the right to privacy.

The rejection of the Spencer case means that Britain's law on privacy and press freedom will not be tested by the Strasbourg court. However, there have been recent developments that may change how complaints against the media are dealt with and these could have important implications for journalists. On 21 January 1998 Sir William Wade, a leading constitutional lawyer in Britain, told a legal conference that because of the Human Rights Act (which received royal assent in autumn 1998) people will now take the media to court over privacy claims rather than going to the PCC. This reinforces the view that the new law will lead to a privacy right being developed by the courts. At the time of writing, no one is certain how the Human Rights Act will affect the media.

Of course, the media should have some right to invade a citizen's privacy, provided there is a justification of public interest in the affair. This can be loosely defined as the public's right to know about something which is being done privately by someone and which is against the general or specific interests of society. This defence is considered in detail in Chapter 3.

## Guaranteeing the quality of information published

A journalist and his or her publisher must be answerable to their consumers for the quality of information that they provide. Clearly truth and accuracy have a part to play in guaranteeing the quality of information (see Chapter 3, p. 31). All journalists and editors have an obligation to be honest with their public about the quality of information provided. However, this guarantee of quality of information is not something that can be instantly provided and some news outlets can be considered more reliable than others.

The BBC World Service, for instance, has a superb reputation world-wide and when changes were suggested in 1996 these were strongly opposed by many who saw the new practices as damaging to the service's unrivalled reputation for unsensationalised, accurate and balanced coverage which had been built up in more than 50 years of broadcasting. BBC Director-General John Birt had planned to cut back programme-making drastically, whilst moving the radio newsroom to a combined newsroom in West London. This would have meant sharing with domestic services and therefore introducing a slightly different approach to the news-gathering. The move was opposed by the former World Service Managing Director, John Tusa, the novelist P.D. James, a Conservative peer and former BBC governor, John McCarthy, Mark Tully and Sir George Solti, to name just a few. A mass lobby was held outside parliament on 2 July 1996 (*Journalist*, August/September 1996: 9). Also in 1996, a sub-editor who was sacked from the *Sport* for allegedly making up quotes was reported in the *Journalist* (The NUJ's magazine) as saying that: 'We did this all the time. I have invented quotes for her often before . . .' (*Journalist*, August/September 1996: 8). The BBC World Service and the *Sport* can be seen as spanning the range of reliability in the British media, from a news service relied on by state leaders to one that is not taken seriously. Yet both have a place in the media market and both employ journalists who take their work seriously.

The decisions journalists make about the extent of their research, and the extent to which they correlate sources, depend on the needs of their audience. The quality of information they provide will vary depending upon the market and its requirements. For instance, readers of the *Sport* appear only to require titillation from stories that do not need to be honest, truthful, accurate or balanced. Their view of the world will only be changed peripherally by what they read and they are unlikely to base decisions of any importance on the stories and information contained in the *Sport*. However, even though readers are unlikely to believe any particular story, the continued diet of stories of a such a titillating nature about supposedly sexually-available women might damage their view of the world and be more likely to lead them to hold women in low esteem. Academics are still researching the notion that our view of normality is affected by what we see in the media, but most of the work is centred around fictional violence rather than supposedly factual stories. It seems to me that the debate about whether *Reservoir Dogs* or *Tom and Jerry* alter our views about the acceptability of violence is an entirely different one from whether a consistent diet of supposedly truthful stories about the sexual antics of other people affects someone's view of what is normal. Publications which do not rely on stories that are true and accurate are not confined to the UK. *Weekly World News* is an American publication that contains truly fantastical stories. Some of the greatest front pages include such shockers as 'Society matron commits suicide – after breaking wind at swanky dinner party' (*Weekly World News*, 26 November 1996: 27) and 'Doc throws up in heart patient's surgical opening – and kills her!' (*Weekly World News*, 22 November 1994: 19). Clearly, the journalist is giving the readers what they want and boosts circulation by so doing. The audience wants largely titillating fiction and that's what is provided. The quality of the information content is very low, but the entertainment value is high.

While this formula works reasonably well with extremes such as the *Sport* and the *Weekly World News*, the majority of news providers lie somewhere in the middle. They want to provide their audience with entertaining stories but they also want those stories to have credibility so that the consumer will continue to consider them as a competent supplier of news. It is here that the temptation grows to provide stories that are not as thoroughly supported by sources as they should be because they are entertaining to the target audience. For a paper such as the *Sun*, which is bought for its entertainment value rather than its ability to inform with a high degree of credibility, it is easier to print stories that are not so well sourced. For the *Daily Telegraph*, which draws an audience that requires a high degree of credibility to its information, an entertaining story that withstood only a cursory analysis would be very damaging to its sales. Its readers would soon switch to another publication if its stories were regularly proved to be wrong.

## Exhibit 4.1 Testing the credibility of news stories

There are two main ways that we can check the information we are given by news outlets:

1 We can test it against our knowledge, our experience of the outlet, and scepticism.
2 We can test it by accessing primary sources and checking the information.

For instance, if a tabloid newspaper reported that a Conservative Home Secretary was going to legalise cannabis, we might well, as readers, be sceptical. After all, the Conservative party has long supported the banning of drugs for recreational use. The paper that the story appears in does not have a good reputation for total accuracy and may well have distorted whatever element of truth there is in order to get a better story. However, if a broadsheet was running the same story, it would be more likely to make us accept the story. This is partly because we would be given more information from a wider range of sources, together with a more detailed analysis of the issue, which might well make the story more convincing. Perhaps the new Home Secretary is a libertarian from the far right of the party who believes there should be no restrictions on the sale of drugs provided their purity is assured.

Television and radio news would be able to go even further in convincing us to accept the story. A short introduction and a quick interview with the Home Secretary saying, 'I believe that making drugs illegal is counterproductive. It sets up a criminal sub-class and robs the Treasury of potential billions in excise revenue. I intend to legalise them all tomorrow and set up a drugs consumer bureau which will ensure the quality of all drugs on sale' might well shock and surprise the electorate but would leave no doubt about the veracity of information. It is the ability to hear, or see and hear, the prime sources that helps make broadcasting so potent in news reporting. Whilst we need to remain aware of the ability of the reporter to pick and choose the sound bites used, we are still able to confirm for ourselves that the words were used and we can make our own minds up about whether the person who spoke them was telling the truth and meant what he or she said.

The need to guarantee the information a source provides raises the following ethical issues for the journalist (these are considered in detail in the chapters indicated):

- Guaranteeing sources for information (Chapter 4).
- How those sources are reported (Chapter 8).
- The reporting of comment as fact (Chapter 7).
- Image manipulation, including video and film editing (Chapter 7).
- Playing fair with interviewees, e.g. using material on/off the record (Chapter 6).
- The selection of news (Chapter 8).
- Bribes and corruption of sources and reporters (Chapter 7).
- Protection of sources (Chapter 7).

It is important to remember that the issues discussed in this chapter will arise only in a democratic society which respects and values freedom of speech. In a country which no longer allows free speech and a free press there will be laws limiting the amount and the quality of information that can be published. What information can be gathered and published is already controlled for the journalist and editor. The only ethical consideration remaining to journalists working in such countries is how to regulate how the information is obtained. But this is really a sterile debate because with strict limits on what information a journalist can gather and what he or she can publish, how they gather it is not likely to be a problem area. The law has taken over the main duties of ethics. However, in a democratic society ethical considerations become an important aspect of the journalist's work. The driving force for the ethical debate within the media is to help journalists perform to the standards needed and expected by the culture in which they work, despite the restrictions laid down by the same culture, either directly by its social expectations or indirectly by government edict.

## Summary

- In the UK, the media has the same rights as individual citizens. However, in some European countries the press has special rights of access to information that is not available to the general public.

- Constraints are put on the gathering of information about some matters, such as those which would threaten the security of the country.

- There are many ethical problems surrounding the publication of certain information, such as that which has been gathered by invading the privacy of an individual or by deceit.

- It is the duty of journalists to be able to guarantee their information. However, there is a tension between providing entertaining stories and stories which have credibility and the journalist needs to gauge the requirements of his or her audience carefully.

## Questions

**1** Do you think journalists should have additional rights to ordinary citizens? Can you think of any dangers or problems that might result if journalists were to have special privileges?

**2** The Internet is a publishing medium which allows open access and reaches a very wide audience. What are the dangers of individuals who are on the Internet being able to publish their views as fact?

**3** Compare the stories published in tabloid newspapers (e.g. the *Sun*, The *Daily Mirror*) and broadsheets (e.g. the *Guardian*, *The Times*) on the same day. Can you identify the target audience for each newspaper? What do you think the target audience looks for in that particular newspaper?

# Chapter 5

················································································

# Professional morality

### Chapter outline

- This chapter looks at what is meant by a good journalist and how this concept varies according to which aspects of the job are seen as the most important.
- It looks at the variety of people and organisations to whom the journalist owes loyalty.
- It discusses some of the methods journalists use when producing stories and the basic patterns of working which underpin professional practice and ethical journalism.
- It looks at how regulatory bodies and other organisations deal with elements of unprofessional practice and some of the guidelines they produce.

What is a good journalist? As this chapter explains, there is no one answer to this question. The kinds of attribute that would be valued by colleagues would not necessarily be the same as those sought by the public or consumers. For instance, an editor would probably value reliability and the ability to produce exciting stories to a deadline. The reader, however, might think that above all a journalist should be highly principled and truthful, even though they appreciate the exciting or controversial stories he or she has written (see section on morality and the consumer, p. 42 in Chapter 3). How then does the journalist decide what is good journalism? Which aspects of a journalist's work are the most important? And how should journalists approach the stories they cover? We need to look at how journalists work in order to help explain why they take some of the decisions they do, and to offer ethical guidance that might help journalists improve their decision-making.

## What is a good journalist?

Some people have attempted to produce a definition of a good journalist. David Randall tells us there is only 'good or bad journalism' (1996: 1). Dismissing liberal journalism, Western journalism and a host of other adjectival journalisms, he goes on to produce a list that he claims describes the 'good' journalist. The list is too long to print here and it does little to help us to decide what a good journalist is, although it certainly contains a number of the functions that most people would happily ascribe to a 'good' journalist. Randall believes that this list is universal, and condemns the cultural differences that can easily be spotted between journalists across the world as being evidence of bad journalism. It seems to me that there are several definitions of a good journalist, depending on where you are standing in both a global and hierarchical sense.

If I were a newspaper editor employing a journalist, I would certainly have a firm idea of the qualities I was seeking in a good journalist. They would include:

- An ability to recognise a good news story.
- An ability to find dramatic and interesting stories.
- An ability to persuade people to talk to them about their experiences.
- An ability to take a good note.
- A willingness to work hard and put in long hours.
- An ability to write well.
- Punctuality.
- Trustworthiness and reliability.
- The ability to use the word processing system used by the newspaper.
- Honesty with their expenses.
- Someone who is cheap to employ.

If you look in the *Guardian* media section or the *UK Press Gazette* – the journalist's trade magazine – you will find jobs advertised for reporters that list many of these qualities, or at least imply them.

However, if we were to ask a newspaper reader what they would look for in a good journalist, we would see some different answers. So long as they found interesting, dramatic and truthful stories and wrote them up well, the average reader would be little concerned with the journalist's punctuality, knowledge of a particular computer system or his or her willingness to work long hours for poor pay. The people featured in the stories would seek yet a different set of qualities. They would want the journalist to be capable of taking a good note, to be accurate and to write well. They would also want punctuality, reliability and honesty. Of course prioritising characteristics can be in the journalist's best interest. Whilst an editor is never going to pay more than he or she needs for a journalist, one who combines workaday values such as reliability and punctuality with professional virtues such as the ability to track down a good story is more employable and is more likely to earn better pay.

Clearly, it is possible to produce a list of characteristics that a good journalist should possess, as David Randall has done, but it is up to each individual journalist to decide which of them are important and which should have priority. The journalist has a moral duty to decide which characteristics he or she will choose to display whilst doing their job and to make an evaluative choice about which qualities are more important. It is tempting to think that one can display a different set of values at different times: one set in the office for the editor and another out on the job with a contact. But this is not really possible. The drive to be loyal to an editor may make a journalist choose to sensationalise a story in order to make it seem more exciting and therefore more saleable, but this cannot be achieved whilst still pretending to choose accuracy for both the reader and the contact. A journalist can either satisfy a moral directive to be accurate or make his or her newspaper more marketable by building up a story beyond the point where accuracy can be guaranteed.

## Journalistic duty

Deciding to whom you owe loyalty is an important component of working out what you should do in any moral dilemma. Clearly, the journalist is working in a field in which there are a number of conflicting duties or loyalties. For instance, journalists have contractual duties as employees, they have professional duties, and duties of responsibility. It follows that the journalist's obligation to choose how he or she performs his or her work may depend on whom he or she feels most loyalty towards: the reader, the employer, and so on.

### The reader

Maintaining trust with readers means dealing fairly with them by providing them with the information they want in a truthful and timely manner. This raises a number of questions. How do journalists decide what information readers want? How do they ensure truthfulness? And so on. Since most of the moral components of the good journalist's approach hinge on loyalty and fair dealing, the journalist who deals fairly with consumers, refusing to trick them or lie to them, stands a better chance of behaving morally than a journalist who treats consumers with contempt.

### The editor

Find and produce stories that sell and which do not get the editors into trouble with consumers, complaints commissions, etc., and editors will be happy. Since keeping the editor happy is usually good for one's career, whether in terms of money, ambition or simply pleasanter working conditions, this loyalty may well take precedence over others.

## The advertiser

Advertisers will be upset when, having paid thousands of pounds for a major campaign in a newspaper or with a broadcast station, they find that the journalists on the same outlet are running derogatory stories about their products. Their objections inevitably get back to the editor and may be bad for business, and bad for the career of the journalist concerned. Although this loyalty rarely outweighs that to the reader or the editor, it does happen and we need to be aware of its potential to distort news selection and to limit the complete truthfulness of a report.

## The proprietor

The proprietor is not only concerned about keeping the advertisers happy but is also keen to boost circulation. He or she may also have private areas of concern (be they political, commercial, or private) that he or she would like to publicise or hush up. Rupert Murdoch, for instance, likes BSkyB satellite television to be promoted in other News International products, such as the *Sun*. He is also prepared to protect his commercial interests by refusing to publish things he fears might be damaging. Consider the refusal to publish a book by the former governor of Hong Kong, Chris Patten. Mr Patten had been commissioned to write a book, *East and West: The Last Governor of Hong Kong*, by one of Murdoch's publishers, HarperCollins. In January 1998, they told him that the first six chapters did not meet 'reasonable expectations' and also leaked a story to a Sunday paper that the book was 'boring'. Mr Patten sued for breach of contract and shortly afterwards received an unreserved apology and an undisclosed financial settlement. He has signed a new contract with Macmillan – not a Murdoch company. The *Daily Telegraph* reported:

> A joint statement issued by lawyers for both sides said: 'It should be publicly recorded that HarperCollins have unreservedly apologised for and withdrawn any suggestion that Chris Patten's book was rejected for not being up to proper professional standards or for being too "boring". They accept that these allegations are untrue and ought never to have been made' . . .
>
> An internal memo, disclosed by *The Telegraph* last week, made clear that the book was dropped at Mr Murdoch's instigation because of its 'negative aspects'. It has been widely assumed that he did not wish to compromise his satellite television interests in China by publishing trenchant criticism of the regime in Beijing. (*Daily Telegraph*, 7 March 1998)

The story was also an embarrassment for the Murdoch-owned *Times* newspaper which had not covered the story. Raymond Snoddy, the media editor of the paper, had to admit that the paper had made an unacceptable error in failing to report the row over the book.

> He said there had been no conspiracy and that he had not been 'leant on' to ignore the story that HarperCollins, the publishing house owned by Mr Murdoch's media group, abandoned plans to publish the book because it criticised China. But Mr Snoddy, widely regarded as one of Britain's most authoritative media journalists, said that the lack of coverage had inevitably resulted in his own reputation, and probably that of *The Times*, being damaged.
>
> He told Radio 4's Medium Wave programme that he believed it to be 'completely obvious' that the decision to ditch the book stemmed from the threat to Mr Murdoch's economic aspirations in China. (*Daily Telegraph*, 2 March 1998)

## Parliament and the law

A journalist should generally abide by the law and has a responsibility to parliament as the central law-making body. Parliament and the law, in theory at least, are the representation of the will of the people in the society in which journalists live. Of course this does not mean that journalists have to obey blindly. A healthy dose of scepticism for those in power and the laws they make can ensure that law-makers have always to justify what they do. But it does mean that journalists cannot behave morally without due regard to the laws and standards of the society in which they are working. Of course, this may mean different standards in different societies. For instance, a female journalist working in a Muslim country might need to change her Western style of dress to avoid offending the local people from whom she is expecting to obtain stories. This is a moral issue in the sense that it is good professional practice. It is much more difficult to get stories from shocked and outraged interviewees than those who merely think you are a slightly eccentric foreigner.

## Regulatory bodies

A regulatory body such as the Press Complaints Commission demands some loyalty, even more so if the body is voluntary and self-regulatory, as is the PCC. If journalists and editors ignored the PCC's codes and its judgements, the PCC would become an irrelevance. And as the PCC would be replaced by a statutory body, something many journalists and editors would not like, there are also political reasons for supporting it. The recent proposition that more people will take media complaints to court rather than the PCC (see Case study 4.2 on p. 53) will naturally have important implications.

## Contacts

Journalists need to deal with their contacts as fairly as possible, telling them who they are, what they intend to do and how they intend to do it. It is in the journalist's best interests to deal with contacts fairly. A contact who has been tricked will probably not speak to that journalist again. A journalist who abuses trust by printing lies or half-truths is not dealing fairly with the contact and is not a 'good' journalist. This is particularly true if the journalist has promised to keep the contact's name secret.

## Him/herself

It is important that a journalist is loyal to him or herself. If journalists are not clear about their reasons and motives for handling stories in the way they do, then work will eventually become very difficult. A journalist has personal desires and ambitions, and often dependants to whom he or she also owes loyalty. Working long hours, for instance, may well support the loyalty felt towards the editor and proprietor but would not be appreciated by a partner or children.

## Other journalists

Most journalists feel some loyalty towards colleagues working for the same employer. However, even journalists from other media or employers deserve some level of loyalty, whether that is expressed through membership of a union such as the National Union of Journalists, support for the NUJ's Code of Conduct, or is a more general sense of loyalty with members of the same profession.

Journalists work as a team, but in competition. They work with journalists for their own paper or broadcasting station but will be in competition with journalists from other outlets, or even, on occasions, from their own organisation. This means they will often do things to mislead other journalists or put them off the scent of the story. For instance, papers run what are know as 'spoilers' to ruin the circulation-boosting effect of an opponent's scoop. A journalist will rarely share information with another journalist, whether it is a contact, a direct quote or another piece of information. The exceptions are on a colleague-to-colleague basis in situations such as press conferences or sports matches where a moment's inattention can mean missing what has happened. Journalists who know each other will then often help each other out. Refusing to share information with a competitor is justifiable provided you do not expect help from them in the future.

Technology has helped change some of the more competitive aspects of journalism. The days when fighting to get your hands on the only telephone was an important part of the job have gone. Lines of communication remain very important to journalists but, with the arrival of the mobile phone, it is no longer necessary to queue up to phone copy over the only working public telephone within a ten-mile radius.

## Professional practice

There are some basic patterns of working that underpin ethical journalism. They are not about the big issues, such as invasion of privacy, or truth, but more about fair professional practice. Good journalists will be aware of these aspects of their work and will understand the implications of how they deal with them.

### Sensitivity

A journalist needs to be sensitive both when gathering stories and when writing them up for publication and the journalist who is anxious to avoid unwitting offence will generally perform better as a journalist than one who does not. Dealing sensitively with those who have been bereaved, voted out of office, sacked or made bankrupt is an important professional function and therefore one that a good journalist has a moral duty to strive for. However, a journalist will sometimes use the appearance of false sensitivity as a technique to ingratiate him or herself in a way that is itself dishonest and therefore morally dubious.

### Meeting people

Most journalists work hard at being personable. They discover early on that being liked is an important part of gaining people's trust and getting them to talk openly. Journalists in television dramas are often portrayed as blatantly nasty, untrustworthy characters. This is far from reality. Who would talk to such a person? Even the rottenest journalists, provided they have any professional ability at all, can produce a veneer of friendliness, and many of the best have considerable charm. It is usually their interest in people that has drawn them to this career in the first place. The gap between fact and fiction works in the journalist's favour here. Those who do not deal often with the media expect a journalist to be sly and seedy and are pleasantly surprised by the personable character they meet and find it difficult not to say more than they intend. Journalists are trained to be friendly, to put people at their ease – it is an important professional skill.

### Causing offence

A journalist should always be aware of the risk of causing offence, whether it is through poor choice of language or sentence construction, or too detailed an approach to the subject. Sometimes a journalist may be reporting on an issue that is likely to cause offence. For instance, trying to alert readers to the horrors of war by printing horrific, shocking photographs could cause offence and the journalist needs to be sure the offence caused is not an end in itself (see the discussion about the reporting of the Gulf War in the Case study 3.1 on p. 46).

What upsets consumers will, of course, vary from media outlet to media outlet. What is acceptable in the *Daily Telegraph* would not be acceptable transmitted on the BBC six o'clock news. The *Telegraph*'s readership is generally intelligent, mature and well-informed. It would not be so easily shocked by detailed descriptions of offensive material, provided it was dealt with unsensationally. The mixed audience of all age groups watching the six o'clock news on television needs to be handled more delicately. For example, in 1995 Rosemary West stood trial for torturing and murdering a number of young women, including her own daughter. The details were so shocking and horrific that the jury, court officers and many reporters required counselling to get over it. The details of the case were not reported extensively on the television news. Even the tabloids carried little detailed evidence of the trial. However, the *Daily Telegraph* carried a considerable amount, certainly enough to give readers a flavour of the true horrors: for example see issues for 11 October 1995; 31 October 1995; 22 November 1995. News editors had to spend a lot of time deciding just how much detail to carry about the trial to give a true picture of the horrors without offending consumers.

Television and radio tend to carry the least detail about stories that are likely to offend because it is more difficult for people to control what is let into their home through these media. National newspapers have to be purchased by the consumer, but even so the tabloids tend to carry little detail because their audiences are much wider and therefore more open to being offended. The broadsheets take a different attitude, but even they rarely put stories such as the West trial on the front page. If they do, it is to use a sanitised version pointing to a fuller report inside. Free newspapers have a similar responsibility to television, since they are delivered to the home without the reader having any choice in the matter.

### Case study 5.1 The publication of offensive material

A case that was taken to the Press Council in 1984 illustrates the point perfectly. The *East Grinstead Observer* carried a front-page report of a court case about a man who had indecently assaulted his seven-year-old step-daughter. A complaint was lodged that the paper had included unnecessarily explicit detail about the case, rendering it offensive. The complainant was particularly upset as the newspaper was a free paper delivered 'unrequested, through his door'. The Press Council agreed that the

report was offensive and upheld the complaint: 'In the Council's view, it is imma-
terial in this case whether the report appeared in a free or in a paid for newspaper.
The Council agrees that the report published prominently as the paper's front page
lead included unnecessarily explicit detail of an indecent assault. The publication
was particularly offensive as the victim of the assault was a seven-year-old child'
(Press Council, 1984: 167) (see Appendix 1, clause 7).

In another case, a complaint was brought against the *Caterham Comet Leader* which
was also upheld. Details of the condition of a man's body found in a wood, reported
in the *Caterham Comet Leader*, were distasteful and distressing. The account published
would have been tasteless and unnecessarily offensive in any type of newspaper but
was particularly so when published in a free newspaper. In such circumstances, an
even greater degree of care and discretion than usual is required of an editor when
deciding whether to publish material which may be offensive. Publication in this case
was an error of judgement. The Press Council welcomed the editor-in-chief's recog-
nition of this, his letter of unreserved apology to the complainant, and his decision
later to publish an apology for the report (Press Council, 1990: 196).

## Interviews

Interviews always require a professional approach. As stated earlier, a journalist has a loyalty to contacts and must treat them fairly. The only exceptions to this that might arise are when subterfuge or deception are the *only*
way of getting a story which is in the public interest (see Chapter 4, p. 50).
The Press Council dealt with such a case in the early 1980s (Press Council,
1984: 188). 'A reporter was justified in posing as a Nazi sympathiser to expose
the activities of a member of an extremist organisation,' it decided after a
complaint was made that a reporter had obtained an interview by subterfuge
for a *News of the World* story headed 'Teacher leads double life as nasty Nazi'.
The reporter said he called at the home of the subject of the article 'posing
as a fellow Nazi, and asked if he (the complainant) could provide contacts
for a trip to Germany'. He told the Press Council that he had paid the visit
because he had received a report that the complainant had taken over as
international liaison officer of the League of St George.

   In another case in the same year, the Press Council decided that subterfuge
was not justified. The *Daily Mail* ran a feature about the Teachers for Peace
organisation and other peace campaigners calling it the 'School's most
sinister lesson'. Whilst the Press Council supported the *Daily Mail*'s right to
criticise the teaching of peace studies in schools, it did not support its
reporter's use of subterfuge:

> Its reporter wrote that he posed as a left-wing English teacher in order to obtain
> information from the Teachers for Peace organisation. The Council has said

consistently that journalists' use of subterfuge can only be justified in pursuit of information which ought to be published in the public interest and only when there is no other reasonably practicable method of obtaining or confirming information. The council is not satisfied that there was no other reasonably practicable method of obtaining such information about Teachers for Peace as the *Daily Mail* got in this case. (Press Council, 1984: 208)

In a majority of cases a journalist should be both fair and honest with interviewees. Most people are not used to being interviewed whereas most journalists are skilled and experienced at interviewing. There are, however, some people, politicians for instance, who are experienced at being interviewed and have a few tricks of their own. An inexperienced, local reporter interviewing a Cabinet minister could use every trick he or she had learned without being able to take unfair advantage of the politician. However, since a local paper is likely to support the status quo, there probably wouldn't be much point in hammering the minister anyway – the paper would be seeking an interview with a celebrity visitor rather than the grilling of a Cabinet minister. Only if there were a local campaign under way about a major issue would a local reporter normally take a minister to task, and then most streetwise politicians steer well clear of such places until the campaign is over. For instance, a town that is reeling from the closure of a defence establishment with the loss of hundreds of jobs is unlikely to receive a visit from any Cabinet minister, never mind the ministers for defence and employment, for some time after the announcement.

Behaving fairly to interviewees requires journalists to make it clear from the start who they are, whom they represent and their reasons for quizzing the interviewees. Good professional practice will mean putting interviewees at their ease, talking them through the situation and making it clear that notes or a tape recording will be taken and seeking their approval for this. For a broadcast interview this is a two-stage process. First, talking through the issue with the interviewee, collecting the facts and deciding on what line to take for the recorded interview and preparing the interviewee. The second stage is recording the interview. Even audio-taping an interview can be an ordeal for the inexperienced, but a television interview with a camera operator, sound technician and interviewer can be a real trial. Good professionals will do all they can to put interviewees at their ease and thus allow them to put their case in the way they want.

One of the huge advantages that broadcasting has as a news medium is the ability not just to transmit people's words, but their demeanour and, to a certain extent, their personality. It is a matter of professional morality to ensure that the interviewees are given the opportunity to present themselves in an accurate light. This does not mean that the reporter needs to alter the image in an attempt to improve it. If, for instance, the interview is with a farmer about farming issues, then interviewing the farmer in his working clothes out in the field or farmyard would be accurate and give the viewer a rounder picture. But to interview the same man in the same position just after he has been elected president of the area Rotary Club would be to give a different impression and it would be important to give him the opportunity to change clothes and setting if he wishes. Only by taking care over these matters can a journalist be sure that he or she is being as truthful as possible with the audience. For a newspaper journalist, this is not so important as the interviewee is not seen. But if pictures are taken, then the same thing would apply.

It can be reasonably assumed, provided all this is done, that the interviewees are happy to see their names and what they say in print or broadcast. There is no need to confirm that they are prepared to go 'on the record' (see below). Provided a reporter has correctly identified him or herself and the reason for the interview, it can be assumed that the interviewees realise that they could end up in the newspaper. Occasionally, however, a reporter may be aware that there are good reasons why interviewees might wish to remain anonymous. Perhaps they are talking about drug dealers setting up in their neighbourhood or perhaps they have committed a crime themselves. In these circumstances, in order to be fair to the interviewees, the journalist should specifically check that the interviewees are happy to have their names used in any published piece.

Sometimes interviews are only given under certain terms and conditions. These place the journalists under a moral obligation to use the information they have gathered only in the way the interviewee has stipulated.

***On the record***. This means that the interview is open and that anything said can be used with the name of the person who said it. It does not mean that quotes can be adjusted to suit the journalist, or that they can be made up. It does mean that things said can be used verbatim or edited to suit the length and style of an article. A journalist is not obliged to use full utterances, but the chosen extracts should be a fair representation of what was said and what was meant and presented in the order that it was said. Often in an interview, people are nervous and their tongues play tricks on them that their brains did not mean. If an interviewee, for instance a politician, were to say something that seemed to support an opposite viewpoint, then it is important that the journalist should check that is what he or she really meant in order to play fair with the interviewee and be honest with the consumers. It would also be wrong to mislead the interviewee about the journalistic status of the interviewer unless there were some overriding reason of public concern involved. A journalist keeping his or her identity secret in an interview can rarely be justified.

**Off the record**. Off the record is an increasingly popular way for those in official or semi-official positions to communicate with the media. Many public servants in such areas as health, education or social services are concerned about developments in their fields and wish to speak out. But they may be afraid to do so because they fear losing their jobs, or making things difficult for themselves. By speaking off the record they can alert reporters to a situation without specific quotes being used or without them being named. Reporters do not have to agree to an off-the-record interview. Often the information is already in the public domain and reporters are only after confirmation and comment. However, sometimes the information cannot be obtained from another source. In such cases journalists should only agree to an off-the-record interview if they are confident they can keep to their side of the bargain, that is promise not to reveal the interviewee's name in print or a broadcast. Of course, if reporters say no to off-the-record interviews, then it is up to the interviewees whether they give any further information, and up to the reporters whether they continue to seek information from the interviewees. Sometimes interviewees will say at the end of an ordinary interview: 'Oh, that was off the record of course.' Clearly it is not right for interviewees to introduce different terms to the way the interviews are being handled *after* the interviews have taken place and the journalists can be morally justified in saying: 'Tough, I'm using it.' However, since this would mean upsetting contacts, the journalists may well need to take a more sanguine view and pick up the interviewees' requests or at least negotiate a compromise. Morally, the reporters are not bound by the late request. Practically of course, they may find it politic to oblige.

**Non-attributable**. This is slightly different to off-the-record statements and is used a lot by politicians and royalty. It leads to such tags as: 'A Whitehall spokesman said . . .', 'A close friend of the princess said . . .', 'An influential member of the Party said'. What the interviewees said can be used in full, but their names must be kept secret.

In the House of Commons lobby, this method allows politicians to talk to journalists without risking their political careers. They can leak information without it necessarily being blamed on them. The main lobby is the twice-daily briefing by the Prime Minister's Office at 10 Downing Street, although other departments and ministers also use the lobby on occasion. Only accredited journalists who are prepared to accept the tight conditions laid down by the Downing Street Press Office are allowed to attend these briefings. The system is controversial with its detractors, who claim that journalists taking part become part of the system they should be criticising. Supporters say it allows them access to information and opinion from important sources they would otherwise be denied. The government finds these lobby briefings useful as it allows ministers to 'fly flags'. This means the minister can suggest that government intends to do something without the source of the information being known. The politicians can then gauge reactions to the idea before deciding whether to make the plan public or to deny it altogether. The lobby can also be used to attack politicians on both sides of the House. Sir Richard Wilson, the Cabinet Secretary, took the unusual step in June 1998 of revealing that he had warned Tony Blair's Press Secretary, Alistair Campbell, to tone down political activity in the lead up to the local elections that year in order to prevent civil servants being dragged into a slanging match with the opposition.

> Sir Richard described Mr Campbell as a 'free bird' who was able to present Government policy in a party political context, unlike civil servants who are constrained by the traditional Whitehall code of impartiality.
> Having monitored the notes of twice-daily lobby briefings for parliamentary journalists, he believed none of the material suggested that Mr Campbell 'comes anywhere near attacking the opposition'. (*Daily Telegraph*, 17 June 1998: 1)

The lobby system has at various times been condemned by journalists and politicians. It can lead to a lack of responsibility on the part of politicians. A politician can leak a story, gauge the reaction and then confirm or deny the story's truth later. This is a useful tool for governments, particularly those with slim majorities. It is also useful to unscrupulous journalists who can provide quotes without having to justify them and without anyone being able to complain of being misquoted. At its worst it allows journalists to take a story and use it uncritically because it is difficult to follow through a story that is not attributed to a source. Such stories can be difficult to attack or defend, prove or disprove. Several attempts have been made over the years to end the lobby system. The *Independent* refused to join when it was first launched but had to review its position later. Although most people agree that the lobby system is far from ideal, no one has yet come up with an alternative which is able to offer all the benefits to both sides afforded by the present system.

## Note-taking

Note-taking is an important attribute of a good journalist. It is certainly important for a journalist to be able to guarantee that what is written as a quote is in fact what the person being interviewed said. Being able to prove it could become very important if the interviewee were to challenge what was eventually published. Fast, accurate note-taking, often in the form of shorthand, is essential if a journalist is going to be able to fulfil the various ethical requirements of the accurate journalist.

## Quotes

The quotes the journalist uses to support a story are the only true record of an interview or report. Watched on television or listened to on the radio, the consumer can be confident that what is heard (supported by voice intonation and facial expression in the case of television) gives them accurate information. A newspaper or magazine is at a disadvantage (in the confidence stakes) because it cannot show, in the same way, that its reporting of the person's words is accurate. For this reason, as well as all the moral arguments about truth-telling, it is important that quotes are dealt with scrupulously. This does not mean that the whole of a twenty-minute interview must be transcribed. Although it is a technique used occasionally in magazines, almost everyone benefits from a little editing. What is important is that quotes are used both accurately, appropriately and in correct chronological order. Mixing and matching what someone has said to put words in a different order, or to cut qualifying phrases away from the main sentence, is to cheat the interviewee. For instance, a union leader who says 'I will have to consult the membership but I believe we will be on strike from next week' is entitled to be angry if he is quoted as saying 'We will be on strike from next week'.

Editing and chronological order are as important as accurate reporting. However, that does not mean that we should not improve people's grammar. What is said in a heated and emotionally-charged situation might sound fine but would look terrible in print. For example, 'The copper just stood there and didn't do nothing to save him' is just the kind of phrase a witness might use, but it could be transcribed to 'The copper just stood there and didn't do anything to save him'. Exchanging the 'nothing' for 'anything' corrects a common grammatical mistake which is barely noticed in conversation but in print makes the speaker seem ill-educated. Changing the 'copper' would, I think, be taking it too far. This word is widely used, so there is no problem about comprehension, yet its choice by the witness says something about the witness's views of the police, and his or her position in society. It helps us gain a better picture of what is going on. A reason for using direct quotations from witnesses is that an accurate report says much more than what they wanted to tell us. Their choice of language and phrasing can help us decide how much we believe them.

Journalists often use the trick of saying: 'Well, would you say that . . .' and then, if the interviewee agrees with what they have said, go on to use it as an original quote. Providing that journalists are aware that putting the interviewees' views into their own words sacrifices accuracy for a sharper sound bite, then it may be a fair exchange. It is a judgement only journalists faced with an inarticulate witness can make.

## Research and cuttings

The pressures on journalists to be more efficient and cut costs has led to an increase in the use of telephone interviews, instead of talking face to face, and the use of press cuttings libraries for research. Although these methods can be useful to overworked journalists working to tight deadlines, the PCC felt it necessary to include a warning about them in its March 1992 report. In relation to cuttings it said:

> Cuttings are an essential part of newspaper research but too many journalists now seem to act in the belief that to copy from 10 old stories is better than to write a new one with confirmation by proper fresh enquiry. In one instance . . . a magazine admitted that because it had been unable to contact a woman who had been attacked by her husband some months previously, it wrote up the story on the basis of newspaper reports, inventing dialogue to put the story into the magazine's style. The result was an article that contained serious inaccuracies and was to a degree fictitious. (PCC, 1992: 2)

In relation to telephone interviews it warned:

> In one article the reporter said of the interviewee: 'Watching her, sitting up in bed . . .' when in fact the reporter had never visited the house. This led the reader to understand that the reporter had been invited into the person's house when in fact what really happened was that a short and somewhat reluctant telephone interview had been given. (PCC, 1992: 3)

The PCC editorial went on to say that such practices could give rise to complaints under clause 1 of the Code that requires newspapers not to publish inaccurate or misleading material.

### Case study 5.2 Journalistic methods and bad practice

Many of the issues discussed above are raised in the 1989 annual report of the Press Council which contains several examples of bad practice. One case concerned the *Daily Mail*. In trying to find information about a reported murder, journalists resorted to telephoning houses near the village murder site at random. Since the call to the complainant came at 1.40am, he was understandably upset, particularly as there was no reason to suppose he knew any more about it than anyone else. The Press Council adjudication said: 'There are rare occasions when a newspaper may be justified in disturbing someone by telephone in the early hours with a request for comment or information. This was not one of them. Such conduct is tolerable when a story is important and urgent, and when the person telephoned is known to be directly connected with the story being covered or, say, an official spokesman. There is no such justification in this case' (Press Council, 1989: 205). In this instance the paper apologised to the complainant.

In another case, a former borough councillor, who had written to a paper, found his letter used as though it were an interview. No contact had been made with the complainant, although the *Milton Keynes Citizen* said it had tried. The Press Council agreed that it was wrong to use statements from the letter without further reference to the writer, giving the misleading impression that he had been interviewed. If the report had made it clear the comments were made in a letter, the readers would not have been misled and there would have been no breach of ethics (Press Council, 1989: 204).

A more recent case of the misuse of an interview occurred in 1998 when the *Sun* newspaper went one step further in misleading the reader. In January 1998, it published a piece about a mother who gave birth at the age of sixty and described it as written by Lord Winston, the eminent Professor of Fertility Studies (*Sun*, 23 January 1998). The following week the paper published an apology in which it admitted that a reporter had spoken to Lord Winston but the article was not written by him (*Sun*, 29 January 1998: 2). To attribute the article to Lord Winston was clearly unprofessional and highly unethical.

## Use of language

Journalists have a professional and moral duty to ensure they use language precisely and carefully. It is very easy to offend people or distort the truth by the poor use of language. The wrong word, an ill-chosen phrase can put a slant on something that might not be intended. Journalists can never use the excuse that they did not mean what was written; their tools are words and they must ensure they use them well. There are numerous examples of the use of offensive language in the Press Council's annals. The Press Council, for instance, made it a rule that the word 'poof' was offensive and should not be used (Press Council, 1990: 189). In another judgement they ruled that the word 'chinky', as a reference to people of Chinese origin, was offensive and should not be used in newspapers (Press Council, 1990: 193). The then editor of the *Star* (which had used the word in a headline), Brian Hitchin, argued that most people thought the headline was very funny. However, the Press Council upheld the complaint: 'The *Daily Star*'s headline was superficially an amusing play on words and rhyme but its use of the derogatory term "chinky" was offensive and is happily outmoded. The temptation to use it should have been resisted' (Press Council, 1990: 193).

Many words of this sort are offensive to different groups in society and the good journalist needs to be aware of this. To use such words in a deliberate attempt to offend or be provocative is one thing, but to use such a word without thought and be offensive by accident is unprofessional. There are a wide range of words and phrases that require care. Racist and sexist language, religious niceties, slang, bad language, sexual and anatomical words should all be thought about before use (see Appendices 1 and 2). How would readers feel about the use of such language? It may be fine to use bad language in a magazine aimed at a readership that expects it (for example, a magazine aimed at young men, such as *Loaded*) but probably not in a local newspaper where readers do not expect to read such language. The BBC issued new guidelines to employees when separate legislatures were introduced for Scotland and Wales. It was concerned with the detail of language surrounding nationhood and its likelihood to cause offence. It warned: 'Words like "nation", "country" and "capital" can be interpreted differently by different audiences. . . . It is better that programmes which are broadcast throughout the United Kingdom talk about things happening "across the United Kingdom" or "UK-wide" when that is what they mean' (BBC, 1999: 5). The guidelines go on to warn against using England and Britain interchangeably.

Pronunciation is as important as language use for broadcasters and can cause offence just as easily. It is important to check you have the right pronunciation.

## Making promises

A journalist should be aware that making a promise binds him or her to a course of action. However, the temptation is often there to agree to do something in order to make life easier. For instance, an interviewee will often ask to be sent a copy of the newspaper in which the interview appears, and the easy course is to agree. However, keeping a check on when a particular article appears and sending it on can be more irksome than it sounds and so a journalist would be well advised to refuse to promise to send a paper.

*Vetting copy*. Reporters are sometimes asked by interviewees to provide them with a copy of the report for checking.

If a reporter agrees to telephone someone and read back the copy, or put a photocopy in the post, that reporter has abrogated editing responsibility to the interviewee. No matter how firmly the journalist tells the interviewee that he or she cannot change a word, inevitably there will be words that the interviewee insists should be changed – the interviewee may claim they are wrong or give a bad impression. The journalist may say that the piece was only offered for checking, but can hardly complain when alterations are offered. In any case, checking is the journalist's job and he or she cannot pretend that a piece is accurate and fair if the piece is to be shown to one or more of the people interviewed before publication. Not to take up the changes asked for would be to invite legitimate criticism. In a Press Council case, the *Daily Mail* had a complaint upheld against it for failing to honour an undertaking. 'As a result of the failure to honour the undertaking the article included items of a highly personal nature which the complainant found offensive, although the intention of the article was to be sympathetic' (Press Council, 1978: 114). The Press Council was here condemning the failure to honour a promise, but it was a promise that should never have been made. Showing the copy to an interviewee is a tacit admission that the piece is Public Relations and not journalism.

*Covering stories*. Promises are often sought about the use of stories. Court cases are a good example where journalists are often approached by people accused of committing a crime, or their relatives, and asked to keep a certain story quiet. However, journalists' loyalty is not to the accused but to the editor, the reader and society in general. Therefore, any approach made to a journalist about a story should be referred to the editor and it should be the editor's decision whether copy is used or not. This is doubly true if a bribe is offered, threats are made or the journalist is somehow personally involved. To allow these considerations to influence whether to submit a story would be highly unprofessional. Some editors are so concerned about undue pressure being brought to bear that they will automatically use such a story even if they wouldn't normally have bothered. Because this is the case, many experienced reporters will advise distressed relatives not to contemplate suppression; that they should contact the editor if they feel they must but that their chances of non-publication would be much better by leaving the matter to the lottery of space and news values. I see nothing wrong with journalists using their knowledge and experience of the system to advise those in distress, provided the reporters then go on to write up the story as though nothing had happened and file it in the normal way. Failing to file the copy would be unethical, unprofessional and could well be a disciplinary offence if discovered.

## Embargoes

Organisations sometimes place restrictions on the publication of their press releases. For instance, government departments often release lengthy documents to the media before the official publication date to give them a chance to read and digest the contents. In return, journalists are expected not to use the material until the date given on the embargo. For instance, the New Year's Honours List is published at the start of the new year, but the list is issued to the media around 20 December. This allows journalists to contact the people on the list for interviews and pictures before the Christmas holiday break – a time when many of the award recipients will be unavailable and when many journalists are also on holiday, leaving skeleton newsrooms to do the work. The embargo lets the newsrooms do the work when the reporters and recipients of the award are available.

Neither the PCC (which embargoes its own quarterly reports) nor the NUJ has specific clauses on embargoes but both have clauses specifying that journalists have a duty to maintain the highest professional and ethical standards. It is unlikely that an embargo complaint would be considered by the PCC but one was dealt with by the Press Council in 1989 when the *Gateshead Post* and *Times* (24 April 1989) broke an embargo by publishing the news that a local firm had won the Queen's Award to industry. The company told the Press Council that it had not been allowed to tell its workforce of the award and the publication of information in a press release a day early was not good for worker moral. The company had intended to break the good news to its workers on the day agreed. The newspapers said that the embargo was inadvertently missed, but the managing director of the company said he did not believe that because it was printed plainly at the start and end of the press release. The Press Council upheld the complaint (Press Council, 1989: 214).

All press releases should be checked for embargoes and any decision to breach them should be considered very seriously. A paper or broadcast station that continually ignores embargoes risks not receiving press releases in advance. Since this facility is often to the advantage of the media, common sense suggests that embargoes should be adhered to unless there are good reasons not to, such as an embargo being used to prevent publication of information already widely known.

## Protecting the innocent: areas for particular consideration

Some people come to the attention of the media through no fault, or only limited fault, of their own. They are often people whose rights are more limited for some reason, or who find it difficult to uphold their rights, such as the users of mental health services and children. Journalists need to be aware that, while not all the people who fall into the groups discussed below are innocent, they are often more vulnerable and less able to protect themselves and their interests, and therefore require special consideration.

### Mental health

The PCC in its January–February 1994 report reminded journalists that although many patients at special hospitals such as Rampton, Ashworth, Carstairs and Broadmoor are convicted criminals, a number have not committed any crime and are not detained for treatment because of an appearance before a court. It explained that the 1959 Mental Health Act requires that all such patients, criminal or otherwise, are designated 'patients' rather than 'prisoners'. The staff serve in their medical capacity and are not prison officers, even though some may be members of the Prison Officers' Association (PCC, 1994: 5).

### Case study 5.3 Mental health and the media

There is considerable concern among health professionals, researchers and patients about the descriptions used in the media of mental health patients and the effects these have on public perceptions (see Philo, 1996). Certainly, considerable thought and sensitivity should be applied to the terminology used. Phrases such as 'psycho', 'sicko', 'nutter', 'maniac' and 'loony' do appear regularly, especially in the tabloid press, but should never be used to describe those with mental health conditions. This was spelt out by the PCC in their January 1996 report when the *Daily Star* was found to have committed two breaches of clause 13 of the Code of Practice (discrimination) (see Appendix 1). The first case involved a patient at Broadoak hospital who cycled up to the late Princess of Wales during a visit and asked for a kiss. The *Daily Star* described him as 'a raving nutter' and a 'loony' (9 November 1995 and 10 November 1995). The commission agreed that 'to describe a person suffering from a mental illness as a "raving nutter" and a "loony" could not in the circumstances of this case be other than pejorative in breach of clause 15 of the code' (PCC, 1996: 17).

In the same PCC report, a complaint about a story in the *Daily Star* was also upheld. The article (*Daily Star*, 26 January 1996) reported that there had been a complaint to the patients' council about beef being served at the canteen at Ashworth hospital despite the BSE scare. The newspaper reported that 'crazies at a top security mental hospital refused to eat beef – because it might send them MAD'. The report included a spoof menu with such items as 'bread and nutter pudding' and 'chicken in a basket case'. The PCC said: 'The commission did not accept the newspaper's response as the descriptions contained in the article were applied to all patients at Ashworth. It considered the language to be pejorative . . .' (PCC, 1996: 19).

The National Union of Journalists released guidelines on mental health reporting on 21 June 1997. Called 'Shock treatment', the leaflet encourages journalists to cover stories about mental health in a more enlightened way. The guidelines advise journalists to avoid words such as 'nutter' and 'psycho' and explain that those who use the services prefer to be called mental health service users or survivors rather than patients. The Health Education Authority have also issued a report, 'Mental Health and the National Press', which gives a number of recommendations. The report showed that 40 per cent of all daily national tabloid coverage and 45 per cent of all Sunday national tabloid coverage of mental health contained pejorative terms such as 'loony', 'mad' and 'crazy' (Ward, 1997: 14). The report recommends that editors should avoid using stigmatising language and not use clinical terms such as schizophrenia in non-specific or derogatory ways.

## Children

Children require special thought when it comes to stories about them or involving them. It is a generally held belief that children should have the right to make mistakes as they grow up. All of us learn, and many of us become better people, by making mistakes. Often one can only know what is right by learning from experience what is wrong. Children always end up touching the hot stove despite regular warnings from parents. How can they really understand the concepts of 'heat' and 'burn' until they have done so? With any luck they will experiment cautiously. But as every parent knows, this is not always the case. So what if they accidentally burn the house down? Is it really necessary to name such an impulsive child? Certainly the story that a child playing with matches has burned down a house is in the public interest, warning all parents of the dangers of leaving children with matches. But should journalists expose the child to the derision of school friends or worse?

Although no one is yet calling for new legislation to extend the prevention of naming minors beyond the courts, there are plenty who believe the media go too far. In a powerful plea for his son to be left alone, the father of a child born to a surrogate mother says:

> Our mistake [in allowing a story to be written about their child's birth] has resulted in Peter receiving playground taunts about his family history. . . . puberty is traumatic enough without the *National Daily* making it worse. . . . I am not suggesting that they [journalists and editors] should censor themselves; but they must remember that innocent young children cannot answer back. They have no power and must rely upon us adults to defend their interests. Where no crime has been committed, where no great injustice is being covered up, where it is merely the interests of the newspaper that are being served – they must think more than twice about whether to publish information that could cause damage to a child. (George X, 1997: 15–16)

George X does not call for legislation to prevent naming, nor does he object to references to his son, provided he is not named.

The law goes to some effort to protect children involved with the courts. The Children and Young Persons Act 1933 section 49 and the Criminal Justice Act 1991 prevent the identification of alleged offenders or witnesses at youth courts if they are under the age of 18. The Children and Young Persons Act 1933 also allows judges to make a section 39 order to protect the identity of children appearing before adult courts 'whether the minor is the subject of those proceedings or is a witness to them' (Carey, 1996: 94). In family matters, the Children Act 1989 puts such cases to the magistrates' courts and specially trained magistrates. The Act states:

No person shall publish any material which is intended or likely to identify:
- any child as being involved in such proceedings, or
- an address or school as being that of a child involved in such proceedings. (Crone, 1995: 127)

The Criminal Evidence and Youth Justice Bill, due to become an Act in autumn 1999, tries to tighten this even further. Initially, the bill attempted to prevent the identification of minors from the moment a crime was alleged. This was opposed strongly by the press and the government quickly amended the bill to prevent identification from the moment an investigation started. This is still too limiting for some. Santha Rasiah, secretary of the Guild of Editors' Parliamentary and Legal Committee told *Press Gazette*:

> ... the Bill still imposes an over-wide mandatory ban on media publication, enforced by a criminal offence of uncertain extent. The Bill will still prevent the reporting of many events, incidents and matters which are of proper interest to the public, at local and national level. The same event triggers the ban on alleged offender, victim and witness. Its chilling effect stems particularly from the restrictions arising from the last two categories. (*Press Gazette*, 5 March 1999: 2)

**Witnesses**. A journalist needs to be particularly sensitive when children are at the centre of a story, either as witnesses to a court case or as the main interviewee in a general news story. Standing in a witness box can be an ordeal for even the most self-confident adult but for a child it can be a nightmare, which is made even worse by excessive media attention. Outside the witness box, using reports from children could put them at risk from threats and attempts at coercion. Care needs to be taken about naming children and good journalists will always ask themselves whether a report could put the child at risk. Furthermore, in sexual abuse stories, naming the witness could allow for jigsaw identification of a victim. The PCC has clear guidelines on dealing with children as witnesses. These are discussed in Chapter 7.

**Offenders**. The automatic assumption is that an offending child will be protected by the law, but of course this only happens when a child is in court. A child accused of improper behaviour in other circumstances is often considered fair game by the media. For example, in the summer of 1996 there were a number of cases where children had been excluded from school but were allowed to return after their appeals were upheld. However, teachers then refused to teach these children.

In one of the early cases, a 10-year-old pupil was excluded from a Worksop school for being unruly in class. He was readmitted only after a compromise scheme was worked out:

Teachers' union leaders, governors and local education chiefs devised the compromise scheme after five hours of talks in Worksop last night to try to break the deadlock which has closed the 190-pupil school. Under the arrangements, Matthew **** will return to one-to-one tuition under a supply teacher but will also mix with selected pupils.

Councillor Fred Riddell, chairman of Nottinghamshire education committee, said the 'mixed menu' education would give the boy the chance to show he was amenable to classroom discipline. However, there is no chance of pupils at Manton School returning to the classroom this week. Today is the school's third day of closure. (*Daily Telegraph*, 31 October 1996)

The *Daily Telegraph* used his name in full in the story but I have left the forename Matthew in the quote only after considerable thought.

Many of these cases seemed to be copycat, in the sense that having seen one school take industrial action to prevent the return of a child, others followed suit. It is entirely possible therefore that the children in the subsequent cases were nothing like as unruly as the first principle-testing case. However, in each case the teachers felt the child should not have been allowed to return because he or she was too unruly to teach, whilst the independent panel which hears exclusion appeals felt the school was wrong to have excluded the child.

At the heart of all these cases was the debate between the school and the local authority about the standard of misbehaviour that was sufficient to merit exclusion. However, in every newspaper report, particularly in the tabloids, the focus was on the children involved. The children were named, their reputation blackened, and they were given little opportunity to put their case. The matter was made worse by television and in several of the exclusion stories, the children were interviewed, albeit briefly. Not surprisingly, they wallowed in the unexpected attention and enjoyed their few seconds of fame. Media coverage of this sort might well damage the future of the children involved and, as the law believes a minor should not be named in criminal proceedings so that their future is not jeopardised, journalists should consider not naming a child as a reasonable practice to follow in all cases where children are portrayed in an unfavourable light.

The *Sun* carried a two-page feature on four children expelled from school, none aged more than 13, on 18 September 1996. It named them, alongside large pictures, and published details of the views of teachers and governors. A one-paragraph response from the mothers was the only defence for the children, yet in two of the cases the children claimed their bad behaviour was triggered by an assault from a teacher – being dragged from a classroom in one case and being picked up in another. The first four paragraphs of the feature made it clear that the *Sun* had no intention of approaching this subject in an objective way and was determined to make it clear that the children were hooligans with no redeeming features:

> When pupils used to step out of line they would get a clip round the ear or six of the best from the headmaster. But today, teachers would risk swift disciplinary action for daring to hand out such punishments. If a head teacher and his governors try to expel an unruly pupil, the parents will often rush to an independent appeals panel – appointed by the local education authority – demanding their child is taken back. *And often they get their way after evidence from all sides has been heard.* (*Sun*, 18 September 1996: 18)

The last sentence is printed in italics in order to suggest a feeling of outrage. Yet why should we feel outraged that an independent panel has come to a decision after hearing evidence from all sides? Regardless of your views on school discipline, the *Sun* did not give the pupils a chance to put their cases, but it did identify them and potentially damage their futures. The story would have had just as much impact without naming them.

The story is, of course, newsworthy. Teachers striking to prevent a child being returned to school by the legally appointed authority raises a number of political issues of which we should be aware and also raises a number of human issues which would be of interest to the average reader. With 12,500 or so exclusions in English schools in 1995 (*Sun*, 18 September 1996: 18), it is hardly surprising that there would be a few cases where the independent appeals panels, to which the pupil and parents can take their case if they think the child was wrongly or unfairly excluded, should decide that the head teacher was wrong to exclude in this case. It is also not surprising that half a dozen or so of these cases should upset the teachers who think the appeals panel has got it wrong. But does the media need to name the children involved in order to examine the issues fully? In other cases, naming works the other way around. In one case:

> A teenage tearaway who has committed a catalogue of 1,000 offences was finally sent to secure accommodation yesterday.
>
> Senior police officers in Durham had expressed their frustration that the 15-year-old – known as Boomerang Boy – was consistently freed by courts almost as quickly as he was arrested. They complained that he was back on the streets committing crime as soon as he was out of the youth court doors. (*Daily Telegraph*, 13 February 1999)

The courts then ordered that, under the Crimes (Sentencing) Act 1997, the boy could be named, but his picture could not be used (see *Press Gazette*, 26 March 1999: 8).

**Victims**. Journalists need to consider carefully how they approach a child who has been the victim of a crime, accident or other event. Sensitivity is extremely important and a good journalist will consider resisting the temptation to squeeze information out of a minor, even if the child is accompanied by a responsible adult. In these cases, it is often the interview itself, rather than the publication or broadcast of the child's name, that involves difficult moral decisions, although naming them should be given serious thought as well.

The PCC offered advice to journalists about identifying victims in an editorial in its October–November 1993 report. The editorial was particularly concerned with the difficulties raised by the publication of pictures and the ability to identify victims even when faces are obscured.

> Editors should consider carefully whether or not their pictures offer clues, albeit unwittingly, that will allow some readers to put a name to the individual concerned. Such clues may be found in unusual hairstyles or in distinctive clothing. They may also be found in pictures that illustrate a particular relationship between the victims and family members, friends or locations. The choice of colour photography instead of black and white could also lead to easier identification in some cases. (PCC, 1993: 5)

The Commission suggested that while black and white photographs may not be the complete answer, silhouettes may reduce the probability of identification. The Commission also suggested consultation beforehand to ensure that the subject chooses hairstyle and clothing with care. The context in which the picture appears may also be an important consideration. Cropping and editing may allow a picture to be used in a way that reduces the potential for identification and electronic manipulation of pictures may also be useful.

In another PCC complaint, a mother said that the *Express on Sunday*, *Daily Express*, *Scottish Daily Mail* and *Daily Record* had all used a story about her daughter that invaded her privacy. The daughter had been diagnosed as suffering from Creutzfeldt-Jakob disease, the human form of BSE, and all of these newspapers ran stories about her and her illness which identified her. The PCC upheld the complaints against each paper saying: 'Publication of the identity of the patient was not essential to informing the public of the vital information about the illness and diagnosis, and indeed any doubts about the diagnosis' (PCC, 1997: 10).

***Children and celebrity.*** Children whose parents are famous have come under more pressure lately and their parents have become more protective. Prince Charles decided that he had no choice but to complain after a story about Prince Harry appeared in the *Mirror* in November 1998. The Prince's anger about the invasion of his son's privacy over a trivial rugby injury was exacerbated by the *Mirror*'s claims that the Palace was trying to censor the press.

The Prince of Wales has reported the *Mirror* to the Press Complaints Commission in an effort to protect Prince Harry's privacy at school.

The spokesman said: 'The Prince of Wales has asked me to say that he is deeply disappointed by the reaction of the editor of the *Mirror* [Piers Morgan] to the simple and straightforward appeal for Prince Harry to be allowed privacy at school. We respect what Mr Morgan says about press freedom. Indeed, we support it. However, this matter is nothing at all to do with press freedom. Instead, it is everything to do with the privacy to which Harry and William are entitled during their education.

'We are therefore making a formal complaint to the Press Complaints Commission which, with newspaper editors, has done a great deal over the years to protect the privacy of Prince William and Prince Harry, and will ask them to deal with it.' (*Daily Telegraph*, 21 November 1998)

Tony Blair, the Prime Minister, also complained to the PCC shortly afterwards about stories concerning his daughter's choice of school.

Downing Street said Mr Blair and his wife Cherie would complain that the stories were 'unfair'.

A statement [from Downing Street] said: 'The PCC makes clear that children should be able to complete their schooling free from press intrusion and that the private lives of children should not be covered simply because of the fame or status of their parents.'

The statement said that Mr and Mrs Blair 'tolerate a great deal of media attack and intrusion without complaint, but they see no reason why their children should not be allowed the freedom from intrusion the PCC claims its members support'. (*Daily Telegraph*, 25 January 1999)

The Prince of Wales finally did a deal with the PCC in which new guidelines were issued to editors. St James's Palace agreed, in return, to be more open with the media.

Some children are, of course, celebrities in their own right. This applies to the royal princes, and Prince William is beginning to find that his good looks are making him a target for a media keen to carve out a wider share of the teenage girl market. Whilst coverage of him at school has been reasonably muted, coverage of some of his recent tours with his father has been extensive. Celebrity of this sort is usually less of a concern than most other coverage of minors. In the main it is accepted, even welcomed. There are always exceptions of course.

### Adult victims

Victims of crime and disaster also need to be handled with care. Women, in particular, are often the victims of sexual violence in circumstances as diverse as being beaten up by their partners in the home to being abused by an exploitative boss. Journalists should be careful not to sensationalise such events. These incidents can often make good copy for the tabloids, with claims and counter-claims of explicit sexual activity. Industrial tribunals are frequently the sources of such stories, with women seeking recompense for sexual harassment or other exploitative behaviour. They then face a further ordeal as the details of their sexual ordeal may be dragged on to the front page of the papers with counter-allegations of sexual impropriety being made to weaken the women's claim for damages. In all cases, the need to satisfy the information requirement of the reader (see Chapter 2, p. 20) must always be balanced by sensitivity to the victim and the need to maintain professional standards (see Case study 5.4).

### Case study 5.4 Reporting crime

The *Sport* had its knuckles rapped by the PCC in November 1991 for publishing an inaccurate report of a rape that could have led to the identification of the victim. The PCC says in its report:

> The *Daily Sport*'s report of a rape trial included prurient and offensive details of evidence, the publication of which was likely to cause additional distress to the victim . . .
> Misleadingly it omitted an important part of the victim's evidence which made it clear that a particular act which had been threatened did not take place. By reporting her attacker's address inaccurately, the paper increased the risk that she would be identified by readers who knew her. This possibility was made more distressing by the paper's unnecessarily detailed account of the attack on her. (PCC, Report No. 4, 1991: 6)

The Commission expressed its profound sympathy with the victim and upheld the complaint.

However, the Press Council rejected a complaint from a woman that the *Redditch Indicator* and the *Redditch Advertiser* had irresponsibly published a picture of her when she was the subject of persistent harassment (Press Council, 1985: 166). The woman was a police officer, although this was incidental. The man pestered her with 5,000 phone calls for which he was jailed for nine months. The two local papers published pictures of her. The court had made no order not to publish photographs and the newspapers in question claimed they had no reason to know that the defendant was unaware of what the woman looked like. Although in this case it is difficult to blame the newspapers which merely made a natural assumption that the defendant knew what the victim looked like, it is a suitable cautionary tale.

### Publishing names and addresses

Journalists like to use names in their stories because they add veracity to the article. Sometimes of course the name is the article. A story about something happening to President Clinton may well be newsworthy whereas if the same thing happens to me, it will not be. Also, if I were to say we should declare war on Australia, then no one would do more than look at me oddly. If Tony Blair were to say it, then there would be banner headlines.

David Randall explains the journalistic requirement to name people very well with an anecdote about his first week in the job:

> . . . by a combination of luck and my determination to make an impact [I] got on to a good story about river pollution. I went off, did the research and then rushed back to the office dreaming of the accolades that would be coming my away when I turned in the story. 'What the hell is this?' shouted the news editor when he read it. 'Where are all the names?' I had been so thrilled with the story I had forgotten to ask the names of the people I interviewed. There were lots of good quotes, but all of them were from 'worried resident', 'water engineer', 'safety inspector' etc. (Randall, 1996: 33)

Randall's story is good lesson for any young journalist to learn. But journalists need also to be aware that there are times when names do not need to be used and sometimes should not be used. It is regular practice for the police and armed services to refuse to give names of serving officers and to ask the media to refrain from publishing them. Since publication could, in some circumstances, put officers at risk from revenge attacks, most media consider complying with these requests if the circumstances seem reasonable. The media is also asked not to publish detailed addresses of such groups and it is often easier to acquiesce about publishing an address rather than a name. Other groups may also need to have their addresses and movements treated with care. In a judgement in 1985, the Press Council upheld a complaint against the *Kent and Sussex Courier* for publishing the address of a bank security guard injured in a raid. It says: 'It was improper to publish his address, thus placing him and his family potentially in further danger' (Press Council, 1985: 165).

The PCC published some guidance to editors about publishing names and addresses in its August 1992 report (see Exhibit 5.1).

Various groups of people and professionals, who might be considered at particular risk if their addresses or their movements are published, include the following:

- People in the public eye.
- Judges and magistrates.
- Police officers.
- Members of the armed forces.
- People accused of serious crimes, and their relatives.
- Aids victims and their care workers.

Journalists should also refrain from publishing the addresses of refuges and shelters for those who have been the victims of domestic violence and

**Exhibit 5.1 Publishing names and addresses**

The PCC places responsibility on journalists to 'discourage, and certainly not encourage, the harassment of individuals named in stories and features in their publications' (PCC, Report No. 12, 1992: 5). The PCC supported the practice of regional papers, which like to publish street names to stress the local relevance of a story, but do not publish house numbers or names in order to reduce unwanted attention and because: 'It reduces the possibility of error: if you do not publish the number, you cannot get it wrong' (ibid.).

The PCC reminded editors and other journalists to use their common sense and careful judgement on the use of addresses:

> It is true that in the case of prominent people addresses are readily available but the press is not under an obligation to make it easy for cranks and criminals by saving them the bother of researching telephone books and directories. Newspapers should not assist in identifying targets for opprobrium, far less for life-threatening attention, and there is a common-sense obligation upon editors to avoid endangering families by publishing actual addresses unless they constitute an essential part of the story. (PCC, Report No. 7, 1992: 5)

The PCC gave as an example the *Evening Standard*, London, which, after giving the address of a prominent individual's weekend home in Wales, suggested: 'He had better not tell the Welsh nationalists or they will come and burn it down' (ibid.: 6). The PCC held this to be an infringement of the person's privacy.

Perversely, the PCC decided that there had been no breach of the Code of Practice in 1999 following a complaint from Eric Forth MP and the parents of the five suspects in the Stephen Lawrence case against *New Nation* and the *Sunday Telegraph*. *New Nation* had published an article giving the suspects' addresses, together with robust comments about enhancing their 'facial features'. The PCC found that the robust comments were on a matter of public interest and dismissed complaints about harassment and incitement to racial hatred. They also dismissed complaints about invasion of privacy against both *New Nation* and the *Sunday Telegraph* saying: 'In view of the wide reporting of the case and the fact that the information about the complainants' addresses was already in the public domain, the commission did not find that there was a breach of the code' (*Press Gazette*, 7 May 1999: 6). One can't help wondering if commissioners were swayed by concern about the opprobrium a decision to uphold the complaint would have heaped on the Commission's head.

abuse. This would put the people seeking refuge and the workers in the refuges in danger. Indeed, the very purpose of the refuges is invalidated if addresses are made public.

## Naming lottery winners

The National Lottery has captured the interest of the nation. Many people want to know more about those who win millions of pounds on the lottery and newspapers often pursue lottery winners in order to satisfy their readers' curiosity.

## Case study 5.5 Winning the lottery

The first rollover lottery jackpot was won on 10 December 1994 by a resident of Blackburn, Lancashire. The media's interest was intense, but the winner did not give permission for his name to be revealed. The organisers of the lottery, Camelot, said the winner had requested that quite detailed information be released to the media but that Camelot decided it would be more prudent to release only information about the region in which he lived, the size of his family, that he was a factory worker, what paper he read and that he watched satellite television.

Two national newspapers, the *Mirror* and the *Sun* (12 December 1994) offered £10,000 rewards for additional information. Camelot obtained a High Court injunction preventing the naming of the winner but this was challenged and overturned. The *Mirror* and the *Sun* then decided not to publish the name and made much about their decision in their papers. The editor of the *Sun* made it clear at the time that he had been influenced by the strength of feeling of readers. However, the *News of the World, Yorkshire on Sunday* and the *Sunday Mercury* all identified the winner the following Sunday.

Although the winner himself did not complain, his MP, Jack Straw, did and wrote to the PCC. Labour's media spokesperson, Chris Smith MP, also wrote, asking the Commission to adjudicate over the practice of offering money for information. There were also 32 letters from members of the public on the issue. The Commission asked editors for their views. The *Sun* responded that whilst they had decided to cease the practice of 'bounty money', they would certainly fight any move for a blanket restriction on naming lottery winners. The editor said he 'would have no hesitation in identifying winners such as the Queen, the prime minister, Myra Hindley or the Archbishop of Canterbury, irrespective of whether anonymity had been requested' (PCC, Report No. 29, 1995: 27).

The PCC condemned the decision of some newspapers to offer rewards and went on to draw up guidelines for the future (see Exhibit 5.2).

The media's treatment of lottery winners has been mixed, but there does seem to be a streak of invasive jealousy about much of the coverage. Mark Gardiner won the lottery on Saturday, 10 June 1995. By 13 June, the *Sun* had branded him a 'Lotto Rat' and exposed his private life to the world. The newspaper claimed he was a heavy-drinking womaniser who had had three wives and two mistresses and was now living with someone else's wife. Another lottery winner was photographed on holiday at an exotic location with a group of friends. Allegations were made about the 'lively' behaviour.

**Exhibit 5.2 The National Lottery: PCC guidelines**

- The press should generally respect the wishes of a winner of the National Lottery to remain anonymous if he or she so wishes.
- The press should not seek to obtain information about winners from the operator of the National Lottery in breach of any duty of confidentiality which the operator owes to winners under the terms of its licence.
- The press should not seek to obtain information about winners who have requested anonymity, from their family, friends or work colleagues through any form of harassment contrary to clause 8 of the Code of Practice (this refers to the old Code of Practice; for the new code, see Appendix 1).
- It may be permissible for the press to identify a winner of the National Lottery who has requested anonymity if such can be justified in the public interest under clause 18 of the [old] Code of Practice; the size of the win alone would not be sufficient justification for such disclosure.
- The press should not offer rewards for information about the identity or private life of a lottery winner. Such offers can only be justified in extreme cases where there is prima facie evidence that a serious fraud or scandal is involved.
- The Commission believes that the press cannot be expected to act as scapegoat in maintaining the anonymity of winners, irrespective of all circumstances, including the actions of Camelot or the winners themselves. Accordingly, this guidance will be applied by the Commission in the context of any future complaints after taking into account the circumstances of each particular case.

# Plagiarism

Plagiarism involves passing off someone else's writing as your own. The most obvious use of plagiarism is when another media outlet has a story that a journalist wants to use. It is very tempting, bearing in mind the pressures of time journalists are often under to meet copy deadlines, to use that story, perhaps rewriting it in order not to breach copyright and to avoid detection. However, the problems with this are twofold:

1 Can it be morally right to take someone else's work and pass it off as your own, thus depriving the original journalist of fees that are rightfully his or hers?
2 What if the original story is wrong? A journalist who copies a story risks repeating any error contained within it. Furthermore, he or she may bow to the temptation to firm up elements left deliberately vague in the original, thus increasing the number of errors. Often sub-editors who have re-written a reporter's copy to make it 'brighter' have been forced to return to something closer to the original because the copy says more than the reporter is able to support and is straying into the area of defamation or sensationalism.

This is not to say that we should not use other media to alert us to stories. Sometimes a newspaper will carry a story that is of such importance that rivals are duty-bound to follow it up. Because of this, national tabloids will often hold a superb story until after the first edition has been printed and then publish the story in the second edition when the time available for the rivals to pick up the story is greatly reduced. All news desks use television and radio news to alert them to a breaking story. Listening to local radio stations can alert local newspaper journalists to any serious accident or blaze in plenty of time for them to ring the appropriate service, get the details and go out and get the story. The television and radio can be extremely useful in providing us with eye-witness information on events such as royal weddings and sporting occasions.

## Personal lives

Many people believe that journalists should be impartial (see Chapter 3). At its most extreme, this view proposes that journalists should not have any personal political views, that they should be aloof from society and act as pure observers. However, journalists do need to be concerned about the society on which they are reporting and commenting. If they are not concerned about it, not involved in it, then they will probably be very poor journalists. Journalism is about people and journalists should be gregarious, and interested in the people and the issues on which they are reporting. This means that many reporters have political ideals and are politically active (though many have also seen far too many politicians to be anything other than cynical about politicians and politics). Furthermore, some journalists have other outside interests and are involved in various clubs and societies, although others find their hours of work militate against joining such groups. Because of this, journalists, more than most professional groups, enjoy each other's company.

In order to keep their personal and social lives clear of professional conflicts of interest, it is important that a journalist should inform the news desk if any story on which he or she is working is likely to produce such a conflict. Having said that, most journalists should be professional enough to avoid the obvious traps. If, for instance, a Labour-supporting journalist cannot interview a Conservative MP and produce a fair and balanced piece, then maybe that journalist should reconsider his or her career. That is not to say that the piece would be necessarily completely impartial. There are bound to be issues on which the Conservative record was not perfect and these should be picked up by any journalist, no matter what his or her political views. Indeed, it is often more difficult for journalists to be certain they have left their personal views on hold if they are supporters of the person being interviewed rather than generally disagreeing with the interviewee. There is the constant fear that one is being too soft, not going for the main issue.

Some personal links are, however, more difficult to deal with. For example, it would not be easy for a journalist to investigate a company whose environmental record is poor if his or her partner worked for the company. Furthermore, if the partner's job was potentially at risk, the investigation might well become too stressful. In a case like this the journalist should tell the news editor the problem and the news editor should then assign another reporter to the job.

## Freedom to publish

I have talked at length about the need for a free press (see Chapter 3), but the phrase 'freedom of the press' also needs to be discussed. It is a phrase used often by politicians, broadcasters and newspaper proprietors who want to use press freedom for their own ends, and therefore their definitions of 'freedom of the press' will differ. Politicians tend to see freedom of the press as the freedom to print the 'truth' about their opponents, whereas printing the 'truth' about them is interpreted as an invasion of privacy. Newspaper proprietors mean freedom to print whatever makes money, but also accept that printing stories about advertisers, if they are derogatory, might damage profits. Broadcasters want the freedom to broadcast whatever will titillate and increase audiences to improve ratings and boost advertising revenues.

In some countries, for example Sweden, the US and Australia, there are very few limits on what may be printed or broadcast. Only decency and public acceptability prevent publication. However, in the UK, whilst paying lip service to press freedom, we have taken the view that there should be limits on what may be printed for a number of reasons. These limits are quite extensive and come under the following headings:

- Coverage of criminal proceedings.
- Protection of individual honour (libel).
- Protection of commercial confidentiality.
- Invasions of personal privacy.
- Security and defence.
- Sedition and blasphemy.
- The public good (decency and good taste).
- Public order.
- Prevention of terrorism.

It seems to many that in the UK freedom of the press is under attack as the number of newspaper proprietors continues to fall, allowing fewer outlets for alternative views. Furthermore, the proprietors who remain have reduced the number of papers they produce. There are far fewer national, regional and local papers than there were a few years ago. In broadcasting, there are more stations, but they are owned by fewer people and tend to have less commitment to news.

## Why the media are in business

It is important to remember that most newspapers and broadcast stations in a market economy are not in business because of high and lofty ideals; they are there to make a profit for their owners and shareholders. This means that costs need to be kept to the minimum, concomitant with providing a saleable product, whilst keeping revenue, through selling advertising space and the product, as high as the market can bear. It is a pressure of a market economy that if a revenue-generating idea proves to be successful, other entrepreneurs will move in to exploit the profit potential, reducing the amount of revenue available to all until the number of competitors in that market place neatly matches the number that can exist and still provide a reasonable return on capital invested. This means that any serious interest that commercially-driven broadcasters and publishers have in information is entirely based on its potential to develop revenue and therefore ultimately to make profits.

With profit as the motive for owning and running a newspaper it can hardly be surprising that proprietors, and therefore editors, want to present news that costs as little as possible to gather, and yet provides the largest audience and thereby the highest revenue return possible. In-depth investigative stories based around issues are not the highest-profile stories. They are also some of the most risky in terms of libel suits. With libel laws in Britain being some of the most repressive in the world, a court system that is extremely costly and juries which, at the moment, are highly unsympathetic to the media, it is a brave editor who will stick his or her neck out to run an investigative story about sharp practice in the City and risk a law suit which could cost several million rather than a kiss-and-tell exposé of some celebrity.

## Separation of publishing and journalism

Journalists are not so directly driven by profit as newspaper proprietors and broadcast stations. They are, of course, concerned that the organisation they work for should continue to operate (as they do not want to lose their jobs) but as long as the journalists feel they are providing their employer with stories that will interest readers, and so continue to make their newspaper or broadcast station successful, then they have fulfilled their function.

Newspaper proprietors and broadcasters are only really interested in the moral aspect of the final product; the means of achieving it are of less importance. Journalists' decisions need to be made before this. They need to be aware of the moral issues surrounding the stories they are pursuing and how they are pursuing them. As discussed, by the time the story is published they may have already considered several different moral problems, starting with whether to cover the story at all. Journalists need to consider the level of protection they can give to a source, the veracity of the information they are being fed and how they would support that information and how far they can morally go in gathering evidence. Only when they have the story does the publisher become involved, yet this is often too late.

The early PCC Code of Practice concentrated largely on publication only. Whilst, because it had been set up by journalists themselves, the NUJ Code saw the need to control journalism and the way journalists behaved, the PCC Code, because it had been established by editors and publishers, concentrated on what was published. The changes that have been introduced since the Code was first written have tended to dilute this concentration on publishing, with the emphasis turning towards news-gathering. This process was speeded up by the death of the Princess of Wales and the subsequent public outcry over her perceived hounding by the press. The strengthened Code attempted to introduce more controls on the gathering of news and this meant that more clauses needed to include the defence of the public interest. The new PCC Code of Practice (January 1998) introduced clauses on the taking of photographs, the use of listening devices and intrusion into private grief, all of which extended controls on news-gathering. At the time of writing, it is too early to tell if this has had any effect on the type of complaints made.

## Guidelines

The PCC issues guidelines on topical issues from time to time as did the Press Council before it. Its reports on the coverage of major events such as the Strangeways riot (PC Booklet No. 8, January 1991) drew the media's attention to important lessons. It is a shame that the PCC does not carry out such full-scale enquiries. The NUJ also puts out guidelines on various issues from time to time. In 1984, in co-operation with the Health Education Council, they issued guidelines about HIV and AIDS, although this did not appear to affect the messages put across in much of the press coverage which represented AIDS and HIV as a 'gay plague' visited upon those who deserved it (Wellings and Field, 1996: 251). Other guidelines include those on sexist language, racist reporting, reporting on disabled people and mental health (see Appendices).

## Summary

- The concept of a good journalist means different things to different people, including the newspaper editor, colleagues, the reader and the person featured in the story.

- There are many people and groups to whom the journalist owes loyalty and who have to be considered in journalists' moral decisions. As well as those mentioned above, these also include regulatory bodies and the law.

- Journalists need to be aware of issues such as causing offence, good interview practice and the implications of making promises when carrying out their jobs.

- Organisations such as the NUJ and PCC produce guidelines for journalists about important issues, such as dealing with children, publishing names and addresses and HIV/AIDS.

## Questions

1 What do *you* consider to be the most important qualities a journalist should have?

2 Find examples of stories where deception or subterfuge have been used. In each case decide whether the use of subterfuge was justified and give your reasons.

3 Name some groups of people who should be treated with particular care in media coverage and explain why.

# Chapter 6

·········································································

# Codes of conduct and regulation

**Chapter outline**

- This chapter explains the moral basis of codes of conduct, their development and the reasons why they are important.

- It looks at the ways codes are enforced through different types of regulatory body and the powers these bodies have.

- It explores the differences in codes and the regulation of the media in different countries.

- It discusses the complex issues that arise in connection with the law, media and ethics.

Virtually all democratic societies insist on some standards of ethical behaviour from their media. Consequently, many countries now have codes of conduct, upheld by professional or cross-industry bodies or, in some instances, by a legally appointed tribunal. Essentially, a code of conduct is a list of dos and don'ts to guide journalists through the maze of moral problems they face from day to day, and, as Nigel G.E. Harris points out: 'one of the most noteworthy features of codes for journalists is just how wide is the range of countries in which they have been adopted. They are found not just in Western Europe and North America, but in countries as diverse as Egypt, South Korea, Jamaica, Mali and Venezuela' (1992: 62). But, as this chapter explains, the content and types of issue covered by codes varies a great deal and their use and effectiveness have varied in the many countries in which they operate. However, before looking at the codes themselves we need to look at some of the fundamental issues that underlie them.

## Personal codes versus public codes

Most people have their own personal code against which they can measure their behaviour. Some people's codes are pretty basic, whereas others have a much stricter personal code. Whatever a person's code is, it has to be self-policing; if it is breached, only he or she will know. Since people generally have a good idea about the motivation of their behaviour and most of the circumstances involved in a particular problem, they can act as both prosecutor and judge to determine whether this act or that breaches their personal code. However, codes which are externally regulated, that is public codes, are more complex. It is no longer a question of acting as your own judge and jury.

A public code involves trying to work to a universal statement which is universally applied; if it is wrong for one person to do something under certain circumstances, then it must be wrong for another person to do the same thing under the same circumstances. This is obviously different from a personal code where an action I may well consider to be wrong would be considered perfectly acceptable by someone else. Because I work for Global News Corporation, for instance, I might consider it morally wrong to be disloyal to my employer by covering a story about corruption in GNC. However, a reporter from another news organisation could cover the same story with enthusiasm.

For the universal application of moral codes, everyone has to be clear about and accept what the code has to say. Because of this, codes tend to be limited to areas of general agreement and phrased in a way that covers all circumstances. So, for instance, a code could stipulate that it is wrong that I should *lie* to get a story about GNC corruption, whichever company I worked for.

## Moral basis of codes

In order to appreciate how universal codes operate we need to take into account whether they have a motivist or consequentialist viewpoint (see Table 1.1 on p. 10). A motivist would argue that a universal code needs to take into account the reasons *why* a journalist would breach the code. An example of this is the public interest. Sometimes journalists breach a code of conduct when writing a story, by using subterfuge for example, but claim that they have done so in the public interest. Often this is accepted as a good reason and no finding of guilt or punishment will follow their act. Kant believed that the essence of morality is to be found in the motive for which the act is done. An action can only be a moral action if it is carried out with a sense of moral obligation. An action which is carried out because one fears the consequences or because it is in one's best interests is a prudential action. This accords well with the public interest defence. Only the wider duty to the public well-being can justify a journalist straying from a code of conduct. A consequentialist, on the other hand, is only concerned about the consequences of someone's actions and not the motive. To a consequentialist, it is the effect of the action that is important.

Contrast the two approaches in the following example. A man has killed an unpleasant miser because he wanted to steal his money. Another man has killed a terminally ill patient who was in considerable pain because he wanted to save them unnecessary suffering. A motivist might say that in the second case the man who killed was more moral than the one involved in the first case because his motives were good. A consequentialist might not be so sure about this. The effect in the second case was to kill a man, but it saved him from continuing pain. In the first case the effect was also to kill a man, but it removed someone who was considered by many to be unpleasant.

Now the moral basis of codes has been discussed we can look at how they have developed over the years.

# Codes of conduct

## The development of codes

The first codes of conduct were drafted in the US in the early part of this century. Britain and other European countries followed in the 1920s and 1930s. The British NUJ code was first suggested in 1935 and eventually launched in 1936 (Bundock, 1957). However, one of the first European countries to start to develop a code was Sweden.

> The Publicists Club [of Sweden], which was founded in 1874 with journalists, news-paper editors and other publishers as its members, had, on a number of occasions in the beginning of the 1900s, served as a self-appointed tribunal to hear complaints against newspapers. (Nordlund, 1991: 2)

The Swedish Press Council was formed on 16 March 1916 at a joint meeting of the Board of Publicists Club, the Swedish Newspaper Publishers Association and the Swedish Journalists Association (now the Swedish Union of Journalists).

In the early stages, codes were relatively brief, consisting of a few paragraphs or so and covering some basic principles. However, with the massive growth of television and radio broadcasting during and after the Second World War, codes came to be seen as more important. Separate codes were set up for print and broadcast journalists in many areas. Although the basic moral principles underlying the type of information to be used and how it is gathered remain much the same for print and broadcast journalists, their application, as we will see later in this chapter, is often very different.

In Britain, independent television was, until recently, covered by three bodies: the Independent Television Commission (ITC) which deals with broadcasting licences and lays down guidelines for commercial broadcasters; the

Broadcasting Standards Council (BSC) which adjudicates on complaints of taste and decency; and the Broadcasting Complaints Commission (BCC) which looks most closely at ethical issues as they affect journalists. The Broadcasting Act 1996 combined the BCC and the BSC into a new Broadcasting Standards Commission that started work in January 1998. This has drawn up a new code of practice. The Broadcasting Act 1990 brought the BCC into being as a statutory complaints commission, and set a framework for complaints.

Section 107 of the Broadcasting Act 1996 says:

(1) It shall be the duty of the Broadcasting Standards Commission to draw up and from time to time review a code giving guidance as to principles to be observed, and practices to be followed, in connection with the avoidance of:

(a) unjust or unfair treatment of programmes to which this section applies, or

(b) unwarranted infringement of privacy in, or in connection with the obtaining of material included in, such programmes . . .

Now we have fewer regulatory bodies monitoring the broadcasting media. The Radio Authority (RA) has control over independent radio, the ITC over independent TV, the BBC governors over BBC TV and radio, and the BSC over the whole industry.

As codes of conduct became more fashionable, often to convince an increasingly sceptical public that the media can work in a moral way, they began to grow and what had been just a few paragraphs in the early codes often became several pages with many detailed clauses. The main reason for this was because professional media bodies were determined to account for every situation that could arise that might result in public outrage. However, conversely, the more complex the codes became the easier it became for the media to wriggle around the words therein. It is difficult to convince people determined to stamp out 'media excesses' that a short code is often better as a method of control than the long, detailed rambling that many codes have now become.

A short code has the advantage of being easier for journalists to remember and use. They are able to measure directly their performance against the principles contained in the code and quickly realise when they are straying from the straight and narrow. For instance, 'thou shalt not steal' only becomes difficult to operate when it is hedged with a number of sub-clauses detailing what is meant under specific circumstances by 'thou', 'shalt' and 'steal'. Similarly, in journalism, if a code says 'journalists shall not represent comment as fact' all journalists would be able to use that to measure their behaviour even though they would not all come to the same conclusions in similar cases. One person's comment might be seen only as analysis and interpretation by another.

Codes are often now more concerned with practicalities than with principles. The Swedish code of conduct, for instance, consists of 19 short paragraphs covering many of the main issues. The British NUJ Code of Conduct (Appendix 2) covers most issues in 13 fairly terse paragraphs. The British PCC Code of Practice (Appendix 1), however, requires a weighty 45 paragraphs in 16 clauses with six paragraphs of introduction to cover fewer issues. The BSC goes even further with 44 paragraphs covering 33 clauses that are only supposed to cover the area of fairness and privacy. The Radio Authority has a more general code which runs to 52 paragraphs covering 19 clauses. The outcome is that the longer codes are now too long to be of use to editors and journalists who do not have time to refer to the code every time an issue comes up. Editors and journalists then have to rely on an understanding of the basic ethical principles, something they were rarely given during training. A short direct code, which they would have time to use, would give journalists guidance on the issues.

### Exhibit 6.1 Amendments to the PCC Code of Practice

By January 1998 the British PCC Code of Practice had been amended 15 times since its inception in 1991:

- Additional paragraph in preamble on the reprinting of adjudications.
- Postscript inviting comments from the public.
- Clause on listening devices.
- Requirement for swift co-operation by editors inserted in preamble.
- Long-lens cameras included in privacy clause.
- Definition of private property inserted.
- Addition to editor's responsibility in harassment clause.
- Payment for articles clause reworded.
- Addition of rules to prevent jigsaw identification in child sex cases.
- Consolidation of the definition of a public interest defence.
- Reference to private property definition added to harassment clause.
- 'Responsible official' changed to 'responsible executive' in hospital clause.
- Alteration to definition of private property.
- Alteration to wording of clause on children in sex cases.
- A considerable rewrite, particularly on intrusion and privacy following the death of Diana, Princess of Wales.

## Codes and professionals

Codes of conduct are introduced into any professional area to give moral guidance. 'They serve an important purpose by setting standards against which conduct can be measured and evaluated' (Gordon *et al.*, 1998: 69). It has been argued above that to be effective a good code needs to offer easy guidance to the people who actually need to use it. But, as we have seen, as codes have developed they have become longer and more complex and one of the problems journalists face is not so much whether they abide by the code of conduct (either the NUJ's Code of Conduct or the PCC's Code of Practice), but whether they know what it says. It is easy to be dismissive of a code of conduct if it is too long and contains complex and difficult-to-follow clauses about ethical matters that rarely interfere with the average journalist's business. For instance, a clause about gaining interviews only by straightforward means is more likely to be remembered, and therefore acted on, than more detailed, but often less used clauses about seeking permission of an authorised person before entering a hospital (see Appendix 1). Bursting into a private nursing home bedroom wearing a borrowed white coat and trying to obtain an interview from a seriously ill patient while pretending to be a doctor is more likely to be debated if thought of as not being a straightforward means of access rather than whether the reporter should have gained permission from an authorised person. The first goes to the heart of the issue whereas the second merely sparks a debate on who an authorised person may be.

Keeping it simple gives the journalist more chance to think about the issues in real situations and less chance of ignoring the issues altogether in an attempt to wriggle around weak wording.

## Codes and public relations

Another important function of codes of conduct is the important public relations role they have. They are introduced to reassure the public that a profession has standards of practice and to imply, at least, that professionals who transgress those standards will be disciplined. Many professions and trades have raced to introduce codes of practice over the past few years in the light of rising consumer consciousness: 'Written codes of ethics suggest that the mass media, and the men and women who produce them, are virtuous servants of society. They imply unified allegiance to professional standards of performance . . .' (Gordon et al., 1998: 65).

A trade or profession feels better able to fend off public criticism if it has a code of practice it can produce to wave at the public in times of crisis. Whether it is travel agents replying to criticisms following a large number of complaints from dissatisfied holiday-makers or insurance companies fearing high levels of claims and complaints following a big storm, the calming influence of a code of practice is very important. A company finds that being able to claim that all will be dealt with according to the code of practice deflects criticism in a way that is difficult to achieve by any other method. It allows decisions to be delayed whilst tempers cool and, more importantly, the issues to be forgotten (and maybe even forgiven) by the wider public.

No industry has failed to notice that codes of practice can add an aura of respectability and fairness without necessarily forcing any real need for responsibility. It is almost impossible to achieve this in any other way. Even government has seen the benefit of introducing codes such as the Citizens' Charter.

## Regulating ethics

We have discussed the moral basis, development, benefits and problems of codes of conduct and will now look at how they are regulated. Although the law is used to support media councils in some countries, it is not a method of regulation that is widely favoured in the UK. It is possible to have methods of control that fall short of legislation and in the UK there are a number of bodies which exist to police codes of conduct and make them effective.

### Licensing authorities

Self-regulation is the keystone of British media regulation for the press yet not of broadcasting. Broadcasting is tightly controlled in two ways: (1) a licence is needed to operate a broadcast station; and (2) there are statutory regulatory bodies to deal with complaints.

Whilst anyone who can raise the money can start a newspaper, to broadcast one must be a 'fit and proper person' (Part 1, Section 3(2)(a) of the Broadcasting Act 1996) in order to win a licence from the Independent Television Commission or the Radio Authority. Once you are transmitting, both these authorities lay down strict guidelines about what the station may or may not broadcast. The Broadcasting Standards Commission, the broadcasting complaints body set up in 1998 by amalgamating the Broadcasting Standards Council and the Broadcasting Complaints Commission, is another statutory body whose rulings can be backed up by the courts if necessary.

Broadcasters are obliged by law (Representation of the People Act 1983 and Broadcasting Act 1990) to be impartial and to provide a range of reports on current affairs and religion in a way that does not apply to newspapers. The Independent Television Commission and the Radio Authority share the power to lay conditions on licence holders. 'News programmes must be provided at regular intervals, particularly at peak viewing times, and be presented live and simultaneously with other Channel 3 licensees' (ITC, 1993: 21). Licensees must also provide current affairs and religious programmes as well as programmes for children. Regional licensees must provide a suitable proportion of regional programmes – many of these are news and current affairs. The ITC's programme code has specific guidance on the portrayal of violence and due impartiality. The BBC has similar clauses in its *Producers' Guidelines*. This means that television and radio are obliged to put out a reasonable amount of impartial news coverage spread throughout the day. Newspapers, on the other hand, have no statutory obligations on the provision or presentation of news at all.

So why are the two media in this situation? Why is broadcasting statutorily constrained when newspapers are given a free hand? How can the government be so supportive of self-regulation for the press yet so determined on statutory regulation for broadcasting? Lord McGregor (former Chairman of the Press Complaints Commission) and others claim to be uneasy about the possibility of legislating for control of newspapers yet do not seem unhappy with the idea of legislating for broadcasting.

Part of the reason seems to be based in politics. Television is seen as too dangerous a weapon to allow partiality and the risk that one political party may be more favoured than another. The Labour party might fear that advertisers would pressurise the independent stations at least towards the political right whereas the Conservatives might fear that the natural liberal inclination of broadcasters would veer news reports to the left. Statutory impartiality allows both sides to claim foul and attempt to edge coverage in their favour by employing PR consultants. The build-up to the 1997 general election saw an unprecedented increase in anecdotal evidence of rising complaints by party spin doctors to broadcasters about bias in one of the dirtiest elections anyone can remember.

However, the more usual argument given for the tight control of broadcasting, and certainly the one that the main political parties support, is that there are only a limited number of airwaves available, whereas, in theory, anyone from any political point of view can start a newspaper or magazine. To run a television station you need to be one of the seventeen licence holders (this includes Channel 4, GMTV and Teletext) or the BBC. Since this clearly limits access to the airwaves, the argument runs, there should be an impartiality rule. This is due to change with the introduction of digital television.

From a more cynical viewpoint, looking at a press with nine mainstream national papers spanning the UK, three national papers in Scotland and Wales, a handful of regional morning papers (Bristol, Liverpool, Leeds, Birmingham) and a reducing number of evening papers, it can be argued that the difference is more to do with being able to control television in a way that would be impossible to do with the press. The press, to be partial for the moment, could hammer any government into the ground before they had a chance to introduce any such legislation. The Broadcasting Act 1996 launched digital TV, with the opportunity for scores of terrestrial TV channels plus the chance for cable and satellite digital broadcasters to offer hundreds of channels, but the control on ownership remains.

Furthermore, the idea that anyone can start a newspaper is nonsense. Several brave attempts have been made since the launch of the *Independent* in the early 1980s. *Today*, the *Sunday Correspondent*, *News on Sunday* and the *North West Times* all failed. Even the *Independent* ceased to be independent. Only the *Sport* and *Sunday Sport* survive outside the big media groups. *Today* went under despite being owned by News International, Rupert Murdoch's international conglomerate that includes *The Times* and the *Sun*. Debilitating price wars, which have included reducing the price of *The Times* to only 10p, would be increased if more competition were to come on to the market, in an almost certainly successful bid to put the newcomer out of business.

## Regulatory councils

Newspaper proprietors have made it clear they dislike, and even fear, the idea of a press regulated by law, and that any government considering it should be wary. What proprietors and editors are prepared to accept is some form of code of practice and an accompanying regulatory authority. There are three types of enforcing body for codes of conduct and ethical issues in newspapers and broadcasting that can be set up, each with their own unique advantages (see Exhibit 6.2).

### Exhibit 6.2 Regulatory bodies and their powers

**A Voluntary regulatory body**: This is usually set up by the industry to consider complaints. It may also be a lobbying body for the industry and have other functions such as training, standards and promotion. Such industry bodies have been formed in many countries, sometimes following pressure from the government. One of the first was Sweden (see p. 173). There is a wide variety of industry-appointed regulatory bodies. Some, such as Sweden's, are true cross-industry bodies with representatives of editors, journalists and proprietors. Some, such as Britain's PCC, are set up only by proprietors. The only power these bodies have is to ask newspapers or broadcasters to publish their adjudications so that newspapers would be obliged to publish any criticism within their columns. Many councils contain members of the public to balance the self-interest of the industry and to add a perspective that only interested but non-expert members of the public can bring.

**Voluntary regulatory bodies with statutory powers**: These councils are similar to voluntary regulatory bodies but have statutory authority to fine or punish transgressors in other ways. Bodies of this type exist in a few countries, for example India, and it was proposed for Britain by the Heritage Select Committee in 1993. Neither the then Conservative government nor the later Labour administration wanted to move away from the present system of press self-regulation.

These bodies are still voluntary, although they may be funded by public money, and various schemes can be suggested to determine the constitution. The one ▶

**Exhibit 6.2 continued**

suggested by the Heritage Committee required lay and professional members. The code of conduct in these circumstances has the support of law and some section of the judiciary is usually used as a court of appeal. Fines, or strict instructions about how and where in a publication the council's findings should be used, are standard punishments. The punishment element and right of appeal against a decision of the regulatory body by a journalist or publication adds a strength to this system that does not exist in the solely voluntary bodies.

**A Statutory tribunal**: Such a body was recommended by Sir David Calcutt QC (Calcutt, 1993) in his review of press regulation. It would have statutory powers to investigate and punish. Such tribunals would have contained at least one judge and would have been closer to courts of law than the arbiters of professional morals that the voluntary bodies can claim to be. Sir David Calcutt, in his 1993 review, found that the Press Complaints Commission was not working and wanted to set up a Press Complaints Tribunal. This would have had three members and would have heard complaints on an adversarial basis and been entitled to punish newspapers and magazines by instructing them how to present adjudications in the paper or magazine, or have the power to fine transgressors.

Both the Independent Television Commission and the Radio Authority are statutory bodies set up by law with powers to punish – either with fines or the withdrawal of the licence if necessary – broadcasting companies which break the rules. The Broadcasting Standards Commission is also a statutory body with the power to insist that its adjudications are prominently published. Even the BBC is awarded its charter under law and has statutory obligations for the standards of its broadcasts. The decisions of all these bodies can be challenged in the courts and they must all report annually on their activities to the Secretary of State for National Heritage.

## Working with different styles of media council

Media councils work in different ways. Those which are true cross-industry bodies tend to have codes of conduct that represent that broad church of views. Codes, such as those in Sweden, often contain more matters of concern about the gathering of news material whilst Britain's press code, drawn up by editors and publishers, is much more about what may be published. Only intense public pressure, particularly after the death of the Princess of Wales, has forced the Press Complaints Commission in Britain to include additional clauses covering news-gathering on private land and the use of long telephoto camera lenses (see Exhibit 6.1). Before 1998 we would have to look to the National Union of Journalist's Code of Conduct to see clauses which emphasised the moral aspects of how stories are gathered rather than worrying solely about whether they are published (see Appendix 2).

The PCC's new code (PCC, 1998) contains much stronger clauses on harassment and privacy.

Often countries have separate bodies for dealing with press and broadcasting and this may even mean different codes. Britain, as we have seen, has several bodies to control broadcasting (e.g. the BSC). All are statutory. Sweden has one code upheld by both broadcasters and print journalists. This is partly, at least, because the code's historical roots lie as a development of print journalism with any additional clauses required for broadcasting being added as necessary. Britain and many other European countries developed press and broadcasting councils at different times and for different reasons. This means that their codes of conduct are often different as well. It is certainly true that Britain's press code and broadcast code are both posited from the position of a publisher or editor, yet many of the really interesting ethical issues occur whether the material is published or not, as Case study 6.1 illustrates.

## Case study 6.1 The ethics of gathering of information

I came across a case of a freelance photographer working in England who would dress as a paramedic to attend the scenes of accidents to allow him closer to the victim. In one incident, an 11-year-old boy was dragged from a canal and resuscitated. He had been dried as he was suffering from hypothermia. The photographer splashed him with water again in order to get a more 'dramatic' picture. This sort of behaviour is reprehensible and would be accepted by very few people, journalists and public alike. However there is no way to censure it. The Press Complaints Commission cannot handle it – it can only censure the newspaper responsible for publication and in this case there isn't one as the photographer was freelance. Even if there were a newspaper involved, it is very possible that it would not be aware of, or condone, this person's practice.

Voice or video recordings made in secret are subject to the same ethical problems. Once a recording has been made, it is too late to decide whether it was ethical to make the recording, we can only debate whether it should have been broadcast or published as a transcript. Does this matter in practice? Can one imagine circumstances when the recording is unethical but the broadcasting or publication is not? Imagine a tape recording of a telephone call by a Cabinet minister exposed him as corrupt. Invading the minister's privacy by listening to the call is difficult to justify, but publishing a story that the minister is corrupt, backed by transcripts of phone calls, is an entirely different matter. The journalist could then justify the invasion of privacy as being in the public interest. Of course in the broadcast area, secret recording is something the Broadcasting Standards Commission is specifically charged to consider.

Many people still blame the paparazzi for the death of the Princess of Wales. Had they not been following her car in order to take pictures, some say, the accident might not have happened. Leaving aside the what-ifs, there is certainly little question that following the crash, a number of photographers (approximately 10 although witnesses differ in their accounts) were at the scene taking pictures before the ambulance and police arrived. This was generally considered so shocking, that no British publication or broadcast used any of the many pictures that must have been taken of the crash site and the rescue. Yet pictures and videos of this sort are commonly used in news reports, from the assassination of President Kennedy to numerous train and plane crashes here and abroad. Even the many documentaries that have since been broadcast, speculating on the cause of the accident, have not been prepared to risk attack by using photographs of the scene.

Few examples show as starkly the difference in ethical approach of the journalist and the public. Few journalists (I have not spoken to one) would find it acceptable for a photographer at the scene of such an incident to report to his or her news desk that he or she had not bothered to take pictures because he or she did not think it was quite right. The photographer's job is to take pictures of news events and that is what he or she should do. That does not mean that common humanity goes out of the window. Of course, the ever-present mobile phones should have been used to call an ambulance and of course basic first aid or rescue should have been carried out to the best of the photographer's ability. But taking photographs only takes a short time.

## Enforcing ethical standards

### Statutory enforcement of ethical standards

State control of ethical standards is usually enforced by either the law or a statutory regulatory body or a mixture of both. Regulation is either by a practitioners' body, such as the *Ordine dei Giornalisti* in Italy, which registers practitioners and can prevent people practising if they are found to be in breach of the code, or it is a statutory industry council made up of a mix of proprietors, editors, practitioners and lay people which is able to condemn bad practice and in some cases level a penalty against the offender. Usually this is a fine. Systems such as this operate in a number of Western European countries and elsewhere. South Africa, Australia and India all have press councils. As explained, nearly every culture finds it necessary to enforce some issue of press ethics by introducing legislation. Most Western-style democracies have developed a cultural ethic for journalists that cover in some way most or all of the issues of truth, privacy, harassment and fairness. In some cases the society concerned will enforce that ethic by legislation and it is one of the more interesting and revealing areas of study for those seeking difference in national cultures and identities.

Swedes and the Dutch, for instance, are generally seen as liberal and free thinking and have very little legislative control of media ethics. Their codes of conduct are controlled by media councils. Yet their journalists stick to the codes of ethics more strongly than journalists do in Britain and journalists in Sweden and Holland are often shocked by the lengths journalists in Britain will go to get a story.

In Britain we have a much more rigid approach to such things. 'There should be a law against it' is our first thought when something displeases us. The only trouble is that when we produce a law against something we then spend much of our time complaining about excessive regulation and trying to find a way around it.

## Regulation versus the law

'I am convinced self-regulation is delivering the goods' (Lord Wakeham, PCC Chairman, in the 1995 *Annual Report*). The PCC in its submission to David Calcutt said:

> British Democracy will be imperilled and freedom of expression put at risk if the Government decides self-regulation of the press has failed and legislates to control it. It is vital to draw a frontier of freedom between the government and the press. The press should be subject, like all citizens, to the law, but never the state.

This is more than a little disingenuous. It is perfectly possible for the press to be answerable under the law but not to the state. We are already tightly controlled in this country – more so than most. All that legislation about what can be published has done is distort our view in this country about what is ethical and what is not. Journalists have become so busy trying to slip around the wording of this law or that that they rarely step back and look at the ethical dimension of what they are doing (as Case study 6.3 on p. 114 illustrates).

It is also worth considering that whilst the press is allegedly free, constrained only by a voluntary self-regulatory body, broadcasting in this country is heavily hedged about by statutory regulatory bodies. They also face even more laws about what they can or cannot broadcast. Whilst an argument for impartiality on television but not in the press can be sustained, it is much more difficult to understand why there should be such stiff regulation on fairness and privacy for television but not for the press. One also needs to consider what part this plays in the general view that broadcasting is more trustworthy than newspapers. If we are concerned about whether something is ethical, we need to deal with it on several levels. This relationship between the law and ethics is very important. Nearly all laws are based on moral principles of social fairness. Yet just having the law can often mask the moral principle and prevent the right moral outcome.

## Self-regulation versus statutory regulation

One way of dealing with the problem of giving teeth to the enforcement of moral judgement without going all the way to law and risking completely masking the ethical principle is to use the law at one remove. This can be achieved by giving a regulatory body statutory powers. A statutory regulatory body is one which is set up under statute; its membership is selected according to criteria laid down by law and its method of hearing complaints and punishing offenders is also laid down by statute. Broadcasting bodies such as the ITC and the Broadcasting Standards Commission in the UK are statutory regulatory bodies.

Sir David Calcutt, in his second report, concluded that this was the only way to deal with the press: 'I recommend that the government should now introduce a statutory regime' (1993: para 9, p. xii). He went on to describe in detail a tribunal composed of three judges which would have the power to require the printing of adjudications and apologies, to impose fines and award costs. The Heritage Committee also recommended a statutory tribunal although theirs was much more like the PCC but with the backing of the courts.

Statutory bodies have clear attractions for politicians in that they can point to a body which can deal with the industry as most statutory bodies have the power to fine transgressors or punish in other ways. Most importantly of all for journalists, a statutory body must have the right of appeal. Whether it is a simple judicial review of the decision or a more formal appeals procedure, an appeals system gives journalists the chance to fight their corner in several different theatres.

At the moment, with a non-statutory body such as the Press Complaints Commission, cases are sometimes not properly tested because it would not be in the interests of self-regulation to pursue many cases. If it were a case that might bring the industry into disrepute, even if it was not in fact unethical, then a self-regulatory body, in order to maintain its position, might feel obliged to bring in a decision knowing that it had no particular impact as the only punishment is the publication of the adjudication. This would give journalists no chance to appeal the decision.

## Statutory regulation versus the law

A statutory body is a much better choice for a government than having a range of laws enforcing ethics. Laws covering all the elements of a journalistic code of conduct would be very difficult to word and enforce. A statutory body similar to the present PCC, but with a different membership and method of selection, is much more manageable. It would not be too difficult to persuade a public, which is often disgusted by the antics of the tabloid press, that this was just a way of giving the Press Complaints Commission teeth. The public is now used to the Press Complaints Commission and accepts that it has industry support. Despite the industry's claims about the 'horrors' of statutory bodies, it is very difficult to portray such bodies as unacceptable when self-regulatory bodies doing the same thing are claimed to be fine. The argument then seems to be that it is all right to have a controlling body only if it is run by the industry it is set up to control. Not making the body statutory would be a difficult case to make, particularly when broadcasters are already under the aegis of statutory bodies, begging the obvious question: what is wrong with statutory regulation for the press if it is all right for broadcasters?

A statutory body would have many of the advantages of the present system with the force of law to back up its decisions. Crucially, it would also offer journalists a right of appeal with a recourse to judicial review of the Commission's judgements. It can only be a matter of time, if the tabloids continue to attract public calumny, before deals are done to accept statutory regulation in exchange for some favour such as a Freedom of Information Act. The alternative is highly restrictive legislation introduced in the wake of some appalling gaffe by one or more of the tabloid newspapers.

## The law and reporting

As has been explained, when societies become particularly concerned about an ethical issue they often include the principle in their law. This has the advantage of short-circuiting any debate about the issue.

There are two classes of law that concern us in Britain: civil law and criminal law. Criminal law is based on the Crown bringing a prosecution against someone against whom a complaint has been made. In civil law claimants (formerly called plaintiffs) make demands for redress in actions against defendants who they claim have damaged them in some way. The civil suits that most concern journalists are those seeking recompense for damage to a person's reputation (libel). In the criminal field there are a number of laws which aim to guarantee a journalist's ethics: protecting the presumed innocence of the accused, protecting minors and victims, data protection, intrusion official secrets, and so on.

## Ethics and the law

There are several good books about the law and journalism such as T. Welsh and W. Greenwood's *Essential Law for Journalists* (1995); P. Carey's *Media Law* (1996); and T. Crone's *Law and the Media* (1995). I do not intend to go into the law in detail, but I do want to look at its relationship with the perception of ethical behaviour. There are a number of views about where the join between law and morality should be. Some people believe that the law has no place in controlling morality, whilst some think it should cover everything.

But the law does have a different effect on people than does a mere code of conduct. Whilst a person's own moral code may supersede the law every time, a professional code does not have the same power. The balance of loyalties and other considerations mean journalists will take many cases on their merits. A code can only be for guidance. This means that when there are conflicts between the law and professional practice, the law will almost always take precedence. The only significant exception to this is confidentiality of sources. Many journalists believe that keeping confidential sources confidential is more important than an instruction from a judge to reveal the source. But this may be more to do with an individual belief in keeping promises made than any strict adherence to a professional code.

However there is a major warping effect introduced by the construction of laws affecting the media that we must understand. There are a number of elements in UK law that supersede potential clauses in a code of conduct which are often included in codes used in other countries. Particular examples are protection of personal honour and presumption of innocence, although there are other areas where the law cuts across codes of practice to their detriment.

The law in the UK is strong in the area of presumption of innocence. The British have traditionally believed in fair trials and have gone to some lengths to protect the fairness and impartiality of the justice system. This is particularly concerned with protecting the jury and being scrupulous about giving the accused a fair trial. Although the right to silence has now been removed, the right to be presumed innocent still remains and is protected by law. Because it is so firmly protected, the British journalist does not consider it to be an ethical issue. After arrest and charge, the accused is protected by the contempt of court Acts which make it an offence for the media to publish anything other than legally limited facts about the accused and the alleged crime. Before arrest (and indeed after the verdict) the accused has some protection under the libel laws.

The protection of personal honour is also something the British feel strongly about. No one likes the idea of his or her reputation being wrongly impugned (as Case study 6.2 illustrates). The laws of defamation seek to ensure legal redress for those so accused. Unfortunately, this means that any moral view on protection of personal honour has been subsumed by the legal requirement.

The same is true about reporting on minors. This is not too surprising if we believe, as we clearly do if the law is any guide, that children are not fully responsible for their actions until the age of 18. We seem to believe that they are still going through a learning process which means their behaviour and relationship with society is redeemable. Although most journalists in the UK would probably accept this argument, they do not automatically consider whether to name when faced with a story about children.

In a PCC case, the *Reading Evening Post* named an 11-year-old child who had been admitted to hospital with meningitis:

> ... while the Commission had sympathy with the newspaper's wish to keep its readers properly informed, it nevertheless considered that in the light of the action taken by the school, publication of the boy's name was not essential for the protection of public health. In reaching its conclusion the Commission took into account that the school was named and that concerned parents unconnected with the school could have made further enquiries. The complaint is therefore upheld, but in view of the sensitive handling of the matter, the Commission decide on this occasion not to censure the paper. (PCC, Report No. 37, 1997: 26)

It is unlikely that this was a deliberate attempt on behalf of the *Reading Evening Post* to stretch the limits of the PCC Code. It was trying to keep readers informed and the idea that the child should not have been named simply did not occur to anyone. Naming youngsters is not an ethical issue for most UK journalists. Whilst most journalists accept the sense in the law preventing identification, they see it as a restrictive area of law to be worked around, not as the first step in an ethical tussle which pits the rights of young people against the right of the public to know.

### Case study 6.2 Libel suits and the press

For most British editors, it is not a debate about the morality of exposing someone's private doings that is the major deciding factor about whether to publish, but whether the person can afford financially to sue. The debate has all too often become 'will they sue?' not 'are we right, and can we prove it?' As the following examples show, things do not always work out for those seeking to protect their reputation by suing the media, and there have been some very expensive failed actions by the those in the public eye.

Gillian Taylforth, the actress in the BBC soap opera, *East Enders*, sued the *Sun* newspaper in 1994 after it repeated a police allegation that she and her boyfriend had committed an indecent act in a Range Rover on a slip road off the A1 in June 1992. She lost in the High Court and was ordered to pay £500,000 costs.

Sonia Sutcliffe, the wife of Yorkshire Ripper Peter Sutcliffe, lost an action against the *News of the World* at a cost of £200,000. And Janie Allen, a South African journalist who lost an action against Channel 4 at a reputed cost of £300,000, has seen newspapers measuring a potential victim's purse rather than their reputation.

**111**

The spectacular collapse of the then MP Neil Hamilton's action against the *Guardian* was blamed by him on the exorbitant cost of such actions, although Alan Rusbridger, the *Guardian*'s editor, said that research carried out as part of the paper's defence showed its original allegations were 'just the tip of the iceberg'. He added: 'This research, together with documents which were disclosed to us by 10 Downing Street as part of the legal process, made it apparent that [Mr Hamilton and Mr Greer] didn't have a leg to stand on' (*Electronic Telegraph*, 'Tory drops libel fight over sleaze', 1 October 1996). The *Guardian* went on to publish further and far more detailed allegations in the days following the collapse of the case. Hamilton continued to protest his innocence but lost his parliamentary seat in the 1997 general election to the independent candidate, Martin Bell, a former BBC journalist, standing on an anti-corruption ticket.

Another Tory MP, Jonathan Aitken, the former Cabinet minister, faced legal costs of £2 million after abandoning his action against the *Guardian* and Granada TV. The *Guardian* produced documents which allegedly showed he lied under oath over details of a weekend spent at the Ritz Hotel in Paris. He agreed to pay 80 per cent of the defendants' costs. The *Daily Telegraph* reported:

> No reason was given for his decision to abandon the action.
>
> Afterwards, Alan Rusbridger, editor of the *Guardian*, said: 'For three years he has lied to newspapers, lied to the Cabinet Secretary, lied to the Prime Minister and lied to his colleagues. Now he has made his fatal mistake by lying on oath to the High Court.' (*Electronic Telegraph*: 'Aitken faces £2m bill in libel defeat', 21 June 1997).

Aitken and his daughter were afterwards investigated by the police over allegations of perjury. He resigned from the Privy Council, was found guilty of perjury and was sentenced to a term of imprisonment.

Since the cost of legal action can scare publishers from telling the damaging truth about the rich, it means they are more likely to write about the less rich, secure in the knowledge that they cannot afford to sue. More and more tabloid newspapers are invading the privacy of ordinary citizens who do not have the money to fight libel actions, rather than celebrities who do. The *Star* (12 February 1996) told the story of a 'do-gooder' who ran off with the wife of his rugby coach friend. The story was based entirely on the comments of a cuckolded and presumably embittered and vengeful husband whose wife of 21 years had ended her marriage to be with her lover, who had also left his wife. The abandoned wife did not want to be involved and told the *Star* she did not wish to comment. There were no quotes from the other parties. What possible public interest could there be in this story? Yet the *Star* ran it across two pages. All the parties involved had their names used, their privacy invaded and their personal honour dragged through the mud. There was nothing defamatory published, provided it was true, but it was an unnecessary and unsavoury report.

## Law replacing morals

If you were to be given change for a ten pound note in a shop where you had only offered a five pound note, would you return the change? Keeping the extra is probably not illegal because there was no intent to steal (the law requires a Kantian-style motive for many actions to become illegal). If you were challenged, you could claim a mistake and hand back the cash with nothing more than a little embarrassment. Keeping the change is unethical by most people's standards: you would have taken what is not yours – a reasonable definition of stealing – but many people would still keep the change because it is not against the law and they can get away with it.

As an ethical issue the duty to protect someone's reputation, unless the public interest demands invasion, remains under all circumstances. However, under a civil law system, if you are too poor, or are dead, then there is no protection. If more laws are introduced as a way of dealing with press excesses, there is a danger that they could persuade editors and journalists, as well as the public, into believing that they have firmed up the journalist's ethical backbone when all that has happened is the law has attempted to replace ethics with a mechanical approach that is bound to be less flexible. Where journalists no longer need to consider what they are doing in an ethical light, they will consider only the law.

Each social community within a sovereign state has different views on what is immoral, whilst facing the same laws as laid down by statute or common practice. In the field of tax, for instance, it is a crime not to pay all the tax due under the law, but for many groups in society it is not sinful to evade paying tax due – provided you don't get caught. Every group in society has its views on morality and the law, formed by the views of its members, and we tend to adjust our moral sense to those of our peers and contemporaries. For instance, it would be completely wrong for a doctor to start a sexual relationship with a patient although this would not apply to someone in a different profession, say a plumber and client. Often there are good reasons for these differences in moral acceptability, sometimes it is just a matter of historical accident.

However, journalists tend to have their own unique view of morality that is different in approach from that of society at large. This is particularly so in the area of privacy. Journalism students may start their course sharing the views of the public that privacy is sacrosanct and that we have no reason to invade it. This makes teaching ethics fairly easy; student resistance to invading privacy is high. By the end of the course their view tends to have shifted emphasis and become closer to that of the seasoned journalist. They now consider press freedom and the public interest to be of considerable importance and if this requires the sacrifice of privacy on occasion, then so be it.

In Britain, newspapers can often seem more concerned with the letter of the law rather than its spirit, grounded in ethical practice. This provides a good example of an area where countries differ. In Sweden, for instance, journalists do not cover court cases in the same way that British journalists do. Whilst this is now partly cultural, the Swedish code of conduct can also explain how this happens. It reminds journalists that 'in the eyes of the law, a person suspected of an offence is always presumed innocent until he [or she] is proved guilty. The final outcome of a case that is described should be reported' (clause 14, Swedish Code of Ethics for Press, Radio and Television). This is very different from what actually happens in Britain. Although the law covers the detailed process of arrest, charge and trial, it does not cover cases that slip outside these criteria. One such example is Fred West who, with his wife Rosemary, was accused in 1995 of murdering a number of young women. Whilst I do not want to appear to be trying to gain sympathy for someone who almost certainly committed or helped to commit a large number of horrific crimes, his suicide does mean that he did not face trial and did not get the opportunity to rebut the charges made against him. When he committed suicide, many of the tabloids consulted their lawyers, found there was now no legal reason not to condemn West and ran appropriate stories. Most of the broadsheets and the broadcasters were more cautious, talking about the man who 'allegedly killed' a number of girls and young women. Nor is this a sterile, legal or ethical argument. Rosemary West was left to face the music with her claimed innocence clouded by the revelations produced on her husband's death.

The law can help guarantee the element of society's moral values that are perhaps not shared by journalists, but the danger is that if the journalists' moral sense in this area is eroded, then they will spend time trying to circumvent the law, because they cannot see it as a moral necessity, just an impediment to publishing material of public interest.

### Case study 6.3 The press, the law and morality

In 1996 Colin Stagg was acquitted of the murder of Rachel Nickell. The *Mail on Sunday* (20 October 1996), however, decided to publish evidence not used in the murder trial against Stagg. The prosecution in that trial had decided not to use much of the evidence (as it did not and could not prove Stagg guilty) after the judge had ruled conversations between Stagg and a policewoman inadmissible because they were not up to the standard of evidence required of a criminal court.

The *Mail on Sunday* ignored any moral requirement to presume someone's innocence solely because the law did not directly forbid them using that evidence – the law could not have foreseen such a combination of circumstances. The newspaper's only moral defence was that Stagg was not actually accused of the crime and that therefore presumption of innocence no longer applied.

The press has a duty to track down wrong-doing and make accusations. However, in the normal course of events, the person so accused would have the option of facing a trial and proving the evidence wrong or, theoretically at least, of suing for defamation. Stagg had already faced trial and been acquitted. The law said he did not commit that murder. He could not afford a defamation case; he is a man of only moderate means. And what if Stagg were to have brought such a case and lose? The burden of proof in a civil trial is not as strong as in a criminal trial. For a criminal trial, the prosecution must prove their case beyond reasonable doubt. In a civil trial, the court is deciding between two opposing claims and will pick the one where the burden of proof is strongest. It would be perfectly possible for a court to decide Stagg had no reputation to lose, without him necessarily being guilty of the offence of murder. Such a decision would leave him in an invidious position. Assuming he could afford legal advice about bringing such a suit, lawyers might well advise him against making a mockery of any claims about justice made by the *Mail on Sunday*.

The then editor of the *Mail on Sunday*, Jonathan Holborow, in a letter to *The Times* (24 October 1996) put the paper's case:

> It seems, apparently, that it is politically and legally correct for newspapers to involve themselves in investigations where, for instance, the Guildford Four or the Birmingham Six were found guilty, and for those decisions to be reversed; but not to look into evidence against an accused, subsequently acquitted, which was never presented to a jury. There is an anomaly in English law here which should be addressed if Justice, which at present has one legal eye peeping out from her blindfold, is to be truly served.

In the same edition, Magnus Linklater puts the opposite view under the heading 'Press excesses are getting worse': 'Yet by any standards the *Mail*'s story was grossly unfair. By presenting prosecution evidence that was never submitted to rigorous testing at the hands of the defence, the impression was given that this was reliable information.'

---

As explained above, both the protection of personal honour and presumption of innocence are covered by law in this country. Yet, as Case study 6.3 shows, both can be trampled by a newspaper which finds a way through the legal maze that attempts to cover an area which should be a moral consideration only. In the Swedish code of media conduct, a person accused of an offence has to be presumed innocent. Would this evidence have been published in Sweden? It seems unlikely. A case like this is pretty rare and neither I nor other colleagues I have asked about it can recall a similar case where disallowed evidence has been used by a paper. There was a suggestion at the time, by the legal luminary Lord Denning, that this publication constituted a contempt of court but no case has been laid against the paper.

## Summary

- Codes of conduct were introduced to give moral guidance to journalists and to reassure the public that those who transgress the standards of practice will be disciplined.
- Broadcasting is tightly controlled by licensing authorities; in contrast the press is subject to self-regulation.
- Different levels of statutory enforcements can underpin self-regulation. Bodies with statutory powers can fine newspapers and make sure the results of adjudications are published.
- There is a danger that if more laws are introduced in relation to the press journalists will not consider the ethical issues involved.

## Questions

1 Produce a short code of conduct for journalists. Can you see any areas in the code that might be open to different interpretations by different journalists?

2 Self-regulatory councils are often condemned for being 'toothless'. How would you provide a council with the power to punish the media when it breaches codes of conduct?

3 Broadcast stations are tightly controlled through licensing and statutory regulatory bodies, but newspapers are not. What are some of the reasons given for this difference? Do you think it is right?

4 Name some of the difficulties and issues that would arise if more laws were introduced to enforce media ethics.

# Chapter 7

................................................................

# Practical applications of the ethical issues

## Chapter outline

- This chapter considers all the main areas of ethical concern for journalists.
- It examines the problems faced by contrasting people's privacy with the need for the public to know.
- It explores the difficulties journalists face in dealing with people's reputations.
- It carries out a detailed analysis of journalists' obligations to various codes of conduct.

Many countries have codes of conduct for journalists and in the previous chapter we discussed how these have developed and are regulated. We also discussed some of the theories that underpin views of journalistic morality. It is now time to look at how codes of conduct, all of which contain Kantian-style universal directives, operate in detail, and their practical applications. There are ten main elements in most codes of conduct, covering:

- Gathering information.
- Dealing with contacts and sources.
- Publishing the information.
- Presenting the information.
- Guaranteeing the quality of information.
- Dealing with any complaints.

I intend to discuss each of these elements and what different codes have to say about them in relation to important ethical topics, including privacy, accuracy and harassment. The wording used in a variety of codes of practice, including the PCC Code, the BSC Code, the NUJ Code and the BBC's *Producers' Guidelines* will be explained. It is interesting to draw comparisons between these different codes of conduct as they highlight the differences in approach to journalism by print and broadcast journalists. They also help

**117**

expose the distorting effect that results from treating journalism as a marketable product rather than something that should be made available to people as part of some democratic responsibility. The other regulatory bodies in this country do not have such far-reaching codes, and I will mention them when applicable.

Both the PCC Code and the NUJ Code are printed in full in Appendices 1 and 2 respectively. The *BBC Producers' Guidelines* is 300 pages long and so I have printed excerpts as comparisons. The entire document is available on the World Wide Web at http://bbc.co.uk/info/editorial/prodgl/contents. htm. The BSC Code is also lengthy and is available at http://www.bsc.org. uk. The ITC code can be obtained at http://www.itc.org.uk. Several other codes are also published in the Appendices of this book for comparison, but all the European codes can be found at http://www.uta.fi/ethicnet/.

## Privacy

'A society which permits individuals to choose how they are to lead their lives is one which will recognise the choice of privacy' (Lord Chancellor's Department, 1993: 9). Invasion of privacy is the issue that probably most concerns the public. It is certainly the issue that has underlined all the major debates on the press of the last ten years or so. Privacy is recognised by psychologists as a basic human need; a drive almost as powerful as sex, hunger and thirst. We all need privacy and we need to be in control of the flow of information about our private selves. It is often said that information is power, but it is just as true that control over information is power.

There are cultural differences in what information should be considered as private. Some cultures believe in keeping names private. In British society names have some power. When dealing with strangers, we expect to be called by our surname and probably a title. Only when we get to know people would we use our forenames. Amongst intimates, of course, we might have a nickname and these 'private' names are often a better reflection of how people view themselves than their 'public' names. However, we may feel embarrassment if this private name were to be released to strangers.

We use privacy in our social dealings as a token of good faith and fair dealing. When introduced to strangers, we will talk pleasantly about the weather, the traffic and other areas of inconsequential nonsense. This is an essential social tool in the building of relationships. It allows us to measure up the other person before we move on to revealing elements of ourselves that are more intimate and not generally available for public consumption. We use gradual invasions of our privacy, which we share exchange by exchange, as the price of a growing bond with the other person. There are several levels of this relationship. For instance, private details of work we might exchange with work colleagues, depending on the nature of our relationship; personal family details would be exchanged with relatives, depending on their closeness and so on.

It follows that if we are using self-inflicted invasions of our privacy as the price of our place in our circle of friends and acquaintances, we can hardly be surprised if people react badly to having their privacy invaded uninvited, particularly if that invasion involves really intimate details (of a sexual nature, for example) as the tabloids often do. The question is not so much about the invasion, but about control over the information. This may be why people will often allow their story to be published for money. Money can also be used as a token to establish our place in society, so one thing of value has only been exchanged for another, and the people selling details about their life have retained control of the transaction.

Because intimate revelations are tokens which people use to 'buy' our friendship, they have currency and we are nearly always interested to hear of people's intimate affairs. Furthermore, this knowledge can help shape our view of society and its boundaries of behaviour. Those of high status and celebrity can be role models; we look to them as major boundary shapers. This is why many of the fiercest rows about privacy have involved the royal family; their marriages and love lives have been laid bare for our inspection under the guise of public interest and many people have rightly asked whether the press has gone too far, too often – especially since the death of Diana, Princess of Wales, in August 1997.

Whilst 'seven out of ten of all complaints made to the PCC concern inaccuracy in press reporting' (PCC, 1995: 7), the complaints that cause the most controversy are the invasions of privacy. Most codes of conduct, and certainly the NUJ's, the PCC's, the BBC's *Producers' Guidelines*, the Swedish code and the BSC's, are concerned with privacy. This is particularly true of the BSC as it only has two functions: to consider cases of unjust or unfair treatment and invasions of privacy. However, writing a universal law to cover privacy is very difficult if we are to allow for the public's 'right to know' in certain cases. There are too many variables around the circumstances of each invasion of privacy to allow for hard-and-fast rules. Clifford Christians advocates three tests for the journalist:

1 Decency and fairness is non-negotiable.
2 'Redeeming social value' should be used as a criterion for deciding when to invade privacy.
3 The dignity of the person should not be maligned in the name of press privilege (Christians et al., 1998: 111).

There have been many serious invasions of privacy by the British press over the past few years and these breaches, especially those involving the Princess of Wales, have led to an outcry to introduce some form of legislation.

## The right to privacy

A number of countries around the world already have legislation to prevent invasions of privacy. France has specific laws. Others, such as Belgium or Italy, have clauses in their constitutions that protect the private rights of citizens. The UN Declaration of Human Rights also has such a clause, as does the European Convention on Human Rights.

People's concern with invasions of privacy is a fairly recent phenomenon. Very little was written about privacy until the end of the last century. One of the earliest definitions of privacy is Thomas Cooley's (1888) 'the right to be left alone'. Concern over invasions of privacy started to grow in Britain, and elsewhere in Europe, after the Second World War. As radio and television gradually took over the alerting element of hard news from newspapers, the tabloids increasingly published gossip and stories involving invasions of privacy. The first British Royal Commission on the Press in 1947–49 says hardly anything about the invasion of privacy. It is concerned with monopoly ownership and accuracy. By the late 1960s and early 1970s, however, it was firmly on the agenda. The Nordic Conference on the Right of Privacy (1967) came to the conclusion that:

> The right to privacy is the right to be let alone to live one's own life with the minimum degree of interference. In expanded form this means:
> The right of the individual to lead his [sic] own life protected against:
> (a) Interference with his private, family and home life;
> (b) Interference with his physical and mental integrity or his moral and intellectual freedom;
> (c) Attacks on his honour and reputation;
> (d) Being placed in a false light;
> (e) The disclosure of embarrassing facts relating to his private life;
> (f) The use of his name, identity or likeness;
> (g) Spying, prying, watching and besetting;
> (h) Interference with his correspondence;
> (i) Misuse of his private communications, written or oral;
> (j) Disclosure of information given or received by him in a condition of professional confidence. (Committee on Privacy, 1972: 327)

In 1972, a committee was set up in Britain under the chairmanship of the Rt Hon Kenneth Younger. This investigated the need for privacy legislation. It found, as had others before them, some difficulty in defining precisely what was meant by 'privacy'. 'The majority of us regard the "Justice" Committee's conclusions as one more indication, and a highly significant one, that the concept of privacy cannot be satisfactorily defined' (Committee on Privacy, 1972: 17). The 'Justice' Committee's conclusion says:

> We have therefore concluded that no purpose would be served by our making yet another attempt at developing an intellectually rigorous analysis. We prefer instead to leave the concept much as we have found it, that is as a notion about whose precise boundaries there will always be a variety of opinions, but about whose central area there will always be a large measure of agreement. (Ibid.: 18)

This Committee came to the conclusion that there were risks in placing excessive reliance on the law in order to protect privacy. It recommended that the then Press Council should codify its adjudications on invasions of privacy and that the then Programmes Complaints Commission – the forerunner of the BCC – should have its power extended to handle complaints about privacy.

The 1947–49 Royal Commission on the Press also came to the conclusion that the law was no place for privacy: 'Quite apart from the fact that we consider the Press Council a better forum for establishing rules of conduct for the press in relation to invasions of privacy, we think it would reduce its status and importance if its jurisdiction over this area of activity were to be removed' (Royal Commission on the Press, 1977: 187). The Calcutt Report on Privacy and Related Matters, set up by the government in 1989 and reporting in 1990, came to similar conclusions, but decided that the Press Council should be replaced by the PCC. It recommended against a statutory tort of infringement of privacy but did want to see the introduction of a criminal offence for physical intrusion. Any person able to prove intrusion would be able to prevent the publication of an article gathered in that way. Taking photographs and the placing of surveillance devices without consent should also be an offence. A public interest defence was available.

The House of Commons' Heritage Committee also examined the issue and came to the conclusion that a protection of privacy bill should be introduced. In 1995 the Heritage minister finally reported that the government had been unable to formulate wording and therefore was not intending to introduce such a bill.

> The Government has long recognised that there is, in principle, a case for the introduction of such offences. . . . The government has, however, so far been unable to construct legislation which, in practice, would be sufficiently workable to be responsibly brought to the statute book. It has no wish to introduce bad legislation. It therefore has no immediate plans to legislate in this area. (*Privacy and Media Intrusion*, 1995: 9)

The Labour government made it clear early on that it also favoured self-regulation and did not intend to introduce privacy legislation. The history of privacy in the UK is summarised in Exhibit 7.1.

**121**

## Exhibit 7.1 The history of privacy in the UK

Privacy has a relatively short history in the UK and there was little concern about it until widespread literacy made reading about your fellow citizens a possibility and photography made picture intrusions a reality.

1926   The Judicial Proceedings (Regulation of Reports) Act limited what could be written about divorces. This was one of the first pieces of legislation determining what could be written about people's personal lives.

1933   Children and Young Persons Act 1933 prevented the reporting of the identity of children (aged 10–14) and young persons (aged 14–17) as alleged offenders or witnesses in magistrates' courts.

1937   Both proprietors' and journalists' organisations passed formal resolutions condemning methods of news-gathering which caused distress to private persons.

1947   The 1947 Royal Commission on the Press paid little attention to privacy. It was suggested to the Commission that intrusions into the privacy of individuals, especially those who have suffered bereavement, was an abuse that should be corrected by legislation. The Commission felt it would be 'extremely difficult to devise legislation which would deal with the mischief effectively and be capable of enforcement' (Royal Commission, 1949: 170) and that it was up to the industry to make condemnation of bad practice effective. The General Council of the Press (as suggested by the Commission) would have a role to play here.

1961   The 1961 Royal Commission on the Press said nothing about privacy. However, a bill was put before parliament by Lord Mancroft in the same year to protect a person from any unjustifiable publication relating to his private affairs and to give him rights at law in the event of such publication. It was given a second reading but was withdrawn at the end of the debate to go into committee.

1967   Mr Alexander Lyon MP introduced a bill to protect persons from any unreasonable and serious interference with their seclusion of themselves, their family or their property from the public. The bill was introduced as a ten-minute bill and there was no second reading.
       The Nordic Conference on the Right of Privacy was highly influential in developing some of the main concerns about privacy.

1969   Mr Brian Walden MP introduced a bill to establish a right of privacy, to make consequential amendments to the law of evidence and for connected purposes. His bill was withdrawn after the second reading debate.

1970   The first stab at a privacy law was attempted by the Justice Committee which investigated privacy and the law and reported back to parliament.

1972   The Younger Committee on privacy concluded that: 'Privacy is ill-suited to be the subject of a long process of definition through the building up of precedents over the years since the judgements of the past would be an unreliable guide to any current evaluation of privacy' (Committee on Privacy, 1972: 206). On the other hand, it pointed out that without precedent the law would remain 'an ill-defined and unstable concept' (ibid.) as it was first formulated. In the end they agreed to three things:

- The restatement of the law of breach of confidence.
- The introduction of laws banning electronic bugging.
- The introduction of a new tort of publication of information gained unlawfully.

A minority report by Mr Alexander Lyon MP favoured the addition of a civil tort for invasion of privacy. He had already introduced a bill to attempt this in the past. Mr D. Ross also issued a minority report favouring a general right of privacy along the lines of Mr Brian Walden's bill (see **1969** above).

**1974** The Rehabilitation of Offenders Act 1974 made it an offence to detail an offender's criminal past after a suitable period of rehabilitation had elapsed.

**1976** The Sexual Offences Act 1976 made it an offence to name the victims and accused in rape cases.

**1977** The 1977 Royal Commission discussed privacy but decided this was not within its remit.

In February, Mr Tom Litterick MP attempted to introduce a Freedom of Information and Privacy Bill. It did not get past its first reading.

**1984** The Data Protection Act 1984 was agreed, giving protection to the privacy of personal data held on computers. The 1992–96 Conservative government had intended to allow government institutions to share computer-held information in a way that is barred under the present Act. This was opposed by those concerned about government invasions. On the other hand, newspaper editors were becoming concerned about the use of the Data Protection Act 1984 as a way of preventing the release of information. They were concerned that changes in the Act could tighten up their access to information about people.

**1988** A Right of Privacy Bill was introduced to the house by Mr William Cash MP to 'establish a right of privacy, to make amendments to the law of evidence, and for connected purposes'. This would have allowed for civil action and had a public benefit defence. Proving something is for the public benefit is not the same as proving it to be in the public interest. The bill did not receive a second reading.

The Sexual Offences (Amendment) Act 1988 removed the right of the accused in rape cases to have his name kept confidential. The right of the victim to keep her name confidential was also brought forward to the moment an accusation was made rather than when the case came to court, as had previously been the case.

**1989** A Protection of Privacy Bill to establish a right of privacy against the unauthorised use or disclosure of private information and for connected purposes was introduced into parliament by Mr John Browne MP. This bill made breaching privacy a civil offence with a public interest defence. It was withdrawn after the committee stage but before the report stage. Breach of confidence law does have some part to play in privacy. The law was best defined in 1990 by the Master of the Rolls Sir John Donaldson in a judgement *Attorney General* v *Guardian Newspapers*.

The Children Act 1989 raised the age at which minors could be identified to 18.

▶

## Exhibit 7.1 continued

| | |
|---|---|
| **1990** | The Calcutt Committee on privacy and related matters recommended that a law should be introduced making physical intrusion an offence, but did not call for a privacy law. |
| **1992** | The Sexual Offences (Amendment) Act 1992 widened the range of victims who are legally entitled to keep their names secret. Both men and women who were the victims of sexual assault, buggery, incest, under-age sex or indecent conduct towards a child now had the right to keep their names secret. |
| **1993** | Calcutt looked at privacy and press self-regulation and reported in January, recommending that the government look at introducing a tort for infringement. |
| | The Heritage Committee discussed privacy and reported in March. They decided that a protection of privacy law should be introduced, with a public interest defence, but that this would apply to all citizens, covering invasions of privacy on a wider basis than just publication. |
| **1994** | The government announced that it had postponed indefinitely plans for privacy laws, despite issuing a consultation paper on privacy. |
| **1995** | In July, the Heritage Secretary, Mrs Virginia Bottomley, presented the government's response to the consultation paper to parliament. There should be no privacy legislation. A few changes to the PCC were suggested, otherwise matters were to remain as they were. |
| **1996** | Diana, Princess of Wales won an injunction to prevent a freelance photographer approaching within 300 metres. Many newspapers, particularly the *Daily Mail*, tried to take the moral high ground by condemning the photographer for his methods and claiming not to use his pictures. |
| **1997** | The death of the Princess of Wales brought howls of general protest about the alleged intrusions of the press. Lord Spencer tried to relaunch his campaign to introduce a privacy law, but was refused by the government who said that it was not the time to rush into things. The government announced it intended to introduce the European Convention on Human Rights into UK law, which some saw as privacy law by the back door. |
| **1998** | In February, Lord Irvine of Lairg, the Lord Chancellor, proposed a new law of privacy that would allow for prior restraint by the PCC and the payment of compensation to those whose privacy was breached. He was immediately rebuked by the prime minister as being out of keeping with the agreed Cabinet line and ordered to reaffirm the government line in the Lords. A week or so later, Tony Blair told the House of Commons that he had taken personal charge of the Human Rights Bill in an effort to prevent a 'back door' privacy law. |
| | The European Convention on Human Rights was introduced into law via the Human Rights Act 1998. It will be some time before the impact of this will be seen in the courts. |
| | The Data Protection Act 1998 also caused some concern now that most newspapers and broadcast operations use computers for writing stories and storing information. |

## The present law affecting privacy

Just because there is no specific law against invasions of privacy does not mean to say that journalists can do whatever they want. Alongside the laws on defamation and malicious falsehood, there are a range of laws which offer a patchwork protection of parts of people's private lives.

The law of breach of confidence was redefined by Sir John Donaldson in 1990 and his views reflect the best state of the law at present. This confirms that there is a right to the confidentiality of information maintained in this country. 'Since the right to have confidentiality maintained is an equitable right, it will (in legal theory and practical effect if the aid of the court is invoked) "bind the conscience" of third parties, unless they are bona fide purchasers for value without notice . . .'. However, he qualifies this by saying that 'the right will be lost or, at all events, the courts will not uphold and enforce it, if there is just cause or excuse for communicating the information . . .', and 'the right will also be lost if the information, which is subject to a right of confidentiality, is published to the world by or with the consent of the confider, but it will not necessarily be lost if such publication is by the consent or with the consent of the confidant . . .' (Lord Chancellor's Department, 1993: 57). In the case of *X v Y*, Mr Justice Rose restrained the publication of a story obtained from health service workers which named two doctors with AIDS. He said that the public interest in preserving the confidentiality of hospital records outweighed the freedom of the press to publish such information.

Court reporting can sometimes protect a person's privacy where a judge has ordered that names should not be used. This usually applies to juveniles so that their privacy is maintained, but it can apply to other cases. Rape victims and victims of certain other sex offences are granted anonymity under the Sexual Offences (Amendment) Acts 1976 and 1992.

It is illegal to intercept communications without the consent of one of the parties. So reading letters or taping telephone calls during transmission are both illegal. The Data Protection Acts 1984 and 1998 put limits on the use of data held on computers and give rights to the people whom the data concerns. The 1998 Act gives people the right to find out what is being held on computers about them, particularly 'sensitive personal data':

(a) the racial or ethnic origin of the data subject,
(b) his political opinions,
(c) his religious beliefs or other beliefs of a similar nature,
(d) whether he is a member of a trade union (within the meaning of the Trade Union and Labour Relations (Consolidation) Act 1992),
(e) his physical or mental health or condition,
(f) his sexual life,

(g) the commission or alleged commission by him of any offence, or

(h) any proceedings for any offence committed or alleged to have been committed by him. (Data Protection Act 1998, section 2)

This could have given problems to journalists writing investigative stories, so journalism is specifically excluded as one of 'the special purposes':

(a) the purposes of journalism,

(b) artistic purposes, and

(c) literary purposes. (Data Protection Act 1998, section 3)

Section 32 of the Act specifically excludes processing of such data if it is undertaken with a view to publication.

The Conspiracy and Protection of Property Act 1875, although intended to apply only to industrial disputes, could be brought to bear to prevent others from persistently following or watching or besetting a person's house, or place of work, or business, with a view to compelling them to do or not do something which he/she has a right not to do or to do.

The Rehabilitation of Offenders Act 1974 offers very clear protection for the privacy of former criminals. When their offence is considered 'spent', after a suitable period of rehabilitation, we may no longer write about their conviction or crime.

The Broadcasting Acts 1990 and 1996 are of more concern to journalists as these gives the most control on privacy of any legislation. The BSC was set up under the Act to consider complaints of 'unwarranted infringements of privacy in, or in connection with, the obtaining of material included in such programmes' (Broadcasting Act 1996, Part V 101 (1)(b)). The Act goes on to allow the hearing of complaints from viewers in this area.

Limits on divorce reporting were set by the Judicial Proceedings (Regulation of Reports) Act 1926 and later Acts. The Children Act 1989 and Magistrates' Court Act 1980 also limit coverage of private family matters being dealt with by the courts. Scotland is very different from England when it comes to privacy and the Scottish Law Commission in 1977 argued that there is scope in Scottish law for the development of a remedy for unjustifiable infringement of privacy. The Criminal Evidence and Youth Justice Bill, which was proceeding through the House of Commons at the time of writing (mid-1999) could add further constraints on the publication of the identities of minors in court cases. The Bill (due to become law at the end of 1999) contains a clause to prevent the naming of minors, whether victims, witnesses or alleged offenders. Following a strong campaign from newspapers and editors, the government agreed to amend the Bill by holding back that clause of section 43 of the Bill. The government would need a specific vote of parliament to activate that clause.

## Privacy, the law and the problems

The issues involved in trying to arrive at a legislative mechanism to protect the rights of citizens against a media that is prepared to make money by exposing the private failings of the public are very complex. The position is further muddied in Britain by having a BSC which has a statutory duty to investigate complaints about invasions of privacy and a PCC which has no statutory duty to do anything. The BBC's *Producers' Guidelines* has a fair bit to say about privacy (see Appendix 5 for Code of Ethics). This is hardly surprising as there is more of a statutory obligation on broadcasters than on newspapers.

> The BBC should respect the privacy of individuals, recognising that intrusions have to be justified by serving a greater good. Public figures are in a special position but they retain their rights to a private life. The public should be given the facts that bear upon the ability or the suitability of public figures to attain or hold office or to perform their duties, but there is no general entitlement to know about their private behaviour provided that it is legal and does not raise important wider issues. (BBC, 1996: 04.htm)

There must, in a democratic society, be a defence for the media which is intent on revealing what those with criminal or anti-social motives are intent on keeping secret. It is right, for instance, that the public should be told about the politician who is taking bribes and those who are offering them because this revelation would be in the public interest. But, most people believe, there should be limits on invasions of privacy, hence the calls for legislation.

One problem that would have to be faced is that privacy varies from person to person; there are some people who are more entitled to elements of privacy than others and some who have less right than others by virtue of the positions they hold. A number of people seek social status by holding positions or offices within their communities that carry increased levels of responsibility and therefore reduced rights to privacy. Our expectations of politicians, teachers, doctors, lawyers, clergy, to name just a few, are much higher than those of ordinary citizens. These groups carry status in society but they pay for that with reduced rights. An office manager who had an affair with his secretary would not be considered anything other than foolish, but a teacher who had an affair with a sixth-former or a doctor who had sex with a patient would, quite rightly, feel the full opprobrium of the community when his or her privacy was breached and the story published. Such publication would be in the public interest.

There are other groups who, through their own actions, are taken into the limelight with the result that they reduce their rights of privacy, for instance those accused of crimes. But there are also those who find themselves in the limelight through no fault of their own – the victims of crime or disaster, for instance. We need, as journalists, to be aware that we should treat these groups separately in terms of the privacy they are entitled to.

If the government were to introduce privacy legislation it would first have to decide whether an invasion of privacy should be a criminal or a civil offence. It could make invasion either a criminal offence or a tort: a breach of duty imposed by law whereby a person acquires a right of action for damages. If the matter falls under criminal law, then journalists could face continual challenge by the police, constantly being arrested and arraigned for alleged breaches of the law. For this reason, parliament would be more likely to make privacy a civil right. If your privacy is invaded, you can sue. The trouble with this is that it is likely to become a rich person's toy. Those who have put themselves in positions of higher social status may have to accept that this must make them more accountable to the society that has granted them that status. Should such people then be allowed to seek less accountability by keeping journalists away with a stream of actions for breach of privacy? Robert Maxwell used this method to good effect to protect his name until after his death by suing any publication that wrote about him and forcing them to defend the actions. He would then hold up the action, as he was entitled to do, for up to five years. The defendants would have to spend many thousands of pounds keeping solicitors at bay without any recompense, either because the cases never went to court or because even when costs were awarded, they never covered the full costs accrued.

What this boils down to is that making it a civil offence will mean that journalists will measure a person's wealth before deciding to invade their privacy. And as mentioned in the previous chapter, this makes it more likely that the 'ordinary' man in the street will have his privacy invaded whilst the rich, famous and influential will be able to avoid exposure of their less worthy deeds by threatening a law suit. It is therefore more likely that such a law would lead to an *increase* of invasions of privacy on people whose privacy should be invaded less, ordinary people without power, money or influence, whilst those with these attributes will be able to bring enough pressure to bear to keep their private lives to themselves even though the public interest may mean that their private lives should be exposed. It could also happen that invasions of privacy, whether of public or private citizens, would continue and that newspapers would happily pay the damages, but would make sure they got their money's worth by really exposing the person's private life.

We also need to consider how a law would operate. Would the invasion of privacy be at publication or before? Could a judge be asked to consider each case before going to press or just to decide whether what is published is an invasion of privacy and whether or not it is in the public interest. If it is the former, this presents a range of new problems. At what stage would a plaintiff be able to bring a case? Could a politician, the minute he or she detected a journalist's presence, serve a suit to prevent the journalist's research? How could a journalist prove that the investigation was in the public interest without doing the research required? Telling a court you think that this person might be doing something anti-social is not going to be good enough, but how can you show your case without investigation?

## Intrusion and harassment

This becomes as issue during the reporting stage rather than at publication. Removing material from someone's dustbin, shouting at them from street corners or telephoning them late at night are all forms of harassment and are an unwarranted intrusion. The NUJ has clauses on this matter, as has the PCC and the BBC, but the one difficulty faced by the PCC is how to enforce its code as the number of freelancers used by the industry grows. Whilst the PCC can insist that a paper which sends a staff reporter to harass someone prints an adverse adjudication of its actions, or the Broadcasting Standards Commission can demand that a TV station which broadcasts a programme containing such harassment publishes a similar adjudication, if freelance journalists are intruding, they may well not be working for any particular paper or broadcast channel and so no one can be taken to task about the matter. With the rise in freelance working, as papers and broadcast stations cut back their staff, this is likely to be an increasing problem, particularly as freelancers have more to gain by being more intrusive and have a higher commercial imperative to get the story. Their loyalties are not so tightly directed to readers and they have little loyalty to editors and none to proprietors. Their loyalties must be directed to themselves, their families and, to a much lesser extent, the readers.

### What do we mean by intrusion and harassment?

First of all, let us look at intrusion. As with many moral judgements, one person's idea of what constitutes intrusion is another person's polite enquiry. The NUJ, BBC and PCC Codes talk about intrusion into people's grief or shock. The BSC's code is about fairness. Intrusion is not specifically mentioned. The NUJ Code says that journalists shall do nothing which entails intrusion into private grief and shock unless it is in the public interest. The PCC's Code only says that such enquiries should be carried out with 'sympathy and discretion', although, confusingly, it does mention intrusion under its privacy clause. This can be difficult to work with as there is a public interest defence to this privacy clause. How can a reporter know if the matter is in the public interest until 'intrusions and enquiries into an individual's private life' have been completed?

We need to separate privacy and intrusion as concepts. Breach of privacy is the publication of private matters; intrusion is the way those enquiries are carried out. Intrusion can be found in far wider circumstances than in someone's private grief. Finding photographers in your back garden is an intrusion. Reporters going through your rubbish bin or standing in your kitchen are intrusions. Intrusion, according to *The Oxford Concise English Dictionary* is to 'thrust oneself uninvited'. This does not alter whether the reporter has a good reason for intruding. This is one of the reasons why the codes concentrate on grief and shock only. At any other time, the codes seem to say, the victims of the intrusion should deal with it themselves. As a way of measuring if the reporter was intrusive, the codes rely entirely on what is published and why.

We need to consider whether the ends justify the means. If a minister of the Crown is having an affair, but the press only discovers this by tracking him 24 hours a day, discovering the place where he meets his lover, breaking into that house and setting up bugs and hidden cameras, are they then morally right in claiming this exposure is in the public interest? Or is this intrusion going too far to be justified? If the answer is that the intrusion (not necessarily the publication) can be justified, does this give the press the universal right to do this to anybody and then decide afterwards whether it is in the public interest to publish? Surely not. The way the story is gathered has a moral element that is separate from the moral element of publication.

The BBC is quite clear where it stands on intrusion: 'The BBC will never plant an unattended recording device on private property without permission of the owner, occupier, or their agent unless for the purpose of gaining evidence of serious crime' (BBC, 1996: 04.htm). Even then, the Controller of Editorial Policy must always agree in advance and will require clear evidence that the crime has been committed by those to be bugged. The BBC also condemns what it calls 'fishing expeditions'. That is, there must be some evidence of wrong-doing by 'identifiable individuals' before secret recording can take place. The only exceptions the BBC allows are when filming is necessary for the purpose of showing social attitudes and the essence of the programme is that people should behave naturally. In this case permission to use the footage has to be obtained from the people involved. If identifiable people do not give permission, their faces should be obscured, a relatively easy task with modern digital editing.

Only 1.1 per cent of the complaints investigated by the PCC in 1995 concerned intrusion, so it is not a large part of their work. However, these were only intrusions that fall into the grief and shock category. In the privacy category, there has been a sharp rise in the level of complaints and some of these are certainly about intrusion. Very few complaints to the PCC concern straight intrusion. Nearly all involve complaints about harassment.

## Harassment

Let us now turn to the issue of harassment. The acid test of harassment needs to be a clear indication from the person to be interviewed that he or she does not wish to be interviewed. Continuing to press him or her for an interview after this is for the journalist to lay him or herself open to allegations of harassment.

The *BBC Producers' Guidelines* has a full page about harassment. Door-stepping is of particular concern – the practice of reporters turning up uninvited to confront and record a potential interviewee without permission, usually on private property. Such invasions need Head of Department permission and should only be carried out if the 'investigation involves crime or serious anti-social behaviour' and the subject of the interview 'has failed to respond to a repeated request to be interviewed' (BBC, 1996: 04.htm).

Media scrums are also of concern to the BBC and the PCC. This is where there are so many reporters that their sheer numbers can be intimidating, even if the objects of their interest are willing to talk. The BBC is prepared to accept pooling arrangements and will withdraw if it is clear the subject is not going to appear. The PCC made it clear in four judgements against different papers covering the same issue that it did not find 'collective harassment' acceptable:

> While in this case the Commission did not find evidence to justify criticising this or any other individual newspaper, it would not hesitate to do so if in a future case it became apparent that an individual newspaper or reporter either played a leading part in unjustified collective harassment or did not desist when personally asked to do so. (PCC, Report No. 37, 1997: 12)

It is often easier to find out what the PCC believes is not harassment than the other way around. A *Sun* picture taken of 'Moors murderer' Ian Brady with a very long-range telephoto lens in hospital was not harassment despite there being PCC clauses both on taking pictures in hospital and of using long-range lenses. The public interest was served, the PCC said in Report No. 31 (1995). Nor was it harassment for the *Daily Mail* to ring Judy Finnegan's mother and, on being told she did not do interviews with journalists on the telephone, send a reporter to her home. Both reporters finished the interview politely on being told by Mrs Finnegan that she did not want to speak to them.

In 1984 the *Daily Mail* had a complaint upheld against it for harassment after its reporters tried to photograph and interview a woman lecturer allegedly involved with a runaway jeweller. The college alleged that the reporter and photographer refused to leave college premises when asked, and followed the woman around the college, even entering a classroom in which she was due to teach. She was forced to leave under a blanket after the photographer and the reporter parked in the car park all day near to her car.

An Act to make stalking and other harassment an offence was introduced in 1997. The Protection from Harassment Act 1997 says that: 'A person must not pursue a course of conduct (a) which amounts to harassment of another, and (b) which he knows or ought to know amounts to harassment of the other' (http://www.hmso.gov.uk/acts/acts1997/1997040.htm). A defence is that the conduct is reasonable or that it was pursued for the purpose of preventing or detecting crime. An offence is punishable by up to six months in prison or a fine.

## Straightforward means

The British NUJ Code is straightforward: 'A Journalist shall obtain information, photographs and illustrations only by straightforward means' (*National Union of Journalists Rulebook*, 1998). The Swedish code has no clause on 'straightforward means of reporting' which suggests that either Swedish journalists are so ethically concerned that such behaviour would never cross their minds (a possibility) or that such material would be unusable in Sweden (also possible). The BBC has no clauses on misrepresentation. Despite its lengthy clauses on subterfuge, the very idea that one of its journalists might pretend to be something else in order to get a story seems to have escaped them. The PCC has several clauses covering the area, as we have seen before. Clause 9, Hospitals, says that: 'Journalists or photographers making enquiries at hospitals or similar institutions must identify themselves to a responsible executive . . .' (PCC, 1998: 19) while clause 11, Misrepresentation, says: 'Journalists must not generally obtain or seek to obtain information or pictures through misrepresentation or subterfuge . . . subterfuge can be justified only in the public interest' (ibid.). Things are different for the broadcaster. Although the NUJ Code applies to broadcast journalists, it is the Broadcasting Standards Commission which protects individuals in this area. The BSC code of guidance (clause 13) says that 'Factual programme makers should not normally obtain or seek information or pictures through misrepresentation or deception, except where the disclosure is reasonably believed to serve an overriding public interest' (BSC, 1998: 12).

Two particularly prominent cases in the UK illustrate the problems journalists face in using subterfuge as a method of gathering information. In one, the feminist writer, Germaine Greer, offered to take homeless people into her home. A *Mail on Sunday* reporter, Martin Hennessey, dressed as a 'down and out' and took her up on her offer. After three days he wrote about his experiences. The PCC's Privacy Commissioner, Professor Robert Pinker, said in his adjudication: 'Journalists should not generally obtain or seek to obtain information and pictures through misrepresentation or subterfuge.' The paper's editor had argued that the method was justified as 'this was the only way in which the article could have been written'.

This example raises two points. The first is whether there is a justification in using non-straightforward methods if the story is in the public interest. If the story were, for instance, exposing corruption or criminal activity, should a reporter feel justified in using such methods to get the story if there were no other way? The second point that requires discussion is at what stage does a story become 'in the public interest'? Does a story about how Germaine Greer treated a 'down and out' fit within the category of public interest? Whilst there might be a story in testing whether her claim to offer a bed to any 'down and out' was true, or only hypocrisy, once the reporter had established that she meant what she said, surely he should have withdrawn and not invaded Ms Greer's privacy, using non-straightforward means to obtain a story that was arguably not in the public interest.

In the other prominent case, which was reported in PCC Report No. 33 (1996), a freelance reporter entered a school to talk to pupils and staff about a story concerning a female pupil's relationship with a teacher. The reporter allegedly claimed she was the cousin of the pupil. Was the story in the public interest? Did it therefore justify the invasion of privacy or was it an unnecessary subterfuge? The PCC decided it was misrepresentation and upheld the complaint. In doing so, the Commission also clarified clause 12(ii) of its Code which the PCC claimed it had interpreted as applying only to children under the age of 16. The actual clause says: 'Children should not be approached or photographed while at school without the permission of the school authorities.'

Utilitarianism morality works well in these circumstances. It calls for the greater good to be the guiding light and we are obliged to use this argument in this circumstance. The effect of using subterfuge is that the reporter does something immoral (i.e., lying), and the subject of the report is usually damaged, held up to ridicule or accused of wrong-doing. Only the fact that the public ought to know more about the activities of such people justifies this behaviour. Providing the public interest is served, it can be acceptable to lie and deceive, as long as subterfuge is the only way of achieving this end. It is important that reporters and their editors remember that the subterfuge they use to obtain material is immoral – the mere act of lying is immoral regardless of the motive and consequences.

Motivists could support the use of subterfuge, provided the motive really is the public interest. Often, of course, this claim to serve the public interest is just a smoke screen to cover the fact that the story is used because it increases circulation figures. The public interest defence was used by the *Sunday Mirror* when, in 1994, it published photographs of Diana, Princess of Wales working out in a private gym. Using subterfuge is extremely dangerous because once the principle is accepted that lying and deceit can be justified by loyalty to the public interest, it is only a short step to justifying it through the reporter's loyalty to the editor or proprietor. In other words, it is but a small step from lying to get a story which is important because it is in the public interest to lying to get a story which is important because it keeps the reporter's paper from bankruptcy or holds its top position in the market. Both *can* be justified on the basis of loyalty, but whereas one may be acceptable to the public, the other may not be.

## Accuracy

Although consumers ask for accuracy, journalists, as we have already considered, can only offer an honest presentation of the information they have gathered, checked as best they can, together with its sources, always remembering that a journalist will have a professional interest to give the consumer as much accurate information as possible. This dichotomy presents journalists with a problem when it comes to codes of conduct. Should they draw up a universal law about accuracy, one that is either so full of caveats and qualifying phrases it becomes almost worthless, or should they draw up a clause they know they cannot follow? Both the NUJ and the PCC opt for the former, producing accuracy clauses full of caveats such as '*strive to ensure* the information he/she disseminates is fair and accurate' (NUJ) or from the PCC a negative approach, '*Take care not to* publish inaccurate, misleading or distorted material'. Of the two, I prefer the positive emphasis even though this is, of necessity, qualified. The Independent Television Commission code is quite definite. It says: 'News in whatever form has to be both accurate and impartial.' The BBC is just as definite. 'Due impartiality lies at the heart of the BBC. . . . The BBC must be accurate' (*BBC Producers' Guidelines*, 1996). This approach means that TV broadcasts will often withhold information because they are unable to guarantee its accuracy. When transmission does finally take place it is often to report that the newspapers have reported that such and such has happened. This allows the TV programmes to maintain accuracy without having to guarantee the actual story. This is a double-edged sword for television. It means that reports are believed, but it also means that stories are lost because they have to have a higher grade of accuracy than newspapers.

Interestingly, the BBC's new *Producers' Guidelines* seem much more interested in impartiality and seem to treat both accuracy and truth as a way of guaranteeing impartiality rather than a direct loyalty to the viewers or listeners. 'Due impartiality lies at the heart of the BBC. It is a core value and no area of programming is exempt from it. It requires programme makers to show open-mindedness, fairness and a respect for truth' (*BBC Producers' Guidelines*, 1996). There is a lengthy clause on accuracy though: 'The BBC must be accurate. Producers in all areas must be prepared to check, cross-check and seek advice, to ensure that the BBC's reputation is not diminished.' The *Guidelines* go on to advise producers on how to be accurate. They remind producers about matters such as distinguishing between primary and secondary sources, warning of the dangers of using cuttings and library sources which might be out of date, the difference between mechanical accuracy and a regard for a wider truth. They also advise producers that it is good practice not to run a story from a news agency unless it can be substantiated by a BBC correspondent or another agency. The BBC is also well aware of the importance of naming sources so that viewers can form their own judgement about the evidence. Reconstructions can be a good way for TV to illustrate what has happened, but the guidelines give appropriate warning about how to handle these events: 'Reconstruction should be identified clearly so that no-one is misled.' The same criteria should be used by both papers and broadcasters when using models to stage events, or when library film or pictures or computer graphics are used. Captions with phrasing such as 'The couple in happier times', 'The couple on holiday earlier this year', 'Actors play members of the gang', 'A computer simulation of the attack', far from detracting from the action, add a sense of credibility and authority without losing the sense of drama.

The BBC's guidelines may be comprehensive, but they are far from being a universal law or a golden mean. The BBC is often seen as authoritative but slightly dull. A good part of this is its inability to bring information which is *likely* to be accurate but which they cannot substantiate.

This is not to say that I have any answers of my own. 'A journalist shall take every care in an attempt to ensure the information he/she provides consumers is as truthful as possible' is as close as I can get. The wording allows for errors but stresses truthfulness. In many ways this is much better than the mere adherence to accuracy demanded by the other codes. It accepts that truth is the more important aim. If journalists are behaving honestly, trying to report the truth, then they should not object to occasionally admitting an honest mistake. In this circumstance, printing a correction is the right thing for the 'good' journalist to do.

## Corrections and right of reply

A correction is used to amend an incorrect fact or false impression that might otherwise blemish the full truth the journalist was aiming to provide the consumer. It is not the same as a right of reply. A reporter should always be prepared to print a correction, and possibly an apology, when he or she makes a mistake or falls short of his or her own standards of truthfulness and the expectations of the consumer. If someone is small enough to make a mistake, they should be big enough to apologise for it. Both the NUJ and the PCC accept this and both have clauses which call on editors and journalists to publish corrections of significant errors promptly and with due prominence. The BBC also considers it important to admit mistakes 'clearly and frankly'. 'Saying what was wrong as well as putting it right can be an important element in making an effective correction. Inaccuracy may lead to a complaint of unfairness. When an error is acknowledged, a timely correction may dissuade the aggrieved party from complaining' (*BBC Producers' Guidelines*, 1996).

A right of reply allows people who think an inaccurate impression has been given about them in an article to seek a response to put the record straight. Many codes of conduct include a right of reply as well as an obligation to print corrections. The fact that a right of reply exists in many countries under statute and works relatively uncontroversially suggests that it should not be a problem to a journalist to print a reply from people who feel they or their ideas were not presented as truthfully as was possible. Again, the NUJ and the PCC agree on this issue and suggest a right of reply should be offered. They differ slightly on what should be offered and why. The PCC only offers replies to inaccuracies. Clause 2 of its Code says: 'A fair opportunity for reply to inaccuracies should be given to individuals or organisations when reasonably called for.' This suggests that only a correction should be offered. The NUJ calls for the right of reply to people criticised, whether or not there was any inaccuracy, provided the issue is of sufficient importance.

The majority of complaints to the PCC are about accuracy (53.9 per cent in 1997, a decrease on 1996's figures of 54.5 per cent), but there is a small proportion about the right to reply (3.6 per cent, the same as in 1996) (PCC Complaints Report, 1996, 1997). According to the PCC's figures, 260 complaints of inaccuracy were investigated in 1995. Of these, only 15 per cent (39) were adjudicated on and only 28 per cent of those (11) were upheld. Of course, in the area of accuracy it is not surprising that many of the complaints were resolved without adjudication. Many newspaper editors will quickly correct mistakes once the matter has been brought to their attention, particularly if it has been brought to their attention on PCC-headed paper. Only 18 complaints about right of reply were investigated. Of these 27 per cent (5) were adjudicated on and one (5 per cent) was upheld.

## Image manipulation

This is an extension of the need to report truthfully. If a picture is taken and then manipulated physically or electronically to show something different, the consumer is not receiving a truthful impression of events. A couple of examples illustrate the damage done to the media's credibility by manipulating images. The *Sun* carried a front-page story about a monk who had fallen in love with a woman and was being asked to give up his post. The picture they had obtained showed the monk in ordinary street clothes walking next to the woman, but with a reasonable distance separating them. The paper admitted in 1993 that the picture was manipulated in order to change his clothes to those of a monk's habit. The impression given by this front-page picture, which was cleverly and undetectably manipulated, was entirely different from the reality. The *Sun* admitted in an official statement: 'We have superimposed the monk's habit to make it clear to the readers that the story is about a monk.' In another infamous example, deputy Labour leader John Prescott had his beer replaced by champagne in a picture used by the *Daily Express*.

Television is also capable of giving the wrong impression. Electronic manipulation by computer or editing can completely alter the viewers' perception of events. During the 1984 miners' strike in Britain, in the crucial political battle between the government of Margaret Thatcher and the miners, public opinion was vital. The miners were seen as doing an important job and were viewed sympathetically by ordinary people. They were also well supported by other trade unionists. But if it could be shown that the strikers were unreasonable or violent, public sympathy would soon ebb away. Several major battles between miners and police damaged the miners' case badly; the television coverage consistently showed the miners' attacks as happening first and the police's 'defensive retaliation' following. Many miners, however, claim that this was a distortion. They say that the police always attacked first, attempting to provoke a violent reaction. Did TV companies, for whatever reason, distort the reality by editing the tape to show the 'truth' as happening as the government claimed, rather than the 'truth' as perceived by the miners? It is probably now impossible to find a truly unbiased witness to give us a credible answer, yet this simple example shows how easy it is to distort the picture to present a new 'truth'.

Digital image processing also allows TV to create images that are impossible to detect from reality. Many feature films and commercials use these techniques to provide us with fictional or constructed realities that are impossible to distinguish from reality. The *BBC Producers' Guidelines* warn that viewers must not be 'misled into believing that they are seeing something which is "real" when in fact it is a creation of a graphic artist . . . on occasion it may be appropriate to signal, verbally or visually, that what is being depicted is an illustration' (*BBC Producers' Guidelines*, 1996).

The Swedish code of conduct has a strong clause on image manipulation: 'Making a montage, retouching a picture by an electronic method, or formulating a picture caption should not be performed in a such a way as to mislead or deceive the reader. Always state, close to the picture, whether it has been altered by montage or retouching. This also applies to such material when it is filed' (Swedish Press Code, 1995). The NUJ agreed at its 1996 conference to campaign 'for the adoption of a world-wide convention for the marking of photographs that have been digitally manipulated'. At its 1998 conference the union decide to change its code of conduct to specifically outlaw the practice of digital manipulation: 'No journalist shall knowingly cause or allow the publication or broadcast of a photograph that has been manipulated unless that photograph is clearly labelled as such. Manipulation does not include normal dodging, burning, colour balancing, spotting, contrast adjustment, cropping and obvious masking for legal or safety reasons' (NUJ Code of Conduct, 1998).

## Impartiality and bias

Impartiality and bias is the big divide as far as TV and newspapers are concerned. Newspapers do not see it as part of their brief to be impartial whereas it is an important ethical area for broadcasting. I've used the point from the *BBC Producers' Guidelines* before, but 'Due impartiality is at the heart of the BBC'. Both history and the law go into making sure that impartiality is a major cornerstone of British factual broadcasting. The Broadcasting Acts insist on it and it is the major regulatory purpose of the Independent Television Commission, the BBC and the Broadcasting Standards Commission.

This means that broadcasting has a duty to be fair to all sides of an argument. This may involve more than two sides. It is perfectly possible that a controversial issue has four or five major strands with protagonists supporting and opposing different strands all at the same time. Television producers must ensure that not only does each protagonist get equal air time, but that the major strands of the debate get a fair hearing. Political matters are particularly sensitive but again, just giving each major party equal time may not be enough. Discussions on the environment, for instance, might involve the Green Party as well as the three main parties. European debates might involve the Referendum Party. These specialist interests should bring new arguments and points of view to the debate. For instance, all three major parties were in favour of staying in Europe in 1996. To get views from a party which wished to pull out (or at least implied that it would be prepared to pull out) one would have to talk to the Referendum Party. But since this party had no policy views in other areas and no MPs, it would not be asked about the economy. 'Reporting should be dispassionate, wide-ranging and well informed. In reporting matters of industrial or political controversy the main differing views should be given due weight in the period during which the controversy is active' (*BBC Producers' Guidelines*, 1996).

Newspapers, on the other hand, are almost always biased and have no legal obligation to present news impartially. They do, however, have an obligation to tell the truth and this should limit the amount of slanting possible, although there is no obligation on a newspaper to present all sides of an argument. Whilst some are better than others at presenting a range of views, very few present all the facts all of the time. It is necessary to read a number of papers and listen to the news if one is to get a balanced view of the news.

## Comment

This sub-section of impartiality is slightly different in that comment in the media is common currency. Whether it is reviewing a film or a book, describing the performance of a sporting team or player, or analysing the ideas of a politician, journalists in all media are commenting about things and presenting their opinions to the consumers. There is nothing wrong with the presentation of comment in the media provided everyone is clearly aware that those views are the opinion of the writer or broadcaster and are not to be taken as fact.

Many newspapers, radio stations and TV channels rely on opinionated writers or presenters to outrage or cheer up their readers or listeners. Indeed, publication of strong and controversial opinion without the need to present a single supporting fact is the historical birthplace of modern journalism, which sprang to cynical middle age from the cradle of political partisanship. Only if comment is mixed in with factual reporting in an attempt to mislead or distort should the journalist beware. Again, truthfulness is damaged if the consumer is led through a series of opinions under the guise of truth.

The BBC and other broadcasters have a legal obligation to be impartial and this can give rise to problems with comment programmes. The *BBC Producers' Guidelines* says that such programmes involve special obligations. Such programmes must be signalled in advance to the audience and editors must ensure that comment does not misrepresent opposing viewpoints. The *Guidelines* suggests that it may be appropriate to offer an opportunity to respond and that it may be inappropriate for regular presenters and reporters to present personal views on such programmes.

The PCC Code of Practice has a clause on comment: 'Newspapers, while free to be partisan, should distinguish clearly between comment, conjecture and fact.' The NUJ Code calls on its members to 'defend the principle of the freedom of the press and other media in relation to . . . the expression of comment and criticism' and to 'avoid the expression of comment and conjecture as established fact'. The Independent Television Commission's code only calls for news to be impartial, which has some place in this section although partiality is not the same as comment. The Broadcast Complaints Commission also has a duty to ensure that TV is impartial. This would also mean ensuring that comment is not presented as fact.

There was a big rise in 1995 in the number of PCC-investigated complaints of comment or conjecture being presented as fact. The number of investigated complaints rose from 3.0% to 11.8%. This represents 57 complaints yet only one case was eventually adjudicated and this was rejected. All other cases were either resolved or not pursued by the complainant.

## Discrimination and bigotry

This is a difficult area where the approach will vary from culture to culture. Words, pictures, expressions, including the choice of copy or video footage and its editing and use, can be crucial in deciding whether copy or video will give a truthful or misleading impression about the views, feelings or approach of a minority or oppressed group. Many a politician has seized on the scapegoat nature of a minority group to place all the problems and dissatisfaction of society at its doors. From the very earliest of leaders through to the modern politician of your choice, there have always been those who have been willing to play on people's fears about other cultures.

Nor is it just politicians. Ordinary citizens are also often keen to blame minority or culturally oppressed groups for their problems and failures. Often this can be explained by ignorance or fear. If we do not know or understand the culture of a minority or oppressed group, it is easy to see its behaviour as unacceptable or 'uncivilised' and therefore not worthy of consideration or respect. Only when we come to understand another culture's ways can we start to realise that it is, like ours, only human and neither totally wrong nor totally right. It should be a part of a journalist's role to give readers the information they need to come to these decisions, not to play on their fears and prejudices. If journalists tell people only what they expect to hear about minority or oppressed groups, then the debate about their position in society is not advanced. It is part of the journalist's duty to help advance society's awareness of such problems by providing people with a wider truth than their existing prejudices.

This determination to inform people and help them overcome their fears does not mean that a journalist cannot write material that is critical of one culture or another. Journalists need to be truthful about a society, cultural group or minority if we are to come to valid conclusions. The public needs to know why this group of people has aroused hatred in another, and the failings and good points of both, if they are to understand difficult and serious situations around the world. We can use Aristotle's golden mean here to try to set the standard somewhere between the frugality of no debate and the excess of printing every offensive piece of bigotry available. The elements of hatred and violence are often used to help define this mean into a universal law. An example of a debate where a lack of sound information stunts understanding is Northern Ireland.

### Case study 7.1 Northern Ireland

The Republicans and the Unionists had been unable to accept each other's view for some time. This erupted into violence in 1967. This 'civil war', politely referred to as 'The Troubles', continued until 1994 when a cease-fire was called by the IRA, the armed wing of the Republican movement. That cease-fire has now wobbled into the Good Friday agreement, although at the time of writing peace and stable government still seem a long way off. For a little more than 25 years, Northern Ireland, and to a lesser extent the mainland of the British Isles, have suffered serious violence from terrorist acts, killing thousands and maiming many thousands more. Yet in Britain coverage of the dispute meant that the tabloid popular press was more concerned with condemning terrorism than investigating its causes.

Reports written in sensationalist and perjorative language after each fatal bomb attack meant good sales but also an inevitable hardening of attitudes amongst readers. There were few attempts to investigate in detail the reasons for the violence and what the IRA and other paramilitaries, both Republican and Unionist, hoped to achieve by it. While the condemnation of needless killing, violence and misery may be an acceptable reason to drop objectivity, the position of those caught in the middle of the conflict was not advanced by the fixed, unthinking stance taken up by the tabloid press. If more time had been spent investigating why a group of UK citizens felt so strongly about an issue that they were prepared to kill and destroy in support of it, it is possible that we might be a little closer to a solution.

The tabloids' approach was compounded by the British government's decision to make it an offence to interview or show IRA members or members of other banned paramilitary groups on television. This simple abuse of free access to the thoughts and opinions of many at the centre of 'The Troubles', made by the British Home Secretary Douglas Hurd in 1988, was carried to extremes in some areas. Introduced to prevent 'terrorists' enjoying 'the oxygen of publicity', it did nothing to prevent the killing and bombing but a lot to ensure that the dearth of good information about 'The Troubles', that had already been started by the tabloids, was not relieved by usually more thoughtful broadcasters.

The BBC is rightly concerned about reporting on terrorism. Its *Producer Guidelines* warn against picking up terrorist language and using it to legitimise activities. Words such as 'execute', 'court martial' and 'liberate' should all be attributed or not used at all.

Many codes of conduct have clauses against discrimination. As would be expected from the BBC, its *Producers' Guidelines* have excellent advice on the use of discriminatory language. This discusses terminology and methods of reporting on issues involving women, Asian, African and Caribbean people and people with disabilities. Religious groups, the aged and a range of people with differing sexual orientation also come under close scrutiny. The BBC accepts that gay, lesbian and bisexual people make up a significant minority who are 'entitled to be served and treated fairly by the BBC' (*BBC Producers' Guidelines*, 1996). The BBC condemns the use of words such as 'queer', 'dyke' and 'poof' in factual programmes.

The National Union of Journalists' Code says simply: 'A journalist shall only mention a person's age, race, colour, creed, illegitimacy, disability, marital status (or lack of it), gender or sexual orientation if this information is strictly relevant. A journalist shall neither originate nor process material which encourages discrimination, ridicule, prejudice or hatred on any of the above-mentioned grounds.' It is an attempt to tap into that golden mean with a universal law.

The Swedish code says: 'Do not emphasise race, sex, nationality, occupation, political affiliation or religious persuasion in the case of the persons concerned if such particulars are not important in the context or are disparaging' (Swedish Press Code, 1995). The British PCC has something similar: '(a) The press should avoid prejudicial or pejorative reference to a person's race, colour, religion, sex or sexual orientation or to any physical or mental illness or handicap. (b) It should avoid publishing details of a person's race colour, religion, sex or sexual orientation, unless these are directly relevant to the story' (PCC Code of Practice, 1996). The British Broadcast Complaints commission has a similar clause for broadcast journalists.

In some countries this area is considered serious enough for laws to be introduced to prevent incitement to hatred. Britain has such laws. These do not apply just to the media, but their general application impinges strongly there. Broadcasting or printing material likely to incite hatred on the basis of race, colour or creed is an offence. Denmark has very strong laws in this area which has led to several clashes between the authorities and broadcasters and journalists seeking to bring reports of neo-fascist excesses in that country.

Despite all these laws and codes, discrimination is still a strong strand running through much of the media. Homophobia is still widely apparent in the tabloid press and racism can also be found regularly, albeit in a slightly more muted form. This is not the place for what would be a lengthy discussion on the representation of women in the tabloid press, but take it from me that it is sexist and discriminatory, from the 'Starbird' through to the *Sun*'s picture file on the agony page.

It is interesting to note that in its entire history the PCC has only found two papers guilty of breaching the discrimination clause and in neither case was this about racism. Either our press is a model of non-racist reporting (difficult to imagine from an industry that gave us 'Kinky Chinky peeked at my jing jong') or the PCC is not able to give the black community the support it deserves. The PCC's view on third-party complaints poses some difficulty here as many of the complaints that would be brought are general and therefore outside the PCC's remit.

## Presumption of innocence

Whether we start with the UN Declaration of Human Rights or in a more lowly fashion with simple fair dealing, few would argue against everyone having the right to be presumed innocent of any crime unless proven guilty by a court of law duly constituted for the purpose of hearing their alleged crime and deciding upon the justice of the case against them. In practice this is often more difficult to achieve. Often, people appear guilty of things for which there is little hard evidence. It is tempting for a journalist to write a story which will present someone as guilty of a crime or misdemeanour. Take an example:

A row breaks out at a supermarket check-out. A man becomes violent and hits another man. There is a struggle. The man who started the fight leaves the supermarket and drives off in his car. A reporter could well use this story, using the evidence from the other person involved in the tussle. This witness would of course claim that he was the injured party. He did nothing to provoke the other. An unwary reporter might be tempted to use the car's registration plate in an effort to help bring the man to justice. This would label the owner of that car as someone who involved himself in violent behaviour. This may not be the case. Perhaps the car had been stolen or borrowed. Perhaps the witness was lying to cover up his own actions.

Many countries have strict laws governing what may be written about crimes and the reporting of them both during court cases and before. Britain, for instance, has a number of laws which determine exactly what can or cannot be written about. Breach of these laws is considered a very serious offence. 'Contempt proceedings are vigorously prosecuted, usually by the Attorney General, with the offender facing criminal sanctions if found guilty' (Crone, 1995: 140).

But presumption of innocence is more than concern about contempt of court, important to the good practice of justice though this may be. It is a matter of ensuring that no one should be falsely accused. Approaches to this vary widely throughout the world. In Britain, the law is very strict, yet every detail of a criminal proceeding from the act itself to the eventual sentencing of the criminal can be and often is covered in detail. British journalists believe that justice should be seen to be done. The tight restrictions of the law can ensure a fair trial but leave loopholes. In a celebrated British case, Frederick West had been arrested on charges of ten murders. He was accused of abducting young girls, abusing them and then killing them and burying their bodies beneath his home. After being taken into custody, but before he could be brought to trial, he hanged himself. Many British papers were full of stories the next day describing him as a 'murderer'. Yet he had not been tried; no evidence had ever been presented to a court.

Britain's strong laws about what can and cannot be covered have allowed themselves to be distorted away from the aim of presumption of innocence into being solely a protection of the court itself and a bar on bringing it into contempt. British journalists do not see presumption of innocence as an area of ethical concern. They are worried solely about committing a contempt of court and the damage to their paper or broadcast station that this would bring. Presumption of innocence does not appear in the PCC or the BCC's Codes of Conduct. Consequently, when the law no longer applies (as was the case following the death of Frederick West), British journalists are not constrained by anything.

In Sweden, however, the opposite is the case. There are few laws restricting what can be written about court cases, yet the code of conduct is strong. Clause 14 says: 'Remember that, in the eyes of the law, a person suspected of an offence is always presumed innocent until he is proved guilty. The final outcome of a case that is described should be reported.' Clause 15 also adds: 'Give careful thought to the harmful consequences that might follow for persons if their names are published. Refrain from publishing names unless it is in the public interest.'

Swedish journalists take this very seriously and so it is unlikely that they would name people mentioned in a story that would lead to them being presumed guilty. British journalism comes from a very different tradition and not publishing a name would be considered the same as failing to find a good source for a story.

## Protection of victims and relatives of criminals

Whilst those accused of crime have the right to be presumed innocent, journalists must never forget that their victims or relatives and friends are also innocent. This group of people is often dragged into the public domain through no fault of its own. Picked, often at random, to be victims, or being related to a criminal, their troubles can be magnified first by being harassed by journalists and secondly by the way their story is subsequently treated by the press or on the airwaves. The BBC has a lengthy section in its *Producers' Guidelines* about reporting crime. Much of it concerns the presentation of programmes such as *CrimeWatch* and *Police Cameras Action* where guidance is given about the presentation of crime and violence in a way that sets it into context and makes it clear that it is an exceptional event. It covers items such as not using incidental music, taking care about camera angles and not using slow motion to linger on dramatic events. It also gives advice on interviewing serious criminals and the need to avoid glamorising their actions.

Friends and relatives of the criminal and the victim are some of the first people journalists approach to get information. These are usually people dragged into the limelight very much against their will. Imagine the shock of Dunblane killer Thomas Hamilton's mother. Almost minutes after the police informed her that not only was her son dead, but that he took 16 children and a teacher with him, the media is on the telephone. No wonder she looked odd on her television interview. She was in shock. This is not so much an invasion of her privacy but merely insensitive behaviour. She is not directly involved with the crime, but with the criminal. Whilst it would be acceptable to quiz her gently about her son, with the same sensitivity that a journalist would use with any grieving person, it would not be right to cause her distress. The BBC says: 'Although full reporting of the facts surrounding notorious criminals may properly entail reporting of their family circumstances, we should always try not to cause unnecessary distress to the innocent' (*BBC Producers' Guidelines*, 1996). The PCC Code of Conduct has quite a strong clause to cover these problems. It says: 'The press must avoid identifying relatives or friends of persons convicted or accused of crime without consent' (PCC Code of Practice, 1998). This does not mean that friends and relatives can be assured of strict anonymity, because this is one of the clauses identified by the PCC as having a public interest defence, but it does mean that a paper has to have a good reason for publishing. The Broadcasting Standards Commission (taking over a power held by the old Broadcast Complaints Commission) has a clause on privacy that would allow it to take a similar line with broadcasters. Friends and relatives would have the right to complain and it would be up to the publisher to prove that publication or broadcast was justified.

## Victims

The only clause the PCC Code has on victims is to say: 'The press must not identify victims of sexual assault or publish material likely to contribute to such identification unless there is adequate justification and, by law, they are free to do so' (PCC Code of Practice, 1998). Since, in most cases, the media is at liberty to do so, being the victim of crime is to lay oneself open to having one's privacy invaded. The BBC does not have much to say about victims, suggesting only that journalists think of ways to minimise distress. The *Producers' Guidelines* merely refer readers to the section on privacy.

Journalists need always to remember that victims of crime are not there by choice and rarely through any fault of their own. If the report will make things worse for the victim, then the journalist should think carefully about how the report should be handled.

There seems to be a growing trend amongst journalists to equate accuracy with giving as much detail as possible. When plans were first drawn up to make it an offence to report the name of a rape victim, many editors condemned it absolutely. Yet some 20 years later, there is little evidence that it has damaged the press's freedom to report the court cases. Except in the case of a celebrity victim, the inability to report the name makes little difference to the newsworthiness of the story. Indeed, the anonymity given to victims seems to have increased the number of reported incidents, allowing more attackers to be brought to justice.

## Chequebook journalism

Many sections of the media, of course, make payments to informants and sources. The NUJ Code has nothing to say about this practice, but the PCC has a fairly lengthy clause covering this area:

(i) Payment or offers of payment for stories or information must not be made directly or through agents to witnesses or potential witnesses in current criminal proceedings except where the material concerned ought to be published in the public interest and there is an overriding need to make or promise to make a payment for this to be done. Journalists must take every possible step to ensure that no financial dealings have influence on the evidence that those witnesses may give. (An editor authorising such a payment must be prepared to demonstrate that there is a legitimate public interest at stake, involving matters that the public has a right to know. The payment or, where accepted, the offer of payment to any witness who is actually cited to give evidence must be disclosed to the prosecution and the defence and the witness should be advised of this.)

(ii) Payment or offers of payment for stories, pictures or information, must not be made directly or through agents to convicted or confessed criminals or to their associates – who may include family, friends and colleagues – except where the material concerned ought to be published in the public interest and payment is necessary for this to be done. (PCC Code of Conduct, 1998)

The BBC also advises against paying witnesses and criminals. 'Programmes should not make payments to criminals, nor generally to former criminals who are simply talking about their crimes' (*BBC Producers' Guidelines*, 1996). Nor does the BBC generally allow witnesses to be paid before a trial. There are one or two exceptions: overwhelming public interest or because the interviewee is an expert witness whose professional opinion is being sought.

The Government was so concerned about payments made to witnesses during the Rosemary West trial that it issued a consultation document seeking views on making such payments illegal (see Chapter 11).

## Protection of sources

Many codes of conduct include clauses on the need for journalists to protect confidential sources. Much rubbish is talked about confidentiality. Reporters are not like doctors, obliged to keep confidential all that is told to them. Indeed, the very opposite is true. Journalists are expected to reveal confidences and report everything they are told. Occasionally, however, it is necessary to get information from sources who would be put at considerable risk if it were known that they had revealed what they knew. They might, for instance, lose their jobs or perhaps face even harsher punishment. These informants might be able to help a reporter to track down a story without the reporter having to use the information actually given by the informant. In this instance, a reporter might decide to guarantee confidentiality to a source. Only if the reporter has given his or her promise, or implied a promise, does the matter become an issue of ethical honour. If reporters are to be reliable and to be seen as trustworthy to the reader, they should also be trustworthy when they give a promise. No reporter should give this promise lightly.

In some countries reporters can be instructed by a court to reveal a confidence and failure to do so can result in severe punishment. Several British journalists have gone to prison in the past for failing to reveal a source. Some countries, such as Denmark, have laws that prevent a journalist revealing a confidential source. This can work in a reverse fashion, allowing a journalist who has not sourced a story properly to pretend that the contact is strong but that he or she is unable to reveal the source as to do so would be to breach the protection of a confidentiality promise.

Protecting confidential sources has a place in most codes. Deontologists say that the rightness of an act doesn't depend on its motives or consequences but purely on the nature of the act itself. You are obliged to keep a promise by the very fact that that is what defines a promise: it is a pledge one keeps regardless of circumstance or consequence. Deontologists would say that it is no good promising to keep a contact secret and then telling a court simply because to refuse to so would mean a jail sentence. If you promise someone confidentiality, you must stick by that. Since it is also in the reporter's interest to stick by this promise, revealing sources is not something that happens regularly. In one recent celebrated UK case, Bill Goodwin won his appeal to the European Court of Human Rights over the issue.

### Case study 7.2 Protecting sources

Whilst working as a trainee reporter for *The Engineer*, he was contacted by a source who gave him some useful material about the financial dealings of a major company which suggested that the company was not as successful as it would have the market believe. Acting like a good journalist, he wrote the story and then contacted the company for its comments. The company refused to comment and, shortly after, *The Engineer* received a court injunction preventing it from publishing the story and demanding to know the name of the source.

The NUJ and *The Engineer* supported Bill Goodwin when he refused to name the source. *The Engineer* paid his £5,000 fine whilst the NUJ helped him to fight through the courts before going to the European Court of Human Rights in April 1996 which ruled that Goodwin's human rights had been violated. This leaves the government in a difficult position but it has made it clear it has no intention of changing section 10 of the Contempt of Court Act 1981 which says: 'No court may require a person to disclose, nor is any person guilty of contempt of court for refusing to disclose the source of information contained in a publication for which he is responsible, unless it is established to the satisfaction of the court that it is necessary in the interests of justice or national security or for the prevention of disorder and crime.' Lord Mackay, the Lord Chancellor, told the House of Lords on 17 April 1996: 'Amending the legislation is unnecessary to give effect to this judgement.'

These cases are not always easy for journalists to fight. Since the court has the right to insist on disclosure 'in the interests of justice', the journalist is forced to show that disclosure is not in the interests of justice – and this is not always easy. In the Bill Goodwin case, none of the company's assertions to the court could be challenged without revealing the name of the source – the very thing Goodwin was fighting against. In an article for *The Journalist*, the NUJ's magazine, Goodwin wrote about his court experience:

> The source must be an ex-employee motivated by revenge, I was told. The information was so sensitive, the courts decided, that unless the informant was unmasked, the company could be forced into liquidation and 400 people would lose their jobs. It was hogwash. But I could not challenge any of these assumptions, based on the flimsiest of evidence, without giving away the source's identity. And because the hearings were 'interlocutory' we could not test Tetra's hysterical assertions in the witness box.

Goodwin's case is an important one in that he was upholding the confidentiality of the source despite not having promised to do so. The promise, in this case, was implied and therefore as binding. The wording of the NUJ Code of Conduct is that 'confidential sources' shall be protected. The implication is that there are sources who are not confidential.

Much of the moral decision-making in this area hinges around the making of specific promises as well as a general method of working that would mean keeping names of sources private. Since a good portion of a journalist's worth is his or her sources, it makes good professional sense to keep sources of information secret as far as possible.

However, this is different from promising to keep a source secret. This is not always as difficult as it seems. Whistle blowers are often reticent about revealing their names. They will give a journalist the story, but will refuse to give a name. Since the journalist now knows the information and is now only looking for a way of guaranteeing the information, it is easier to make a decision about promising to keep the name secret. There are times when keeping a source secret may not be the moral thing to do: information from someone who is about to commit a major crime or threaten life is information that may well need to be passed on to the authorities and a journalist may have to decide that he or she will breach any undertaking to keep the name of such a person secret. This is one of the reasons why this moral tussle must remain in the hands of the journalist and not the law. Only the journalist is in a position to explore the motives of the informant and decide whether his or her identity should be kept secret. The law is too unwieldy a weapon to use in this kind of decision-making. There is much agreement in the industry over confidentiality. The BBC says that promises of confidentiality given to a source must be honoured. It recognises that such promises may put the journalist into conflict with the court and recommends that journalists should not enter into such undertakings lightly. The BBC recommends a number of general principles which are good advice for all journalists:

- The possibility of agreeing *from the very beginning* with a contributor not to use his or her name unless forced to do so by a court.
- It may be possible to establish a source's authenticity without knowing his or her name or having any way to find it out.
- No document, whether paper or electronic, should identify the source.

The last point is extremely important as the court can demand the production of documents, notebooks, tapes and videos relating to the case. It is always good practice not to keep records of confidential sources and discussions alongside ordinary notes. Any such notes you are forced to keep should be destroyed as soon as possible as the court may order their confiscation and destroying material after such an order is a criminal offence in itself. The name or ways of identifying the source should not be shared with colleagues who may be ordered to reveal it.

The NUJ Code of Conduct says that 'a Journalist shall protect confidential sources of information' while the PCC says that journalists have a moral obligation to protect confidential sources of information.

### Requests for unused material

This is not the same as not revealing sources and the issues are mainly those of protecting journalists in difficult positions. If it becomes widely known that journalists supply untransmitted video or still pictures to the police, their position on newsworthy events such as demonstrations and riots could be put at risk. Some violent elements may well seek to ensure that video and still pictures do not find their way to the police by attacking the photographers and film crews at such events.

Material that is transmitted or published is, of course, already in the public domain and there is therefore little increased risk in co-operating with the authorities. Unpublished material is a different matter. The NUJ has supported photographers facing court orders for their unpublished material by sending the material abroad to safe places provided by the International Federation of Journalists.

The BBC is also concerned and says in its *Guidelines*: 'The BBC will not voluntarily allow access to untransmitted material when to do so would endanger people who work for the BBC or when it would make it more difficult to gather such material in the future' (*BBC Producers' Guidelines*, 1996). The BBC is also concerned that allowing access to untransmitted material could point to the identity of a confidential source and says that all such requests should be refused. It does occasionally allow viewing, but insists on a court order for such material to be removed.

## Bribes, corruption and conflicts of interest

No journalist should take a bribe or inducement to write a story a certain way or to prevent publication of a story. This would include commercial pressure from advertisers or proprietors to distort or spike a story and possibly any other gift or freebie. The NUJ Code of Conduct says: 'A journalist shall not accept bribes nor shall he/she allow other inducements to influence the performance of his/her professional duties.' The British PCC's Code has nothing to say on the subject but does talk about the inadvisability of journalists who work in the financial sphere cashing in on their own advice by taking early advantage of confidential information. The NUJ is also concerned about this. The Swedish code does not have a specific clause about bribery either. However, as we have seen, both the PCC Code and the Swedish code are aimed at published material. Since they both have clauses which seek to bar inaccurate or misleading reports, both do have a way of preventing bribery.

It is important that journalists should be seen as providing truthful information. To alter the balance of a story for financial gain would be to make void that essential pact with the reader. Whether untruthfulness is caused by laziness or incompetence, or by a more reprehensible desire for financial reward, doesn't really matter that much. The effect is that the reader can no longer rely on the impartiality of the report and the publication's purpose is no longer served. So although neither the PCC nor the Swedish codes have clauses on bribery, their clauses on accuracy are sufficient to deal with the problem, should it arise, because the offending material should not be published.

The pressures from advertisers tend to be not so much what is written, but whether it is written at all. The Royal Commission on the Press (1949) said: 'We have had evidence . . . that the direct influence of advertisers on the policy of newspapers is negligible.' Whilst there may be even today little evidence of *direct* influence on *policy* there is plenty of anecdotal evidence of indirect influence on the type of stories used and the way they are handled.

### Advertising as editorial

The increase in the number of advertising features used by the regional and national press has started to distort the way a number of reporters view their responsibilities. Constantly writing material that is, to all intents and purposes, advertising copy means that many reporters view their role as putting the advertiser in the best possible light for an article which is intended to look like part of the editorial with all the qualities that that implies about accuracy, comment, and so on. Because the advertising feature purports to be editorial, the reporter should maintain the standards that apply to editorial. This does not always go down well with advertisers or with advertising departments which tend to see the reporter's concerns as being over-scrupulous. But where material is masquerading as editorial, then the editorial standards need to apply or the paper risks damaging its editorial reputation. Advertising features are not a problem for television, although the growth of programme sponsorship could become one. The use of brand labels in programmes is a problem, however, and although the BBC no longer goes to the lengths of obscuring brand names, it does attempt to avoid using them.

*Other conflicts of interest*. Other conflicts of interest, apart from advertising and the misuse of information, can arise, particularly for broadcasting journalists where the need to be impartial is so important. Promotional activities, advertising and political activity can all be hurdles for the journalist, especially those in broadcasting. The NUJ Code of Conduct prevents journalists from endorsing material in advertising unless they are advertising the publication for which they work. The BBC also has much to say about advertising and promotional activity. It tells its staff that all such work is unacceptable when it might compromise public trust in the integrity of programmes. It might be possible for a journalist to support a worthy cause, but to support a commercial organisation would be putting impartiality at risk. The same applies to political parties. The BBC is also concerned about its staff training people on how best to use the media and this is also proscribed, presumably for fear of seeming to offer an unfair advantage.

## Protection of minors

Many countries have strong laws to protect minors. There are two main elements about dealing with minors that need concern us.

1 Not taking advantage of those who may be too young to make legitimate judgements.
2 Protecting the reputation of someone who may be too young to know better.

The PCC Code of Conduct in Britain is fairly strict:

(i)  Young people should be free to complete their time at school without unnecessary intrusion.
(ii)  Journalists must not interview or photograph children under the age of 16 on subjects involving the welfare of the child or of any other child, in the absence of or without the consent of a parent or other adult who is responsible for the children.
(iii)  Pupils must not be approached or photographed while at school without the permission of the school authorities.
(iv)  There must be no payment to minors for material involving the welfare of children nor payment to parents or guardians for material about their children or wards unless it is demonstrably in the child's interest.
(v)  Where material about the private life of a child is published, there must be justification for publication other than the fame, notoriety or position of his or her parents or guardian. (PCC Code of Practice, 1998)

Despite this strong clause, the PCC does not prevent the naming of children in situations where it is their own fame or notoriety that is the issue.

The clause quoted above is built on the back of British law that largely prevents the naming of children involved in crime. There can be exceptions, at the discretion of the judge, but these are rare. The two young killers of Jamie Bulger, a young boy who was led off to be killed in humiliating circumstances, were 10 and 11 years old and the judge took the unusual step of naming them only after a guilty verdict had been delivered and, in part at least, to protect some other children whom rumour had named as possible suspects. The Crime (Sentences) Act 1997 section 45 has increased the power of judges to name young offenders if it is seen to be in the interests of justice to do so.

The naming of juveniles is another area where the law has skewed ethical values. Whilst most reporters accept that not naming juvenile offenders is right, they name youngsters involved in other situations without a thought (see Chapter 5, p. 80). Naming the children of the famous has also become increasingly unacceptable. The death of the Princess of Wales brought dealings with minors into sharp relief and the PCC has had a number of complaints from famous parents whose children's privacy has been invaded (see Chapter 5).

The PCC Code of Practice instructs journalists that:

1 The press must not, even where the law does not prohibit it, identify children under the age of 16 who are involved in cases concerning sexual offences, whether as victims or as witnesses.
2 In any press report of a case involving a sexual offence against a child:
   (i) The child must not be identified.
   (ii) The adult may be identified.
   (iii) The word 'incest' must not be used where a child victim might be identified.
   (iv) Care must be taken that nothing in the report implies the relationship between the accused and the child. (PCC Code of Practice, 1998)

Broadcasters in Britain face a much more difficult test. Until recently both the ITC and the BSC were likely to look at complaints in this area without actually giving much guidance to journalists. It remains to be seen whether the new Broadcasting Standards Commission will introduce a code of conduct which is clearer in this area.

The Swedish code does not carry any particular reference to minors but it instructs journalists to avoid the use of names in any case where it would protect minors. There are therefore two main elements that a journalist needs to consider when dealing with minors:

1 Whether or not to name a minor in a story.
2 Whether or not to interview a minor in pursuit of a story.

The aim in point 1 is to ensure that a minor who makes a mistake by breaking the law or committing some other act that is both newsworthy and anti-social does not have his or her adult life blighted by this childhood slip. This upholds the generally accepted principle that childhood is a time to learn and a time to make mistakes and that only when a certain level of maturity is reached should people be held fully accountable for their actions. This is continued in point 2. Journalists should be careful in interviewing minors so that they do not put words into the child's mouth. Very often children make good witnesses and can provide good information. They are often very observant, have better memories than their elders and have the time and inclination to put these to good use. But they can also be easily led in their desire to give a person whatever it is the child thinks he or she wants. This is particularly true in what may be to them an exciting and glamorous opportunity to be interviewed by a journalist, particularly if that interview is being televised.

To ask young people to describe something they have seen is unlikely to lead to problems but to ask children to explain their actions without an adult they trust to help and guide them is perhaps to expect too much of them. As always, discretion is required when dealing with any story involving minors. Asking schoolchildren on the way into school what they think about having to wear school uniform might be fine, provided the head teacher is aware of the identity of the suspicious character skulking outside the school gates soliciting the pupils. Asking them about drug dealers or bullying could put them at risks of which they are innocently unaware.

The PCC Code of Conduct warns about jigsaw identification. This is where one publication may name the accused adult, but not mention the relationship to the victim, whilst in another publication or radio bulletin the relationship is mentioned but the accused is not named, making it possible to identify the child victim of an incestuous sexual assault. The PCC has evolved a system for dealing with this and it takes it very seriously. The former Chairman of the Code of Practice Committee, the late Sir David English, then Chairman and Editor-in-Chief of Associated Newspapers, wrote to providers of training in journalism in February 1996 expressing concern that a number of trainees taking the April 1995 National Certificate Examination in Journalism seemed unaware of the clause on jigsaw identification:

> This is a matter of grave concern and I would ask you to make absolutely clear to those in your charge
> - The code of practice is a foundation stone of successful self-regulation in newspaper and magazine publishing.
> - There is nothing optional in the code – it sets out standards of conduct and practice which all publications and their journalists must follow.
> - The provisions in the code relating to cases involving a sexual offence against a child are being applied by radio and television as well as the press. Only if we all follow the provisions meticulously, can the risk of jigsaw identification be avoided.

He went on to detail the code which says that the adult should be identified and not the child, the offence should be described as 'serious offences against young children' and the word incest avoided. Nothing in the report should imply the relationship between the accused and the child.

This clause was a development of the old Press Council's guidelines on jigsaw identification of rape victims. This followed the Ealing Vicarage rape in 1985 in which the daughter of a vicar was savagely raped by three men who were later imprisoned. A series of reports in different newspapers led to the woman being clearly identified, even though no paper actually named her. The Press Council called a meeting with representatives from the Newspaper Publishers' Association (NPA), the Newspaper Society (NS), Scottish Daily Newspaper Society, the Guild of British Newspaper Editors (now just the Guild of British Editors), the Association of British Editors, the BBC, ITN, IRN and individual editors of national newspapers, the Metropolitan Police, the Association of Chief Police Officers and the Association of Chief Police Officers (Scotland) to discuss the issue. The conference came up with guidelines that specified the following:

- At the time of the offence no more details leading to identification of the victim should be published than would be permissible during the trial.
- The name and address of the victim or her relatives should not be published.
- The relationship between the victim and any other person named in the story should not be published.
- Premises where the crime took place should not be identified.
- The police could ask for such information to be published for operational reasons. (Press Council, 1989: 241)

Since these guidelines were drawn up in 1989, the law has changed again and the Sexual Offences (Amendment) Act 1992 now makes it an offence to publish the name, address or picture of an alleged victim of any sexual offence, not just rape, from the minute a complaint is made. Once an arrest has been made, the Act strengthens this to include a clause which prevents the media publishing any matter 'likely to lead members of the public to identify a person as the person against whom the offence is alleged to have been committed'. The PCC no longer specifies the guidelines on rape and so it seems that another 'Ealing Vicarage' rape scenario is possible.

There are other examples where naming children may well be detrimental to their interests and journalists should always ask themselves whether naming the children advances the story (see Chapter 5).

## Protection of personal honour

Who steals my purse steals trash; 'tis something, nothing; . . .
But he who filches from me my good name
Robs me of that which not enriches him,
And makes me poor indeed. (Shakespeare, Othello, III, iii, 155–61)

There are very few countries in the world with a free, uncensored media that do not have laws preventing the defamation of citizens. Italy includes it in its constitution whilst America, Britain and most of Europe, Asia and Africa have laws of libel: laws, either civil or criminal, often both, which prevent the publication of information about a person likely to damage his or her reputation amongst 'right-thinking' members of the society. The UN Declaration of Human Rights includes a clause giving the individual the right to protect his or her personal honour.

We put a lot of store by our status within the society in which we live. Not only does it directly affect our ability to feed, clothe and house ourselves and our families, but it goes to the very core of our being – we are our social status, if you like. Many people have committed suicide rather than face the disgrace that damaging personal revelations would bring.

There is a certain crossover with privacy here. How much can we invade a person's privacy in order to see if his or her personal honour is worthy of his or her reputation? Most laws of libel allow the publication of material about a person, providing it is truthful and it has not been published with malice – two important tests that no journalist should miss. Since the penalties for a lost libel action can be high, few journalists will risk a libel action if they believe the subject has the wherewithal to bring such a lawsuit. The effects of impugning someone's reputation should never be underestimated and journalists should take all possible steps to ensure they do not do so in error or needlessly. Publishing reputation-damaging information without checking it is about the worst offence a journalist can commit. However, once those tests are made and the journalist is sure the information is true, the right to publish under the law exists.

In a recent British case, a woman was due to be elected deputy mayor of the City of Liverpool – an honoured and honourable position. A journalist learned that in her youth she had been arrested on several counts of prostitution. These charges were revealed in the press. Her status was irrevocably damaged and she was forced to resign the position. The facts were true and printed without provable malice. The offences were committed when the woman was young, but adult. Should her honour have been protected or was it important, as some claimed, that the citizens of Liverpool were informed of the background of the person who was due to become their mayor?

So concerned have British juries become in recent years about the kinds of stories being written about individuals that they have paid out fantastic sums in damages. *Private Eye* was involved in one such case when a jury awarded Sonia Sutcliffe £600,000 leaving *Private Eye's* astonished editor, Ian Hislop, to tell the television cameras that if that was justice ... "I'm a banana." In another case, The *Sun* paid massive damages to rock star Elton

John. They later published a front-page apology under the heading 'Sorry Elton', but it is still doubtful whether the damage done to the star by these revelations was undone by the payout and the apology. We spend a lifetime building up a reputation that can be destroyed in just a few careless moments.

## Summary

This chapter examined the practical application of individual areas of ethical concern, as laid down by most codes of conduct, with particular reference to UK codes such as those of the PCC, BSC, NUJ and the *BBC Producers' Guidelines*.

## Questions

1 List some of the significant differences between codes designed for broadcasters and those designed for print journalists?

2 Why is privacy probably the most important and difficult ethical area for journalists to define?

3 A person's reputation can be damaged without a newspaper risking a law suit for libel. Try to find examples in the papers and decide whether they were fair.

4 Is it always necessary to use the name of the subject of a story published in the public interest?

5 What problems are presented by people asking to see copy prior to publication?

6 Is it the consequences or the motives one should consider before breaching a code of practice clause in the public interest?

# Chapter 8

...............................................................................

# Deciding what to publish

## Chapter outline

- This chapter will look at the decision-making process when journalists are deciding what stories to use for publication or broadcast.
- It will consider whether journalists can be impartial, should be impartial and why broadcasting is different from print in this respect.
- It will look at the pressures that working in a commercial market bring to the journalist's work and the dangers of other threats or bribes.
- It will consider how journalists try to cope with conflicts of interest with their work and their personal lives.

All newspapers and broadcast outlets have to make regular decisions about what to publish. I have looked in detail at what makes news and therefore what influences editors in their decisions on what to publish. Newsworthiness, the space available and a balance of stories all play their part in deciding what is used, but we must also remember that the suppression of stories or the exaggeration of stories (either in the way they are written or by the way they are used) can be determined by the personal views or political stance of the editor or publisher. This is particularly true in newspapers and magazines where there is no legal obligation to remain impartial.

## Fairness and balance

Objectivity or impartiality is one of the most difficult concepts for journalists, and the public they serve, to grasp. In a *Times/Mirror* survey of the media in eight countries, lack of objectivity appeared as one of the three major criticisms in all but three. Other criticisms were invasion of privacy, sensationalism and emphasis on bad news. So it seems that consumers, at least, think that objectivity is important.

Objectivity is generally taken to mean being uninfluenced by personal views or feelings. There seems to be a view held by most consumers and many journalists that somehow the reporter can set him or herself apart from events he or she is recording to become merely a reporting machine, relaying only supportable facts. I wrote at length about this in Chapter 3, but it is worth reminding ourselves how this concept of objectivity and impartiality became a consideration in the writing and presenting of news.

Objectivity has an interesting history in British and international journalism. Newspapers started in Britain as propaganda sheets and it was only with the growth of popular newspapers during the late nineteenth century that objectivity started to become professionally fashionable. One of the earliest books on journalism ethics, *The Ethics of Journalism* by Nelson Crawford (1924/1969), devoted three chapters to the study of objectivity. Theodore L. Glasser believes that objectivity grew more as a market imperative than an ethical goal. It was efficient for agencies and reporters to distribute only the bare facts, leaving interpretation to be added either by editors or by readers. 'To survive in the market place, and to enhance their status as a new and more democratic press, journalists – principally publishers, who were becoming more and more removed from the editing and writing process – began to transform efficiency into a standard of professional competence, a standard later – several decades later – described as objectivity' (Glasser, 1992: 181).

It is certainly the case that the move towards a less partisan style in the late nineteenth century began to gather momentum during the early part of the twentieth century as a desirable aim. So much so that when radio and television came along, many countries included clauses about impartiality within their regulatory remit. This view that the broadcast media should be impartial by statutory obligation still stands in Britain. The Independent Television Commission's programme code contains a number of requirements including: 'News in whatever form, has to be both accurate and impartial' (ITC, 1995: 26). The Independent Television Commission took up several cases of alleged breaches of impartiality which it noted in its 1995 report. Granada TV was required to broadcast an apology over a *This Morning* programme which 'adopted a campaigning position over the release of Private Lee Clegg, then serving a prison sentence for the murder of a joyrider in Belfast. Private Clegg's case was a controversial matter as defined by the Broadcasting Act, therefore requiring due impartiality to be exercised in any broadcast treatment of it' (ibid.). Several other items that were judged to break the impartiality regulations were also broadcast by various franchise holders. In addition, the Broadcasting Act 1996 includes clauses on fairness, which are supervised by the Broadcasting Standards Commission. Yet if we contrast this view on impartiality with the behaviour of the newspapers, we see an entirely different standard being applied. Most newspapers came out strongly in favour of the early release of Private Clegg at the same time as *This Morning* adopted its campaigning attitude, yet if anyone had complained to the PCC, he or she would have been quickly informed that the PCC's Code says that: 'Newspapers, whilst free to be partisan, should distinguish clearly between comment, conjecture and fact.'

## Bribes, partisanship and corruption

It is worth reminding ourselves that taking a bribe in order to use or suppress a story would be immoral unless of course the reporter is totally honest with the reader about it, in which case it is arguable that it is a bribe. What may not be so clear to those outside the industry is the range of 'bribes' on offer to journalists and the difficulty many have with dealing with them.

Being slipped a £50 note in order to suppress a story is extremely rare these days, although a hundred years ago it was standard practice for some of the more unsavoury press. It was in answer to a request for a suppression fee that the Duke of Wellington made his famous statement 'Publish and be damned.' But being offered 'freebies', from a bottle of scotch at Christmas to sunshine holidays, or free dinners, theatre tickets, books, records, CDs or loans of cars is common. Many new products are launched at lavish receptions with free food and drink to put the journalists in a receptive frame of mind.

Dealing with these freebies is difficult. Many media outlets would not review books, CDs, restaurants or holidays at all if the product was not provided free – they would not (so it is claimed) be able to afford it. Even if they could or did, the journalists themselves would not be paying.

The freebie is a vexed question that has bothered journalists for years. Some see no problem in accepting hospitality, provided it does not alter what they would have written without it. Others argue that journalists should be squeaky clean and that all freebies are tainted. Some American and Scandinavian papers refuse to have anything to do with freebies and, at the time of writing, the *Independent* in Britain is reviewing its attitude to freebies. The *Independent* has already banned free holidays, paying for those it reviews.

Of course, the difficulty is deciding whether a freebie alters a journalist's view of the product. Some financial institutions are legendary for the lavish scale of their trips, which their PR departments claim are to allow journalists and company personnel to get to know each other. One cannot help thinking that this could be done just as easily over a glass of wine at home.

The real danger of freebies is that the journalist is unable to bring the full range of sceptical faculties to bear, which is why companies are so generous. As a young editor on a cash-strapped weekly, the records that companies happily sent me each month meant I was able to run record reviews. I enjoyed listening to the music and writing the reviews, but would I have been more critical if the records had been paid for out of my own personal resources? And what about the record company? As far as the records went, I was never aware of pressure to write pleasant reviews. Presumably, they took the view that merely advertising the existence of a new record was enough to entice fans to buy it; my opinion probably did not count for much.

But there have been more serious suggestions of companies trying to bring pressure to bear for good write-ups. Football clubs have banned reporters from the press stand, forcing them either to buy a ticket or not attend, because of a report the football club disliked. The same has been known to happen at press premières of films. There are those who say that the only way to do reviews of things like cars is to accept loans of cars. Because all the cars tested are on loan, they are all measured to the same standard and the fact that no payment is made does not become an issue. An interview with former BBC2 *Top Gear* front-man, Jeremy Clarkson, reported in *Private Eye*, gave an insight into the perks and problems of free loans:

> Clarkson tells the *Eye* that he has not one Jaguar but four on indefinite loan. 'I've got lots of cars on free loans,' he cheerfully admitted to the *Eye*. 'If they're really good I just don't give them back. Everybody does it. We've all got Jags.' But he insists this would never influence his judgement. 'I'm quite straight. You don't last very long in this business if you start taking corporate backhanders.' (*Private Eye*, 19 March 1999: 7)

The NUJ Code of Conduct states: 'A journalist shall not accept bribes; nor shall he/she allow other inducements to influence the performance of his/her professional duties.' The BBC's *Producers Guidelines* takes a similarly robust view:

> The BBC has a duty to be honest with its audiences. They must be sure that the products or services featured in BBC programmes have been selected for editorial and not promotional reasons. This requires great care from programme makers as commercial interests do seek to influence the editorial process. The BBC has an obligation to resist such pressures and to be able to demonstrate how it does so. (*BBC Producers' Guidelines*, 1996)

The guidelines lay down firm rules:

- No BBC programme must ever accept reduced cost or free products or services in return for an on-air credit or any visual or verbal reference to the provider.
- Any reference in programmes to products or services must be for sound editorial reasons only.

However, even the BBC accepts that in order to use the licence-payers' money wisely there may be occasions when products or services can be used free or at reduced prices. Consumer programmes reviewing products may accept freebies, provided it is made clear that this does not allow a right of preview or guarantee a favourable mention. The BBC makes it clear that staff should not accept personal benefits under any circumstances. The PCC makes no mention of bribes in its Code, but as I have discussed before, it is a Code aimed at publication, not news-gathering.

A freebie is not the only way that journalists can be influenced. Threats, either direct ('you write up that report about my brother and I'll come round and sort you out!') or indirect, can have a similar effect. Pressure from advertisers, real or potential, is one of the major sources of undue influence. Often editors worry that writing up a story which is likely to show an advertiser in a bad light will cause the advertiser to withdraw the advertising, so consequently the story is dropped. The Royal Commission of the Press (1947–49) spent some time examining this area. It came to the conclusion that attempts to influence by individual advertisers were infrequent and unsuccessful. The Commission had no evidence of concerted pressure by advertisers for a particular policy but noted that: 'So long as newspapers do not pay without advertising revenue, a newspaper may well think twice before it adopts any policy which is likely to reduce advertisers' demand for its space' (Royal Commission, 1949: 143). Finding proof in this area is almost impossible, but going purely on intuition and anecdotal evidence, it seems to me that things have worsened since the 1949 Royal Commission and that editors and proprietors are now much more likely to allow pressure from advertisers, either real or anticipated, to influence editorial decisions. I can certainly recall a case that happened to me. Writing an advertising feature about a chain of shops, I was rung by one of their managers asking to read the copy. I refused and was told that if I didn't read it to them, they would pull their advertisements in the paper. I refused again and reported the incident to my editor who, to his credit, supported my stand. The advertisements were not used, but I am always glad it was the editor who had to face a fuming advertising department and not me.

Sometimes, of course, reverse influence is the case. A paper may want to show an advertiser (or a linked business) in a good light. The *Sun*, for instance, so regularly puffs BSkyB, its sister satellite TV station, that *Private Eye* has started a special column to mock better (or should that be worse?) examples.

## Conflicts of interest

Just how impartial should journalists be in their personal lives? This is a subject that is not often talked about amongst journalists. It tends to be accepted automatically that although a journalist may belong to a political party, he or she will write fairly about a range of political issues.

The only sensible response that can be made to this dilemma is for reporters to ensure that they avoid working on any story which would bring a conflict of interest. Someone who feels strongly about animal rights, for instance, would ask not to go on a story about intensive farming, unless the angle the paper wanted specifically included a view of intensive farming from an animal rights sympathiser or, of course, if the reporter worked for an animal rights magazine.

Whilst this is a fairly clear and easy moral decision to take, it is often more difficult when other community interests are involved. Any journalist working on a paper or broadcast station with a clearly defined community is going to find some difficulty as he or she becomes involved with that community. Every local journalist knows the problems of being asked to do PR for his or her children's school fête or for the charity committee to which they belong. Gradually, as one becomes part of a community in this way, pressures, usually very subtle, build up to push certain stories or suppress others.

The moral stance in these types of conflict is for the journalist to be honest with the editor and to explain his or her stance. The editor can then decide whether to use the story, spike it, or put someone else on it. Often, of course, there is little problem. If a parent writes the story about a planned school fête, then it is no more likely to be biased than if an impartial reporter were to write it and it might be more accurate. After all, plenty of PR material is used in papers these days with only a light edit. If there were suggestions that the fête committee were on the fiddle, however . . .

## Suppression

Editors and journalists sometimes have to decide when not to publish a story. Brian Whitaker, in *News Limited: Why You Can't Read All About It* (1981), goes into this in depth and his book is well worth reading. In one example he explains why no local newspaper is likely to go upsetting the local *status quo*:

> It is in coverage of council affairs that local papers are usually at their worst. You only have to read the papers to learn that councillors are as public-spirited, well-informed, thoughtful, eloquent, dedicated and high-principled a body as you could ever hope to meet – but then a paper does have to be responsible. To reprint verbatim the speech of Councillor X, a former mayor who has served the borough for nigh on 50 years, would let the world know that the old boy has completely lost his marbles – and that would be cruel. To record the number of times the mayor has to be corrected on procedural matters by the clerk would imply that he is not fit for his office – and that would be disrespectful. To list the financial interests of all the members who get business from the council would suggest that they are out to feather their own nests – and that would be a slur. In short, to tell the truth, the whole truth and nothing but the truth about the council would be nothing less

> than to embark on a campaign to discredit the whole of local government – and that would be grossly irresponsible. (Whitaker, 1981: 39)

Few local newspapers or radio stations are going to risk retaliatory action by local advertisers, who might damage revenue, or local dignitaries or business people, who might hit circulation figures or the ability of reporters to report on local stories. Whilst national and some regional media outlets are better able to withstand these pressures, they have to be certain that the story (or a succession of such stories) will increase circulation more than the damage such attacks might do to revenue. Sometimes, of course, there may be a more noble reason to suppress a story. Kidnaps are rarely reported in Britain before the police have caught the perpetrators. Fortunately, this is a very rare crime in Britain anyway, but it can be argued that the responsible position taken by the media has helped. If a kidnap happens, the police will keep the media informed provided they agree only to use the story once the police approve – usually after the victim has been freed. This gives the media good information on what happened without using the story and endangering the victim's life.

Stories can also be suppressed, or the information that is known limited, during wars. In the Gulf War, for instance, the media was briefed away from the front line to prevent stories about planned attacks being transmitted back home being intercepted by the enemy. Although a story that the SAS were just about to launch an attack across the front line at such and such a place with 200 men set to target a military base at X would be good copy, it would not improve the chances of those 200 soldiers returning alive. Journalists have to decide whether to protect those lives, even though it may mean using the story later or with only part of the information, or not. This is a complex exercise in utilitarianist logic. The high risk of harming 200 people outweighs the small risk to millions of readers. But what about loyalty to the reader? Does this go by the board because of our loyalty to the subject of the story?

Sometimes, of course, stories are suppressed because they do not suit the purpose of the media outlet carrying them. The *Daily Express*, for instance, is much keener on using stories that show the Labour party in a bad light than those that are unhelpful to the Conservative party. The *Daily Mirror* takes the opposite view, whilst the *Sun* does not carry stories which suggest that BSkyB is anything less than the perfect TV station because both are owned by Rupert Murdoch's News International.

## Advertising as editorial

A considerable amount of editorial these days turns out to be advertising and this presents editors and journalists with problems. Pressure from advertisers to cover a particular story or not cover a story can put journalists under pressure over their choice of loyalties. If it puts a reporter's job on the line, it can hardly be surprising if loyalty to self and family means journalists give in to the pressure to print what they are told. If an editor is supportive, then they may well see their loyalty to the reader to tell the truth as paramount. The water becomes a good deal muddier when an advertiser takes what is known as an *advertising feature*. These can take several forms.

An *advertorial* is a small advert supported by accompanying editorial copy, usually describing the advertiser and its wares. This is an attempt to add editorial authenticity to an advertisement. The entire space, including that used for editorial is usually bought by the customer and then filled with the advertisement and the editorial. Often this editorial is written by a journalist. Journalists generally do not like writing these kinds of items because of the pressures to write supportive material.

An *advertising feature* or *advertising supplement* is usually editorial copy about a topic which is supported by adverts on a similar theme. The advertisers are told what the subject area of the adverts is beforehand. An advertising supplement on health and beauty in a woman's magazine, for instance, might well attract advertisers in the health and beauty field. Occasionally, an advertising supplement is just a very large advertorial, where there is only one advertiser whose products are at the centre of the editorial material. Many of the larger retailers use this method of promoting their wares in the quality monthly magazines in the run-up to Christmas. Advertising features are also often written by journalists. These do not tend to be quite so difficult as the subjects are much more general and it is easier to write something fair and truthful. Often though, there is pressure to add the names of advertiser to the copy. Sometimes copy for ad features comes from the PR or advertising agency. This has then to be edited and laid out in the newspaper's standard style. Journalists who do this work are also under pressure to present the material in a favourable light.

Advertisers also latch on to editorial by *sponsoring pages or programmes*. In broadcasting this tends to be confined to drama programmes or weather broadcasts, but it can only be a matter of time before food shows are sponsored by food manufacturers and motor shows by car makers. Newspaper pages tend to be limited in their sponsorship more by lack of opportunity than by principle. Favourites for sponsorship are the TV page, weather and wedding reports.

All of the methods mentioned above for displaying advertising as editorial copy are favoured by advertisers as it lends their adverts the authority and credibility that goes with the editorial. They become more believable. Finance companies are particularly fond of taking advertising supplements in the tabloid nationals; local papers often have ad features for local pub openings. These methods have become more and more popular over the last few years as it means adverts are more likely to be read. This adds to the journalist's fear of undue influence. If a big retailer is supporting an advertising feature, how can the journalist write a true review of that particular product? Often the product the journalist is writing about is known to the journalist only through the press information material sent by the manufacturer. How can the journalist give a fair assessment from the manufacturer's own press information?

The pressures for a journalist to write a piece that is supportive of the advertiser regardless of the real situation is extremely strong. The NUJ takes the view that journalists' duty is clear: they should write an accurate, truthful article. But loyalties are often stretched when reporters are asked to produce stories to advertising briefs. In one provincial newspaper I know of, reporters are expected to write restaurant reviews from a copy of the menu and perhaps a quick telephone call to the restaurateur. They are also expected to ring back and read the copy over the phone for approval. Regular checks with my students over the years show that in their experience on work placements this practice is growing. This makes a nonsense of any pretence that such features are attempting to be truthful. No reporter can give a truthful report of food they have not tasted in a review they have to approve with the advertiser. Yet readers are often misled into believing that such reports are as ethically sound as the material in the rest of the editorial sections of the paper. Most readers are unaware of the difference between editorial and advertorial copy. Both the Newspaper Society and the NUJ advise that advertorials and advertising features should be clearly marked as advertising or advertising features, and journalists involved in editing and laying out such copy should ensure this happens.

## Summary

- This chapter looked at the decision-making process journalists go through before deciding what stories to use.

- It considered whether journalists have the right to be impartial and why broadcasting is different from print in this respect.

- It looked at the pressures on journalists to print or not print certain information for fear of upsetting advertisers or because of other threats or bribes.

- It considered how journalists try to cope with conflicts of interest with their work and their personal lives.

## Questions

1 To what extent can consumers expect the journalist to be completely impartial, reporting without fear or favour?

2 Do you think the journalist's approach is likely to be different between broadcasting and print or between national newspapers and regional newspapers?

3 Journalists work quite closely with some contacts such as politicians or local business people. Do you think this damages their ability to report fairly on these issues?

4 We would all recognise a £50 note in a brown envelope as a bribe. But is the judgement of journalists affected if they accept a free lunch or a book, a CD or holiday abroad to review?

# Chapter 9

·············································································

# Presenting the information

### Chapter outline

- This chapter examines how the editing process of a newspaper can add deliberate bias in line with the newspaper's political allegiance or accidental bias in order to present the story in a more exciting way.
- It considers how TV also attempts to present stories in the liveliest way possible.
- It looks at how reporters can consider 'enhancing' their stories in order to ensure publication.
- It discusses how taste and decency need to be considered when preparing items for print or broadcast.

Newspapers and broadcasting are about more than gathering information, they are also concerned with how the information is presented. The target audience plays a major part in decisions made here. Should a newspaper choose a highly graphic approach suitable for an audience that is wary of too much printed word or should the emphasis be on presenting large blocks of text in a way that can be easily assimilated? Should broadcasters aim at a lively production with short takes and plenty of action or can the target audience appreciate longer, more static displays? The journalist also needs to consider such subjects as taste and decency. At what stage does an image become merely distasteful and no longer enlightening? In addition, there is the new opportunity to bias or slant the information that its presentation offers.

## Presentation of material for print

Moral problems do not end when the text is written. Source-checking should continue throughout, but there is also a new range of problems. Once copy is written and presented to the editor or sub-editors, further decisions are made about its future. A decision will be taken about where the story is to be displayed. Other decisions will be taken about how it is to be displayed and how it is to be angled.

It may well be that the story already has the correct angle, but if not, it may well be rewritten. New angles are added for several reasons. The most important is the market approach of the product. If a newspaper sees its target audience as middle-aged women with middle-class traditional views, it will target the type of news it uses and the way it presents it to be attractive to that audience. Take a look at the *Daily Mail* to see how this works. A newspaper may also choose its news and the way it presents it in order to pursue a political or commercial agenda. The *Mirror*, for instance, likes copy that embarrasses the Conservative party whereas the *Mail* prefers to attack the Labour party.

During this editing process inaccuracies or bias might well be introduced into copy that had been error-free. This might be accidental, in the attempt to make the story more lively. Often a reporter will have been ambiguous because it has not been possible to guarantee the accuracy of a particular fact yet an editor might well rewrite the careful phrase into something more dramatic, but less accurate. Occasionally, in order to make a story 'stand up' or appear more dramatic or exciting, facts will be stretched and distorted. Stories are also presented in a different style. A single piece of copy might be split into several smaller articles, each with their own new introduction. Headings have to be written, along with other pieces of copy, that give the opportunity for further errors to creep in. Headline writing is a difficult art. They have to be bright and lively yet still reflect the story accurately. They must also be accurate in themselves. All this in just half a dozen words or less. Whether it is 'MPs in a new sleaze wheeze' or 'Minister in new sleaze claim' (to give two invented, but plausible, examples), the temptation to go over the top is high.

Finally, pictures are added. Choices here add a new dimension to the decision-making process. Pictures need to be closely linked with the story. Some will have been taken especially for the story and care needs to be taken to ensure that the picture is of who or what the journalist thinks it is and that the caption accurately conveys this. Often picture captions carry names that are spelt differently from the way they are in the story. Library pictures are also a danger area. It is all too easy to get a picture from a library of the wrong person. On 20 June 1996, the *Guardian* carried an obituary of Vivian Ellis, the writer of the song 'Spread a Little Happiness'. Unfortunately it used a picture of Vivienne Ellis. Wrong sex, wrong person. I did not get to see the correction carried later in the week, but I assume there was one. All very embarrassing and potentially libellous in some instances.

The choice of picture offers yet another opportunity for presenting the story in an untruthful way. Even a picture of a politician giving a speech can give very different slants to a story. The way the picture is cut, the gestures the politician is using or the facial expressions can all give a perception that is wrong or at least misleading. Politicians learn early on to take extreme care with facial gestures whilst sitting on platforms. A row of photographers is just waiting for that funny gesture, the drooping eyelids, the whispered aside or the signs of momentary boredom. Many politicians have woken to find their breakfast spoiled by a picture of themselves on the front of the newspapers apparently deeply upset, when all they actually did was briefly rub their eyes at the end of a long and tiring conference. Smiling for six hours solid in case your picture is being taken is hard work.

## Presentation of material for broadcast

Broadcasting brings its own problems in terms of presentation of news packages. Just as newspapers need attention-grabbing headlines that scream drama and sensation, so broadcasters needs to grab the viewers' attention. The easiest and most attractive way of doing this for television is with good pictures. Desperate to provide interesting film to go with news reports, broadcast editors will often try to build up the drama that seems to exist in video footage, whether it actually does or not. Film from the House of Commons, for instance, shows smiling politicians posing on either side of whoever is speaking. Often we find that the only people in the House are those crowded around the spokespeople on the front bench as this makes the shot look good for TV.

Covering disasters provides excellent picture coverage and the only ethical debate is about how to cover it. Often TV will show foreign news, not because it will particularly interest viewers as such, but because it offers great pictures. We seem to get extensive coverage of hurricanes when they hit the US, for instance, because the US networks are there to take the pictures and the pictures make good TV. In other words, the pictures are available cheap and are dramatic viewing. We rarely see pictures of such hurricanes as they rip through the Caribbean as this would require a film crew to be sent out especially, at high cost.

Providing good pictures is not so easy on an issue-based subject. Politicians have long realised this and try their hardest to produce photogenic ideas that reduce issues to images that can attract audiences both on TV and in still pictures. PR companies will always try to present ideas as photogenically as possible. This has the effect of reducing political debate to the level of jousting – plenty of action and drama but not much understanding of the underlying principles. Party conferences become places to attack the opposition rather than develop ideas because idea generation is represented in the media as political drama rather than political debate. Discussions become wrangles, debates become clashes and passionate exchanges of views become party splits. Television, forced by its regulators to be impartial, needs to present an often complex issue, give detailed information about it and present the two or three different viewpoints that surround it in a 30-second (or even 15-second) package that needs to be exciting and visually attractive. It may be accurate, but is it truthful? Whilst such packages are usually unbiased, they are rarely able to tell the whole story.

Even current affairs documentaries which allow for a more measured approach can suffer from the same problems. Fans of *Drop the Dead Donkey*, the realistic C4 sitcom set in a TV newsroom, will have seen several episodes wrapped around the dubious antics of ambitious tabloid TV reporter Damian Day as he attempts to spice up his reports. In one memorable incident, his news editor accuses him of using an apparently abandoned teddy bear as a symbol of pathos in a number of packages from disasters around the world only to find that Damian has the teddy bear in his bag, ready for the next assignment. Yet the news editor feels unable to sack him for this unethical approach. As the station's most popular reporter, Damian is looked on with favour by managers with both eyes firmly on the viewing figures.

## Taste and decency

We have already considered taste and decency in news presentation in Chapter 3, but it is worth remembering that the ethical decisions in the presentation of such images needs to be considered. Pictures, whether for print or broadcast, carry more potential for upsetting readers or viewers than is normally the case for text. Many good pictures can be offensive. Several of the award-winning pictures from the Vietnam War contained stark and disturbing images that many will have found upsetting and offensive. A police chief's street execution and a naked young girl fleeing a napalm raid are images that were widely used at the time and since, and stick firmly in my mind. They are offensive in the way that any picture of violence and destruction is offensive, but they say more about the war and what it meant than even the best of writers could have managed.

## Summary

- **This chapter looked at the editing process of a newspaper to explain how deliberate bias is added in line with the newspaper's political allegiance, or in order to present the story in a more exciting way.**
- **It discussed how TV also attempts to present stories in a visually exciting way and how this might distort the information.**

- It examined the pressures on reporters to 'enhance' their stories in order to ensure publication.
- It reminded us of how taste and decency need to be considered when preparing items for print or broadcast.

## Questions

1 Look at a copy of today's newspaper. Look at the stories with pictures and other display items. Are they really the most important stories or are there others on the page?

2 Watch a TV news bulletin or a documentary. Is the main story used because there are pictures or because it is the most important news item? Analyse the script of a documentary and decide whether the piece was used because it provided us with considerable information or because the filming was exciting/sensationalist/human etc.

3 Try to find examples in print and broadcast of stories that have been built up out of proportion by using design devices and pictures.

# Chapter 10

......................................................................................

# History of media regulation

### Chapter outline

- This chapter details the history of self-regulation in the UK.
- It considers the development of press regulation culminating in the Press Complaints Commission.
- It explains the changes in broadcast legislation that led to the establishment of the Broadcasting Standards Commission.
- It explains how governments over the past few decades have viewed the media and its regulation.

Press regulation first became an issue abroad. Sweden has had a press council from the beginning of the century: 'The Publicists Club [of Sweden], which was formed in 1874 with journalists, newspaper editors and other publishers as its members, had, on a number of occasions in the beginning of the 1900s, served as a self-appointed tribunal to hear complaints against newspapers' (Nordlund, 1991: 1). Even before this, the Swedes had been adjudicating on complaints in an informal way. Other European countries had also considered the subject and some had rudimentary laws by the middle of the 1800s.

The first codes of practice were drafted in America in the early 1920s with quite a number being produced in the period 1921–23. Nelson Antrim Crawford published a number of them in his book, *The Ethics of Journalism* (1924), one of the first books published in the field. European countries followed with codes of conduct in the 1920s and 1930s.

Although codes of conduct did not appear in the UK until the 1930s, concerns about the way the British Press conducted its business were not limited to this century. Sensationalism in pursuit of readership, and therefore profits, is a technique as old as mass readership. Ever since universal education opened the media up to a mass audience, the media has been pursuing readers. Talk of golden ages of the Press when everything was done by the book and ethics were the first consideration is just that – talk. As Raymond Snoddy says in *The Good, the Bad and the Unacceptable* (1993: 19): 'When you get down to the fundamentals of questionable journalism – sex, violence, sensationalism, bias, inaccuracy and forgery – it is remarkable how little has changed.' He illustrates this with a story taken from the first issue of the *News of the World* in 1843, telling of the trial of Edward Morse, a chemist who drugged a young girl before violating her and dumping her in a canal. Not that the *News of the World* was the first newspaper to realise that sex and violence sell newspapers. Throughout the eighteenth and nineteenth centuries, the Press suffered many of the same complaints to which it is prey today. Yet as more and more people learned to read, it became more and more popular.

There should be no surprise about the importance of the Press during the early part of the century. Until the late 1930s, the Press was unchallenged in terms of its ability to bring up-to-date news to its readers. During and after the war, radio and then television were allowed to develop freely. The war had seen a halt of TV development, but radio had become extremely important as a way of bringing news to people during a period of considerable national anxiety. Many serious threats existed: the potential for invasion; the risks to troops fighting abroad, many of whom were the loved ones of those at home; and then the day-to-day weariness of living under a war economy.

Paper rationing meant that newspapers were not able to continue publishing large numbers of editions, whilst the fast-growing BBC was able to bring people news of the war as and when it happened. Radio's power as an alerting medium is unsurpassable by print and it can be no surprise that by the end of the war many households were using the radio as a major source of immediate news as well as entertainment.

This put the Press under considerable pressure. Publishers were used to competing with each other to get the story first. Trying to use this method of fighting back against radio, and later television, was doomed to failure. Even with limits placed on the times early TV could broadcast, fixed newspaper edition times meant the Press could not compete with regular bulletins and news flashes. The Press had to move from being an alerting medium to become more of a reflecting medium.

Newspapers were soon trying other methods of holding readers' attention. For the quality papers this was the in-depth analysis of the headlines provided by the radio. It was a successful system for their educated readership, who wanted up-to-date and accurate information and who were keen to find out the full background. The majority, however, were unwilling to spend the time and effort learning the background, or were not interested. The papers which aimed at this mass market took a different approach. The selling power of gossip, titillation and sensationalism had always been appreciated and used to sell papers, but now the differentiation between people-orientated papers and issue-orientated papers became even starker.

It is difficult to tell whether the gossip about members of the royal family and celebrities led to the personality-orientated culture that boomed during the 1950s and 1960s or whether this culture reinforced and made popular what the popular papers had started. Either way, it ensured that papers stayed far more popular than many in the industry had feared during this difficult transition to an electronic media age. The circulation figures of both tabloid and broadsheet rose during the 1940s and although they fell back during the 1960s and 1970s, in a slump which continues to this day, the decay in circulation was considerably slower than many predicted.

Concerns over journalistic morals had first been raised in the middle of the nineteenth century, although not strongly enough for them to be dealt with on a formal basis. However, contemporary mentions about accuracy and invasion of privacy show that these were starting to become real public concerns. The first signs of a determination to do something about journalistic ethics in the UK came in the 1930s. The National Union of Journalists (NUJ) decided at its annual conference in 1936 to introduce a code of conduct. There had been talk of such a code for a couple of years, from a number of sources.

The Institute of Journalists (IoJ), a rival trade union at that time, wanted to go even further and agitated within the industry and parliament for a State Register of Journalists. This would have meant that anyone calling him or herself a journalist would have had to be registered and qualified by diploma. The NUJ strongly opposed this move and when a parliamentary bill was drafted by the IoJ, the NUJ at its 1937 conference decided to oppose the creation of a statutory body for journalism. The motion to oppose 'was carried amid cheers and without a single vote being recorded against it' (Bundock, 1957: 150).

The NUJ felt that licensing would limit the wide and theoretically free access to the media. The war ended this element of debate and licensing has not been an issue in Britain since then. Whilst some European countries do license journalists, it is generally viewed in this country as a gross interference with the freedom of the Press. Journalists in the UK are not generally considered to be professionals as journalism is 'the exercise by occupation of the right to free expression available to every citizen' (Robertson, 1983: 3).

## Towards regulation

The 1947–49 Royal Commission on the Press was set up by the government with the object of 'furthering free expression of opinion through the Press and offering the greatest practicable accuracy in the presentation of news, to inquire into the control, management and ownership of the newspaper and periodical press and the news agencies, including the financial structure

**175**

and the monopolistic tendencies in control, and to make recommendations thereon'. The Commission was initiated by the NUJ. Two MPs, both journalists, moved a motion in the House of Commons on 29 October 1946 calling for a Commission to investigate the Press, having regard for the monopolistic tendencies in control of the Press. The demand for an enquiry had been developing throughout the union for the previous two years, as Maurice Webb, a member of the NUJ's National Executive Council explained to the House.

The 1947–49 Royal Commission was chaired by Sir William David Ross, and reported its findings to the government in 1949. The Commission made a number of recommendations, including the idea of setting up a General Council of the Press to represent the common interests of the Press as a whole, in particular 'the problem of recruitment and training, and the problem of formulating and making effective high standards of professional conduct'. In its report, the Commission said:

> It is remarkable that although a number of organisations exist to represent sectional interests within the Press, there is none representing the Press as a whole. It is not that those engaged in newspaper production are unaware of the Press as an entity: they are on the contrary acutely aware of it and jealous for its independence and its reputation. It is the more surprising that there is no one body concerned to maintain either the freedom of the Press or the integrity on which its reputation depends: no single organisation expresses the common interest in these things of the men who share responsibility for the character of the Press; and there is no means, other than *ad hoc* machinery created to deal with particular problems, by which this common interest can be translated into action. Indeed, the Press has taken fewer steps to safeguard its standards of performance than perhaps any other institution of comparable importance. (Royal Commission on the Press, 1949: 165)

The Commission went on to recommend that the General Council of the Press, by 'censuring undesirable types of journalistic conduct should build up a code of conduct in accordance with the highest professional standards' (ibid.: 170). The report then listed objects later adopted by the Council:

1 To preserve the established freedom of the British Press.
2 To maintain the character of the British Press in accordance with the highest professional and commercial standards.
3 To consider complaints about the conduct of the Press or the conduct of persons and organisations toward the Press, to deal with these complaints in whatever manner might seem practical and appropriate and record resultant action.
4 To keep under review developments likely to restrict the supply of information of public interest and importance.
5 To report publicly on developments that may tend towards greater concentration or monopoly in the Press (including changes in ownership, control and growth of press undertakings) and to publish statistical information relating thereto.

6 To make representations on appropriate occasions to the Government, organs of the United Nations and to press organisations abroad.

7 To publish periodical reports recording the council's work and to review, from time to time, developments in the Press and factors affecting them. (Ibid.: 174)

The 1947–49 Commission wanted a general council to encourage 'the growth of the sense of public responsibility and public service amongst all those engaged in the profession of journalism whether as directors, editors or journalists and of furthering the efficiency of the profession and the well being of those who practised it' (ibid.). Although the Press Council was proposed in the 1949 Commission report, nothing was done immediately. By 1951, the two main newspaper proprietor organisations, the National Publishers' Association (NPA) and the Newspaper Society (NS) had prepared draft proposals. These provided for voluntary organisations with twelve editorial members and twelve managerial members charged with preserving the established freedom of the British press. The inclusion of lay members on the Council (20 per cent was proposed by the Commission) was opposed by all the proprietorial bodies and their views were endorsed by a majority of non-proprietorial bodies. The organisations involved in the talks were:

- NPA (Newspaper Publishers' Association)
- NS (Newspaper Society)
- SDNS (Scottish Daily Newspaper Society)
- SNPA (Scottish Newspaper Publishers' Association)
- NUJ (National Union of Journalists)
- IoJ (Institute of Journalists)
- GBNE (Guild of British Newspaper Editors)

As the talks continued, a private members' bill proposing a general council for the press was presented in the House of Commons by Mr C.J. Simmons and had its second reading on 28 November 1952. The debate was adjourned, but sparked considerable interest, and in February 1953 an agreed draft for a council emerged. Lay members were excluded and there was no independent chair. The Council held its first meeting on 21 July 1953. The objectives of the new Press Council are shown in Exhibit 10.1.

The new council's objects excluded the Commission's proposals for the Council to deal with complaints. It also ignored proposals for an independent chair and some lay membership. The Commission had wanted the Council to censure undesirable conduct by journalists and build up a code based on the highest professional standards, detailing its work in an annual report. The Council did, however, accept in its procedures that people might complain: '. . . provided that in dealing with representations which it may receive about the conduct of the Press or of any person towards the

**Exhibit 10.1 The objects of the new Council**

1 To preserve the established freedom of the British Press.
2 To maintain the character of the British Press in accordance with the highest professional and commercial standards.
3 To keep under review any developments likely to restrict the supply of information of public interest and importance.
4 To promote and encourage methods of recruitment, education and training for journalists.
5 To promote a proper functional relation among all sections of the profession.
6 To promote technical and other research.
7 To study developments in the Press which may tend towards greater concentration or monopoly.
8 To publish periodical reports recording its own work and reviewing from time to time the various developments in the Press and the Factors affecting them. (General Council of the Press, 1954: 32)

Press, the Council shall be required to consider only those from complainants actually affected and shall deal with such in whatever manner may seem to it (the Council) practical and appropriate' (ibid.: 33). The Commission had also suggested that the Council should examine the practicability of a comprehensive pension scheme, to promote the establishment of common services and to act as a representative of the Press to government and intergovernmental bodies. The new Council ignored these recommendations.

The new body was made up of the fifteen editorial representatives and ten managerial representatives from the following groups: national newspaper editors (NPA), provincial newspaper editors (NS and GBNE), Scottish newspaper editors (SNPA and SDNS), the NUJ and the IoJ. It was funded by a levy of one twenty-fifth of the Council's expenditure for every seat. Colonel the Hon J.J. Astor of *The Times* was elected the first chairman and Sir Linton Andrews of the *Yorkshire Post* the vice-chairman.

The first Council came across many of the same problems that tax the PCC today. Crime, sex and scandal were all there to be reported. In addition there were some problems we no longer face.

> Reports of proceedings against homosexual suspects caused some public protests. In the view of the Council, such reports, carefully sub-edited in accordance with the law against indecent mention of physiological details, did a useful public service. If a great evil is rife in our midst, the facts should be made known in order that a search for the right means of reform might be encouraged. (Ibid.: 9)

The determination of what is right and wrong has certainly changed even if the self-righteous and pompous justification of its exposure in the papers has not. A quick flip to the Press Council Report of 1990 shows how things have changed with a judgement headed: 'Poof and Poofter offensive'.

'Although the words "poof" and "poofter" are in common parlance, they are so offensive to male homosexuals that publishing them is not a matter of taste or opinion within a newspaper editor's discretion,' the Council said (Press Council, 1990: 189). What a difference 36 years makes.

One of the first privacy cases dealt with by the new Council was the publishing of a series of articles by John Dean, the ex-valet of the Duke of Edinburgh. The Editor of the *Sunday Pictorial* justified publication, saying he was satisfied with their authenticity and that there was nothing derogatory in them (General Council of the Press, 1954: 37).

In April 1955, Colonel Astor resigned from the Council because of ill-health and Sir Linton Andrews took over the chair.

With the Council less than two years old the prime minister was asked in the House of Commons (on 13 July 1955) whether he intended to take steps to establish a press council with statutory powers to deal with complaints. Sir Anthony Eden replied that he found it very hard to see how statutory powers could be effectively arranged. The Council had hit trouble with its first report. Attacking the use of the phrase 'private and confidential' by 'many a fussy little jack-in-office [who] would like to set up his own Official Secrets Act' (ibid.: 6) was seen by some as a doctrine allowing them the right to publish anything. In its second report, the Council went to some lengths to define the difference between arbitrarily labelling something 'private and confidential' and the times when the Press might consider itself to be bound by such a description (General Council of the Press, 1955: 7).

Four complaints were received on this question. First, a ballot by the Educational Institute of Scotland on the question of a strike fund was published despite the papers being clearly marked 'Private and Confidential. Not to be communicated to the Press.' The Council agreed that marking it 'Private and Confidential' did not prevent a newspaper publishing it if it considered the subject was one of general importance and interest. Secondly, the town clerk of Poole council asked the Press Council if the *Poole and Dorset Herald* was justified in printing a document sent only to the members of the authority and then refusing to disclose the identity of the person from whom the document was obtained. The Press Council agreed it was so justified. Thirdly, the County Councils Association wrote to the Press Council asking if editors would feel themselves duty-bound to uphold the confidentiality of papers so marked that had been sent with other documents to the press. The Council pointed out that whilst embargoes should be upheld, any editor would weigh in the balance the public interest and would not feel bound to keep information marked confidential private. Fourthly, Llanelly Town Council ran into similar problems as Poole over the publication of a report on council house rents in the *Llanelly Star*. The town clerk received a similar reply.

The second report also raised concerns about the naming of children in court cases (ibid.: 29). Several complaints had been received by the General Council from readers. Editors by and large agreed with the complainants. Either a name was printed in error, or the editors felt obliged to print something they were not expressly forbidden to do. At this stage, the 1933 Children and Young Persons Act allowed the court to prevent identification and forbad the use of photographs. But if a judge forgot to direct the court in this matter, as often happened, the names could be and often were published. The General Council wrote to the then Home Secretary, Major Lloyd George, in December 1954. He wrote back in April 1955 without a final answer. He said he fully agreed with the Council and that he was intending to contact chiefs of police to seek their co-operation in ensuring the court's attention was drawn to suitable cases (ibid.: 34).

The General Council also came under attack from some editors. One certainly took exception to the mild criticism that was all that was available to the Press Council. Alastair Grant, Managing Editor of the *Highland Herald* sparked a row after Inverness magistrates complained to the Press Council when only one of three cases brought against coal merchants for selling underweight, dealt with by magistrates on the same day, was reported in the *Highland Herald*, something they felt was unfair. A copy of their letter, written by the Town Clerk, was sent to the *Highland Herald* by the Press Council. Mr Grant responded: 'Fortunately, town clerks or town councils have quite definitely not the right to instruct him [the editor] in the matter, nor, as you know, has the Press Council, and I resent this ill-advised attempt to do so.'

The Council expressed its regret over Mr Grant's attitude 'towards the council's efforts to investigate a complaint'. 'The Council looked on this attempt to brush aside the complaint without a word of explanation as high-handed, unworthy and a misuse of editorial power.' This brought an explosive response from the editor, who published a letter to his readers in the paper four days later describing the Council as 'a vague and powerless body' and accusing it of inaccurate reporting. The Council responded with a resolution regretting the publication of a 'totally misleading article about the recent complaint'. It went on: 'The paper now gives as its explanation the exigencies of space changing from week to week. The Press Council regrets it has needed so much effort to get this explanation. It deplores the offensive manner in which the editor has treated a proper request put by the Press Council in the interests of the Press as well as the public' (ibid.: 47).

By the third annual report, the Press Council had settled in. Sir Linton Andrews, the Chairman, reported: 'Our first and second reports described the Press Council as an experiment. It has become an institution. No one expects it to give up. After three years of conscientious effort the Council is recognised by a large and increasing number of people as a professional court of honour, a safeguard of press freedom and press fairness' (General Council of the Press, 1956: 1).

The third report, published in the mid 1950s, makes fairly depressing reading. It seems some things never change. A long report on the difficulties between the Press and the Royal Family ended with three suggestions:

1 An improvement in quality and supply of news be sought from the palace press secretariat.
2 Newspapers refrain from offering large sums to former palace servants for their stories.
3 Royal news should be handled with discretion at all times. (Ibid.: 13)

In parliament in 1956, the Earl of Selborne attempted to introduce a bill to set up a Press Authority which would supersede the Press Council and be 'empowered to receive complaints about the conduct of any newspaper or news agency' (ibid.: 36). This bill sought to set up a three-strong authority, with its members nominated by the Lord Chief Justice and the Lord President of the Court of Session, which would have the power to license newspapers and therefore control them. This was roundly condemned by the Press Council, which called it misguided and reactionary: 'This measure would not defend but abolish freedom of the Press, one of the proved historic safeguards of the British people' (ibid.). The Council felt the clauses were too widely drawn to be helpful and that therefore the right to appeal was not useful: 'The right to appeal to the High Court would be nullified because a verdict could be reversed only if it ran contrary to clauses of the bill so general and so far-reaching that the most outrageous decisions might be held to be justified under their authority' (ibid.).

A veto proposed by the Earl of Selborne on 'disrespect or discourtesy to the Royal Family' would see many of today's newspapers in the dock for revealing the affairs of 'descendants of Her late majesty Queen Victoria' and their 'spouses' (ibid.). The move was similar to one suggested by Sir David Calcutt in January 1993. He suggested nominations from the Lord Chancellor; three people sitting, selected from a panel. He did not however suggest licensing newspapers (Calcutt, 1993: xii).

The 1957 Council report tells of hard times in Romford. The *Romford Recorder* of 4 January carried a heading 'MPs too kind to themselves'. The House of Commons Committee of Privileges decided that the heading was a contempt of the House but not of such a nature as to make it necessary to take further action. The editor asked the Press Council to consider whether this was a danger to press freedom. The Press Council felt the House's 'leniency' explained the editor's concern that he had not been given a fair hearing but they felt his treatment was not unfair (General Council of the Press, 1957: 33).

Mr George Murray took over the chairmanship of the Council following the resignation of Sir Linton Andrews in April 1959. During this period several matters had been vexing the press. Contempt of court had become a serious issue with a number of papers running into difficulties with the courts. There was also concern about the right to be admitted to the meetings of public bodies. The 1959 printing dispute had led many local authorities to exclude journalists from meetings. A young and enthusiastic MP called Margaret Thatcher, the Conservative member for Finchley, won a good place in the private members' bill ballot and moved the second reading of the Public Bodies (Admission of the Press to Meetings) Bill in February 1960. Henry Brooke, the Minister for Housing and Local Government, made it clear that he would not be content until all local authorities gave full facilities to the press and the bill passed into law in June 1961.

The 1960s started with a black year for the media. First the *Empire News* was absorbed into the *News of the World* in 1960, despite having a circulation of 2,100,000. It was closely followed by the *News Chronicle*, the *Star*, the *Sunday Graphic* and the *Sunday Dispatch*. The *Sunday Telegraph* was launched in February 1961.

## Another commission

In 1961, a second commission was set up. This was

> to examine the economic and financial factors affecting the production and sale of newspapers, magazines and periodicals in the United Kingdom, including:
> (a) Manufacturing, printing, distribution and other costs;
> (b) The efficiency of production; and
> (c) Advertising and other revenue, including any revenue derived from interests in television;
> to consider whether these factors tend to diminish diversity of ownership and control or the number and variety of such publications having regard to the importance, in the public interest, of the accurate presentation of news and the free expression of opinion. (Royal Commission on the Press, 1962: 9)

The Commission was chaired by Baron Shawcross and it came to the conclusion that there was no acceptable legislative or fiscal method of controlling the economic forces to ensure diversification of newspapers. It also, in passing, pointed out that the General Council still had no lay element. It was critical of the industry's poor response to the recommendations of the 1947–49 Commission: 'Had they been carried out much of our own inquiry might have been unnecessary . . .' (ibid.: 101). It went on to say that whilst it agreed with the previous commission that 'there are important advantages in a body of this kind resting upon a voluntary basis and deriving its authority not from statute but from the Press itself', it felt that if the Council did not gain sufficient authority from the Press then the case for a statutory body was a clear one (ibid.: 102).

The Commission recommended that all parties reconsider the recommendations of the 1947–49 Commission urgently and reconfigure its constitution (ibid.: 117). The Commission said that: 'We recommend that the government should specify a time limit after which legislation would be introduced for the establishment of such a body (an authoritative general council with a lay element as recommended in 1949) if in the meantime it had not been set up voluntarily' (ibid.). The Commission also recommended that the General Council should act as 'a tribunal to hear complaints from journalists or editors about pressure from advertisers (ibid.: 102). It suggested that it might be possible to extend this to complaints from editors and journalists who have been improperly obliged by their employers or superiors to suppress opinion, distort the truth or otherwise engage in unprofessional conduct (ibid.).

At the end of the day, very few of the Commission's recommendations were acted upon. The General Council changed its name to the Press Council in 1963 and allowed the appointment of five lay members out of twenty-five. Mr George Murray gave up the chairmanship and the first lay chairman was elected to serve from January 1964, together with the new lay members. Membership was now structured as follows: independent Chairman (Rt Hon The Lord Devlin PC); five representatives from the NPA, three from the NS, one each from the SDNS and the SNPA, two each from the PPA and the GBNE, four from the NUJ, two from the IoJ and five lay members.

1966 was a big year for the Press Council with the 'Moors murders' trial. Ian Brady and Myra Hindley were both found guilty and sentenced to life imprisonment for murder. The chief witness for the prosecution said he had been in receipt of weekly payments from a newspaper under a contract to provide information. The judge, Mr Justice Fenton Atkinson, said in summing up that he did not think that the evidence had been substantially affected, but asked the then Attorney General, Sir Elwyn Jones (later Lord Elwyn-Jones), to consider the matter. He decided there was no evidence that any testimony was affected and that he would proceed no further. The Press Council however decided to issue a declaration of principle:

1 No payment or offer of payment should be made by a newspaper to any person known or reasonably expected to be a witness in criminal proceedings already begun in exchange for any story or information in connection with the proceedings until they have been concluded.

2 No witness in committal proceedings should be questioned on behalf of any newspaper about the subject matter of his evidence until the trial is concluded.

3 No payment should be made for feature articles to persons engaged in crime or other notorious misbehaviour where the public interest does not warrant it; as the Council has previously declared, it deplores publication of personal articles of an unsavoury nature by persons who have been concerned in criminal acts or vicious conduct.

In making this declaration the Press Council acknowledges the wide support given by editors to the broad principles set out.

The Council does not intend that the principles enunciated shall preclude reasonable contemporaneous inquiries in relation to commission of crime when these are carried out with due regard to the administration of justice. There may be occasions on which the activities of newspapers are affected by over-riding questions of public interest, such as the exposure of wrong-doing.

No code can cover every case. Satisfactory observance of the principles must depend upon the discretion and sense of responsibility of editors and newspaper proprietors. (Press Council, 1967: 9)

The Press Council decided to set up a complaints committee during this period. In the summer of 1967 the Press Council moved headquarters from Legatee House to 6 Salisbury Square, just five doors up from its present location at number 1, although it moved to 81 Farringdon Street in between.

1967 saw a lot of parliamentary activity. Concerns over the commercial future of Fleet Street were raised in both Houses over the Economist Intelligence Unit report (Press Council, 1967: 138), commissioned by the Joint Board of the Newspaper Industry. This report had predicted the failure of four national newspapers by 1970 if nothing was done. A huge row broke out in parliament during February 1967 over the *Daily Express*'s alleged breach of a D-Notice. The editor of the *Daily Mirror*, Mr Lee Howard, resigned from the D-notice committee over the issue. This was also the year that introduced the Criminal Justice Act, which limits what reporters may write about committal proceedings. This was opposed fairly strongly by the press at the time although the then Home Secretary, the Rt Hon Roy Jenkins, reminded the House that the Tucker Committee, which had been set up by him to consider restrictions on the reporting of committal proceedings, had recommended no reporting at all.

A select committee report in 1968 recommended the rescinding of all resolutions prohibiting the reporting of parliamentary procedures. Technically, all parliamentary reporting had been illegal since 1762. Colonel Willie C. Clissitt OBE handed over the secretaryship of the Press Council to Noel S. Paul, a former features editor on the *Liverpool Daily Post* in 1968 while Lord Devlin handed over the chairmanship to Rt Hon The Lord Pearce in September 1969. Back in parliament, the Freedom of Publication (Protection) Bill was lost for the fourth time at its April 1970 revival by Mr Jasper More, MP for Ludlow.

In 1972, the government set up the Privacy Committee under the chairmanship of Kenneth Younger. This thoroughly investigated the desirability of introducing legislation on privacy but, on a majority decision, recommended against adding to existing laws. The Committee did however recommend that as far as technological surveillance devices were concerned, these should be generally restricted, such restrictions applying equally to the press and general citizens. The Committee also recommended a number of changes to the Press Council. It wanted the Council to increase its lay membership to half and introduce an independent element into the method of appointment of lay members. It felt it should do this at an early date. It also suggested that the Council should codify its declarations on privacy. The Committee also urged newspapers to give adjudications similar prominence as that given to the original article (Committee on Privacy, 1972: 13). The Press Council decided in 1972 to double the number of lay members but allowed the other recommendations to lie on the table.

## Broadcast concerns

Until now, not too much notice had been taken of broadcasting regulation. This is not to say that there were no critics. Winston Churchill had accused the BBC of bias as early as 1953 but most of the complaints tended to be about sex and violence on entertainment programmes rather than concerns about news programmes. Mary Whitehouse, the leader of the National Viewers' and Listeners' Association was building her reputation as a campaigner for cleaner television, although looked at from our position today it is difficult to see what she found to criticise.

Generally, it was accepted that broadcast news both on radio and TV were of a high standard – a view that largely holds good today. Any complaints that were made were investigated by complaints panels set up internally by the BBC (Programmes Complaints Commission) or the Independent Television Authority (Complaints Review Board for Independent TV). They would publish their findings in the *TV Times* or *The Listener*. The BBC's Complaints Commission in particular had been criticised for not having a broad enough base (Press Council, 1972: 94).

The passing of the Sound Broadcasting Bill through parliament in 1972, which allowed the setting up of a range of local commercial radio, coincided with the Younger Committee's recommendations on broadcasting which attempted to strengthen the two bodies. It asked the BBC to extend the powers of the Complaints Commission to cover privacy and to amend some of its procedures. The Committee also asked the ITA's review board to publish its adjudications and extend its procedures to commercial radio, if and when the Authority took responsibility for the new services (Committee on Privacy, 1972: 14).

In the Second Report from the Select Committee on the Nationalised Industries in April 1972, Tony Benn (who had earlier been Postmaster General) said that the debate on broadcasting should move beyond who controls what to look at the broader question of broadcasting's role and status in society now it was the dominant medium. Some parliamentarians were becoming concerned that the controls of the Television Act and the BBC Charter might not be enough to prevent television overpowering parliament itself.

On 14 May 1970, John Stonehouse, the then Postmaster General, announced that he had invited Lord Annan, Provost of University College London, to head an independent committee of enquiry, the Committee on the Future of Broadcasting, to look at the long-term future of broadcasting after the Television Act and the BBC Charter expired in 1976. Almost immediately, a general election was called which unexpectedly gave victory to the Conservative Party under Edward Heath. They decided not to rush into a new enquiry and instead the Sound Broadcasting Act (1972) changed the name of the ITA to the Independent Broadcasting Authority and allowed the introduction of the first independent radio stations. Regulation of these came under the auspices of the IBA. January 1972 also saw the Minister for Posts and Telecommunications relax the rules on hours of broadcasting. This opened up programming, allowing lunchtime news reports on TV for the first time.

## More changes at the Press Council

In 1973, The Press Council changed its constitution again. This time, a three-person body called the Press Council Appointments Commission, chaired by Lord Redcliffe-Maud, was set up to appoint lay members. The Council was now thirty-strong with ten lay members. The Complaints Committee was made up of six lay members and six professional members and was chaired by the chairman of the Press Council, now Lord Shawcross who replaced Lord Pearce in 1974.

In 1974, yet another Royal Commission was set up with Sir Morris Finer as chairman. Sir Morris Finer died in 1975 and was replaced by Professor Oliver McGregor (who as Lord McGregor of Durris became the first chairman of the Press Complaints Commission in 1991). The Commission investigated a wide range of press topics, but devoted a whole chapter (20) to the Press Council. It rejected the notion of a communications council set up under statute (Royal Commission on the Press, 1977: 96). A communications council would have combined press and broadcast whilst the statutory suggestion would have removed the element of self-regulation.

The Commission reiterated its belief in self-regulation but again made it clear that the Press Council had to be seen to be working if legislation was to be avoided. It said that it believed the Press Council should show a determination to be independent of the Press: 'The public will not believe that a council dominated by journalists and others from the Press can keep an effective watch on the standards of the Press or can deal satisfactorily with complaints by citizens' (ibid.). It continued the attack on the problem of too few lay members on the Council. It expressed its concern about the large number of criticisms it had received about the Council's self-satisfaction over the press's alleged less than rigorous standards. It said that the Press Council's rejection of those criticisms and opposition to extending lay membership on the grounds that it was a voluntary, self-regulating body on which lay membership was unsuitable was inconsistent.

The Commission reported in 1977 with the following list of recommendations:

1 There should be equal numbers of lay to professional members on the Council with an independent chair.
2 The Appointments Commission chair should be the Press Council chairman.
3 There should be a right of reply.
4 There should be a fast-track conciliation service.
5 The legal waiver should be reconsidered.
6 There should be a code of conduct.
7 The Press Council should be provided with sufficient funds to advertise its services.
8 The publishers' organisations should be approached to agree that adjudications should be published in full on the front pages with a similar prominence to the original story.
9 The Press Council should undertake a wider review of the record of publications of journalists concerned in complaints.
10 The Press Council should undertake to investigate and monitor the press more often on its own initiative.
11 The Commission expressed its concern that there was no right of complaint over inaccuracy and that often opinion was based on inaccurate fact. It recommended that contentious opinion on the basis of fact should be grounds for censure. (ibid.: 236)

In 1976 the Press Council decided to codify its adjudications to form a basis of precedence to their work on complaints and codes of practice.

There was something of a sea-change at the Press Council in the year 1977, partly at least because of the Royal Commission. Kenneth Morgan, who as NUJ General Secretary had often attended Press Council meetings, became

Deputy Director. The Secretary became the Director and in October 1978 Patrick Neill QC took over as chairman from Lord Shawcross. In May 1980, the NUJ quit the Press Council in exasperation over its refusal to consider many of the reforms suggested by the 1974–77 Commission, although the Press Council had increased its membership to thirty-six to allow equal lay representation. By now, Kenneth Morgan had taken over the directorship of the Press Council, a position he was to hold until is closure. He was also to become the first Director of the Press Complaints Commission. The Rt Hon Sir Zelman Cowen was appointed chairman in 1984; he handed over to Louis Blom-Cooper who took up the reins in January 1989.

## Regulation for broadcasters

In February 1974 the Labour Party was returned to power and broadcasting was moved to the Home Office, following the abolition of the Ministry of Posts and Telecommunications. Roy Jenkins, Home Secretary, appointed the former journalist John Harris, now Lord Harris of Greenwich, to be Minister of State responsible for broadcasting. On 10 April 1974, Jenkins announced the revival of the Annan Committee to consider the future of the broadcasting services in the United Kingdom. New legislation was needed to extend the life of the Television Act which would otherwise have ended control in 1976. There was some concern amongst ITV circles about the sixteen members of the Annan Committee: 'Not a single one of the sixteen members was identifiable as what might be described as an ITV viewer and, to judge an industry with a multi-million pound turnover, fifteen out of sixteen had no first-hand experience of business' (Potter, 1989: 225).

The Annan Committee presented its report to parliament on 23 March 1977 and the government issued a white paper shortly after. This recommended a number of new bodies: Local Broadcasting Authority (for local radio and cable), an Open Broadcasting Authority (for the new fourth channel), a Public Enquiry Board (to hold public meetings every seven years), a Telecommunications Advisory Committee and a Broadcasting Complaints Commission.

The Labour government lost the election in 1979 and the Conservatives took over, issuing a new broadcasting bill in February 1980 which received assent in November to become the Broadcasting Act 1980. It was followed by the Broadcasting Act 1981 that consolidated the 1973, 1974, 1978 and 1980 Acts. The Act did little to change the main structure of broadcasting and introduced only one new body: the Broadcasting Complaints Commission, which had been strongly advocated by Lord Annan and which had received strong general support. It was set up to consider and adjudicate complaints of unjust or unfair treatment in television and radio programmes or of unwarranted infringement of privacy in, or in connection with, the obtaining of material included in programmes. Its first chairman was Lady Pike. Geoffrey Robertson said: 'its work since inception has been unimpressive' (1983: 163). He was far from being the Council's only critic. A second council was set up in 1988 to keep a closer eye on the standards of broadcasters. It was seen very much as Mrs Thatcher's baby, her committee to reduce the amount of sex and violence on TV. Lord Rees Mogg, the former *Times* editor, was made its first chairman. The Broadcasting Standards Council was to monitor the portrayal of violence and sex and matters of taste and decency. This would include bad language and the treatment of disasters in radio and TV programmes or broadcast advertisements.

The Council was set up initially on a non-statutory basis pending legislation that arrived in the shape of the 1990 Broadcasting Act. The first director of the BSC was Colin Shaw, the former Director of TV at the Independent Broadcasting Authority and former Chief Secretary at the BBC where he had worked for almost twenty years.

## All change

By the end of the 1980s, as Fleet Street publishers moved out to Wapping and Canary Wharf, it was clear, even to the most stubborn editor, that the writing was on the wall as far as press behaviour was concerned. The editors met in November 1989 at the Newspaper Publishers' Association in London and issued a communiqué which accepted the need to improve methods of self-regulation. They declared their unanimous commitment to the Press Council and to a five-point common code of practice (Press Council, 1989: 340). One of the main reasons for this was the avoidance of legal control rather than any real attempt to clean up their act. Nevertheless, a committee was set up under the chairmanship of Andreas Whittam-Smith, then editor of the *Independent*, which drew up a new code of conduct (the Editors' Code of Conduct). Many of the papers backed up the new code by appointing ombudsmen to 'represent their readers' to the paper. The *Sun* was one of several which made considerable play of appointing a 'readers' champion' to support the new Code of Conduct.

Also, by 1989, some of the Press Council reforms had been put in place. But there were still problems and, after the appointment of Louis Blom Cooper, the Press Council set up its own review body to consider the way forward. This recommended a new code of conduct (the Council had not had one until then) and the addition of a hot line for complaints. These improvements were an acceptable way forward for the NUJ which rejoined the council in 1990 after gaining the approval of its Annual Delegate Meeting. The government had also been concerned by the growing public anger about an over-sensationalist press and in 1989 had set up a committee under the chairmanship of David Calcutt QC (now Sir David) to investigate privacy and related matters. This concentrated entirely on the Press. Broadcasting already had the BCC with its statutory duty to investigate privacy invasions.

Although the committee came up with helpful suggestions on dealing with minors in criminal cases, its recommendations on privacy were less welcome to the industry (Committee on Privacy and Related Matters, 1990). These were not a surprise, however, coming on the top of several royal scandal stories and the Gorden Kaye incident. The actor Gorden Kaye was seriously ill in hospital having suffered a severe head injury during a hurricane in London. On 13 February 1990 *Sunday Sport* reporters Gazza Thompson and Ray Levine managed to get into his hospital room, photographed him and even tried to interview him. The subsequent report provoked howls of protest around the country, which was not helped by the insensitive attitude of *Sunday Sport* editor Drew Robertson, who failed to accept a reprimand from the Press Council and printed a huge article condemning the Press Council as a waste of space in robust and, many felt, unnecessarily crude language. He was later sacked by the board of directors which was surprisingly sensitive to the dangers of the situation. This incident had almost led to immediate legislation and so it was no surprise when Calcutt published strong recommendations on privacy and called for the scrapping of the Press Council and its replacement with a Press Complaints Commission (ibid.). There was some bitterness in the Press Council about this move as most of the proposals for a PCC were included in the Press Council's own review body recommendations. The Press Council also felt that Calcutt's recommendation to remove the duty to defend press freedom from the PCC was ill-advised. Its other concerns about the proposed body were:

- It would not take third-party complaints.
- It was not allowed to investigate of its own cognisance.
- It was lacking in lay membership.

Although the new body was opposed by the Press Council, employer groups had already set up the Press Standards Board of Finance (Pressbof) to fund the development of a PCC with a new code of practice. Its constituent members are: the NPA, the NS, the PPA, the SNPA and the SDNS. The Press Council voted not to give up its jurisdiction, supported mainly by lay members and the trade unions. However, because of Pressbof, the new Press Complaints Committee was the body with the funding and the Press Council was forced, reluctantly, to close in December 1990, its officers and offices being taken over by the Press Complaints Commission.

Calcutt had recommended that this should be the industry's last chance to be self-regulatory and warned that if the media continued to misbehave, then statutory regulation should be introduced. He suggested a probationary period of one year but no criteria were laid down about good behaviour.

The new PCC started work in January 1991. It was dominated by industry representatives, mostly editors, which did its new reputation little good. The Calcutt Committee had recommended removing the right of the constituent bodies to elect representatives in order that the Commission be seen as truly independent of the industry. It also recommended that the Appointments Commission should have 'explicit freedom to appoint whoever it considers best qualified' (ibid.: 69). The Press Complaints Commission's constitution decided on a slightly larger committee than envisaged by Calcutt – sixteen rather than twelve – and also decided that the press representatives should be editors or senior journalists. To date, no press representative has ever been anything other than an editor. This was outside the spirit of Calcutt and angered many within the journalists' unions who saw this as a way of excluding trade union involvement with the new body. This is one reason for the NUJ's antipathy to the PCC.

Even the five lay members appointed to the first council were not seen as totally independent and were labelled 'toffs and profs' by Paul Foot. The Commission was chaired by Lord McGregor and he brought with him some of his team from the Advertising Standards Authority (ASA). They had considerable experience of dealing with complaints but things did not always run smoot' ly with the change-over to a new system. By the end of the year, the Director, Ken Morgan, the former Director at the Press Council, had left and his place had been taken by Mark Bolland from the ASA. There seems little doubt he was forced out, but neither side is prepared to talk about why.

The PCC's refusal, backed by Calcutt, to base its work on the precept of defending the freedom of the press was seen by many as unfortunate. How, they argued, could a journalist's conduct be measured if the freedom of the press was not seen as one of the goalposts? Surely the only defence for invasions of privacy was the freedom of the press to write of matters in the public interest? Nevertheless, a code of practice was drafted under the chairmanship of Patsie Chapman, then editor of the *News of the World*. This was to prove a later source of embarrassment to the Commission when the first complaint to be dealt with was against the *News of the World*. This code of practice did contain (as it obviously had to) a public interest defence against issues of intrusion and invasion. With royal scandal following royal scandal through the early 1990s, as well as a series of indiscretions by politicians, the debate about press excesses continued. The election of 1992 must have its part to play in explaining why these did not spark the introduction of laws on privacy.

Despite the claimed expertise of the former ASA staff, who spent some time rebuilding the complaints systems used by the PCC to follow the model used by the ASA, the PCC quickly showed itself to be ineffectual and self-serving and a few spectacular invasions of privacy by the tabloids led to further calls for legislation. Two major royal stories of 1992 in particular explain why David Calcutt was asked to prepare a second report on the press, and in particular the effectiveness of the Press Complaints Commission.

The first, the taking of photographs of the topless Duchess of York whilst on a private holiday, shortly after her formal separation from the Duke, showed how the public could both condemn and be titillated, self-righteous and hypocritical. Amidst widespread condemnation of the pictures, published first by the *Daily Mirror* (on a Wednesday) and then by *The Observer*, both papers sold out. The *Daily Mirror* went so far as to produce a new run on Thursday morning for the city. These also sold out. Stung by the attacks these publications drew, the papers were far more circumspect when tapes purporting to be of a telephone conversation between the Prince of Wales and Lady Camilla Parker Bowles were made available to the media after publication in an Australian newspaper (owned by Rupert Murdoch, the owner of News International, publishers of the *Sun*, *Today* and *The Times*). Most papers became terribly self-righteous about the story, condemning it on the one hand as an invasion of privacy whilst, on the other, giving a brief synopsis of its content; enough to tantalise without being enough to explain what was in the conversation. Only *The Sport*, *The Observer* and a handful of provincial papers published the conversation in full, exposing it as childish and smutty. The Press Association (PA) refused to circulate the transcript generally and sent it only to papers that specifically asked for it. Most papers ignored the obvious story about where such a tape had come from in order to maximise the sordid nature of the conversation. In this incident, as in the abdication story of the 1930s, limited publication gave the story more impact than full publication would have done, with the added benefit of allowing the media to pretend that they were behaving responsibly.

The *Daily Mirror* followed a similar line when budget papers were leaked to it in November 1996. Refusing to run the story, it returned the papers to the Chancellor amidst much smugness about its responsible stand. The next day it was stung badly enough by criticism of its news sense to crow that it had not run the leaked documents because they were not interesting enough. This was probably true. The story about handing back leaked documents was better than publishing the less than damaging leaks.

In its October 1992 report the PCC spelt out some of the reasons why it felt it had been effective and was becoming more so. It contended that there was a lack of statistical evidence of serious criticism from readers. It also claimed that there was a scarcity of complaints about intrusion into privacy and few about harassment. The PCC submitted a 76-page dossier to Sir David Calcutt, including detailed statistics, to support its view that 'there is no case for statutory intervention in one of our greatest liberties – the freedom of the press' (PCC, Report No. 14, 1992: 5). This presented an interesting can of worms that Calcutt spent some time opening. The original Calcutt report had quite specifically denied the Press Complaints Commission the chance to champion press freedom and indeed this was one of the reasons why many people opposed the change-over from Press Council to Press Complaints Commission. Yet in April 1991, by special resolution, the Press Complaints Commission added a clause to its objectives about press freedom. By June 1991, the Commission was including as its duties: 'The duty to promote generally established freedoms including freedom of expression and the public's right to know, and the defence of the Press against improper pressure from the Government and elsewhere' (PCC, Report No. 1, 1991: 4). Calcutt records in his report that Lord McGregor had assured him 'That it was not part of the Commission's responsibility to be a campaigning body' (Calcutt, 1993: 16). This was followed by an article in *UK Press Gazette* headed: 'Calcutt test passed – now for Press Freedom' (ibid.) which contained an interview with Lord McGregor, allegedly taking a contrary view. Calcutt records his subsequent conversation with McGregor in which McGregor claims he was misrepresented in his views (Calcutt, 1993: 17).

'Calcutt 2', as the new review was quickly called, sparked the PCC into a short burst of activity and the following month's report also contained an editorial spelling out how the PCC was making its existence more widely known. It was certainly possible to complain that the Commission had not been good at making itself better known to the public. It now announced that it had produced a 'How to Complain' leaflet and information sheets about the Commission. One thousand copies of a small poster had been mailed to libraries and newspapers were donating advertising space for the PCC. The Commission announced its intention to be listed in all the main UK telephone directories from the following year, something it does as a matter of course now. The Commission boasted about presentations explaining its role to MPs, editors, students and consumer groups, although anecdotal evidence suggests these were not as widely available as the PCC would like us to believe.

Sir David Calcutt was unconvinced by the Commission's case and reported in January 1993 that in his view the PCC should be wound up and a statutory body put in its place. He recommended that the only way forward was a statutory Press Complaints Tribunal, which would be able to carry out its own inquiries, draw up a code of practice, impose fines and costs, and award compensation, and to require a response to its inquiries. He also recommended criminal legislation for physical intrusion and a new tort of infringement of privacy and called for tighter restrictions on the reporting of court cases involving minors (Calcutt, 1993).

Shortly after the report was delivered, the Secretary of State for National Heritage, David Mellor, who had already warned the press about drinking in the 'last chance saloon', found he had been drinking there himself and he was forced to resign as allegation after allegation made his position untenable. This underlined the high-risk nature of being the Secretary of State responsible for trying to reign in the media. The National Heritage Committee on Privacy and Media Intrusion was set up in July 1992, running parallel with Calcutt's, and returned its conclusions to the House in March 1993. It was chaired by Mr Gerald Kaufman and came up with a number of recommendations concerning the future of the PCC and the basis of press self-regulation. It said that the approach should remain voluntary and that Calcutt was wrong to seek statutory control at this stage, but that he was right to want to ditch the PCC. The National Heritage Committee made forty-three recommendations including the following:

- Editors' and journalists' contracts of employment should include reference to the code of practice.
- Newspapers should appoint readers' representatives.
- A Protection of Privacy Bill should be introduced.
- A Press Commission should replace the PCC, with the power to impose fines and order compensation.
- A statutory Press Ombudsman should be appointed, with power to supervise the wording and position of retractions and apologies and impose fines and order the payment of compensation. (National Heritage Committee, 1993: xxiii–xxvi)

The government had promised in 1990 to bring in new laws on privacy, as recommended by Calcutt, but by the 1992 election these had still not been introduced. The government issued a consultation paper on the infringement of privacy at the end of July 1993 which had some fairly strong things to say about the issue but very little about the PCC. Lord Mackay, the Lord Chancellor, launched the paper with the view that it was time for a new right of privacy. This was supported by the National Heritage Committee. It was opposed, though, by various editors and was strongly attacked in the media. Surprisingly, the government announced an indefinite delay in the publication of the promised White Paper on privacy in March 1994.

The National Heritage Committee was not the only one trying to get in on the media ethics act in 1993. The European Commission had also been becoming more concerned over the last few years and wanted to have its own code of ethics developed.

# The Press Complaints Commission today

The PCC has spent most of its life trying frantically to change its processes in a bid to keep up with a constant stream of criticism. The ink on both the 'Calcutt 2 report' and the National Heritage Committee report was barely dry before Pressbof issued a statement entitled *Strengthening Self-regulation* on 4 May 1993. This announced a series of measures designed to 'reinforce public confidence' in the authority of the PCC. The independent PCC quickly welcomed Pressbof's statement. First it agreed to change the membership: 'Since it was set up in January 1991, the Commission have operated with complete independence. However, to meet any misconceptions regarding their independent status, the membership of the Commission will be altered to ensure a lay majority consisting of an independent chairman, eight non-press members and seven editors' (PCC, Report No. 17, 1993: 5).

Secondly, the PCC was offered, and agreed to accept, the final ratification of the Code of Practice. Despite consistently claiming that one of the strengths of the PCC was that the Code was drawn up for editors, by editors, the PCC now has the final say in ratifying the Code. By the end of 1998, the Commission had yet to use its power to veto a change publicly, but with substantial changes made in 1997, following the death of the Princess of Wales, it can be assumed that planned changes in the Code are notified to the Commission chairman before publication to ensure that the Commission will not be put in the embarrassing position of having to refuse publicly to ratify a Code change. Lord Wakeham made it plain early on that he was unhappy with some elements of the Code and that a major re-write was both needed and planned. His chance came with the death of the Princess of Wales and a new Code was introduced in January 1998. The next change was to set up a help-line for members of the public who feel the Code is about to be breached with regard to their affairs.

The Commission also boasted about the lengths it had gone to publicise itself. It claimed that £250,000 worth of advertising space had been donated and that 130,000 copies of the 'how to complain' leaflet had been distributed in the previous twelve months. In addition, the Code committee had tinkered almost endlessly with its definition of private property (June 1993, October 1993, February 1995). It had also taken to doing its own investigating and commenting on matters, although it was difficult to tell whether this was a deliberate policy or merely Lord McGregor taking any opportunity to gain publicity to show the effectiveness of the Commission.

Towards the end of 1994 the industry tired of McGregor's eccentric approach. When the Commission should have been stifling public outrage under the guise of sober reflection and adjudication of the issue, McGregor was on the front steps of Salisbury Square addressing the TV cameras about the press 'dabbling their fingers in the stuff of other people's souls'. When it could and should have spoken out, McGregor was nowhere to be found. Those close to him during this time believe his illness had started to affect his judgement. He died in November 1997.

A carefully concealed, collective sigh of relief was uttered when McGregor's period of office ended in December 1994 and he was replaced by Lord Wakeham, the former Chief Whip for Margaret Thatcher, Secretary of State for Energy and Leader of first the Commons and then the Lords. He was undoubtedly seen by both government and the industry as a safe pair of hands to guide the PCC on the tightrope between the government and the press with diplomacy and statesmanship. Acknowledged by all as a smooth and talented political operator, he was welcomed by an industry well aware that failure to walk this tightrope effectively would be certain to force the government, albeit unwillingly, to introduce press legislation.

Lord Wakeham set about a major, if subdued, shake-up of the PCC. He started by replacing some of the members of the Commission. His intention was to ensure that a majority of individual members of the PCC were independent of the press and that the whole of the Commission operated as such. He also reformed the method of appointing PCC members. The PCC's articles of association had been changed in 1993 to reflect the concerns of Sir David Calcutt over appointments to the Commission. Unfortunately, the PCC had been operating in breach of those new articles ever since. As Lord Wakeham pointed out to the Secretary of State at the Department of National Heritage on 19 June 1995: 'If this is not open and independent, doubt will naturally be cast on the integrity of the appointments. I was therefore deeply dismayed to discover that the PCC's appointments system was operating in breach of its own articles of association' (Department of National Heritage, 1995: 26). He immediately dealt with this.

Until Wakeham, the Appointments Commission had been appointed by Pressbof. Wakeham changed this so that he now appointed the Public Nominees – the three independent members of the Appointments Commission. He is the fourth commissioner and the chairman of Pressbof is the fifth. Several changes in the Secretary of State at the Department of National Heritage had delayed the government's response to the National Heritage Committee's report but finally the Rt Hon Virginia Bottomley JP MP stayed long enough to produce, on 17 July 1995, a document setting out the government's policy on privacy. This made it clear that although the government had no objection to criminal legislation on invasions of privacy in principle, it felt it had 'not been able to construct legislation which is . . . workable in practice. Accordingly it has no immediate plans to legislate in this area' (ibid.: 9). Intriguingly, despite this inability to construct legislation in the criminal area, the consultative document had been able to include a hypothetical civil remedy, including a definition of privacy. In a far from subtly worded hint as to what awaited the industry, should it drag its heels over change, the report made the industry an offer it could not refuse: 'The industry has indicated that it wishes to adopt a tighter form of words on privacy in its code. The government welcomes this. It believes it may be helpful for the industry, in refining its code, to see what a hypothetical civil remedy might look like. Annex B accordingly sets out how legislation might have been framed . . .' (ibid.: 16).

The government's response to the National Heritage Committee's report deals with four main issues:

- Should regulation be voluntary or statutory? The government is in no doubt: 'It believes that, in principle, industry self-regulation is to be much preferred.' It also feels that this applies to the National Heritage Committee's plan for an ombudsman (ibid.: 5).
- Should criminal law be introduced? The government says it still believes in self-regulation and, in any case, legislation is too difficult to construct (ibid.: 13).
- Should a civil remedy be provided with a statutory right of privacy? The government feels not. Self-regulation should continue (ibid.: 16).
- Has the PCC gone far enough with its reforms? Certainly not. The government 'looks to it [PCC] to make further improvements to ensure self-regulation can be made to work and to carry public confidence' (ibid.: 8).

The government was very clear about what it expected Lord Wakeham to deliver with his cleaned-up PCC. Chapter 2 of the government's response laid out a number of suggestions. Some of these had already been put into operation by Wakeham, but others are still undone.

**Appointments**: The government had welcomed Wakeham's change to the appointment system, allowing wider lay membership of the Appointments Committee and the move to a lay majority on the Commission itself.

**Press hotline**: This would allow editors to discuss sensitive stories with the PCC before publication. At the time of the government's response to the Heritage Committee this was still planned, but now seems to be working, at least on an *ad hoc* basis. Lord McGregor had opposed this as smacking of pre-publication censorship.

**Improvements to procedures**: The government welcomed Wakeham's plan to accept and investigate appropriate third-party complaints. It also called for the adoption of citizen-charter-style performance targets and the publication of fuller summaries of adjudications.

**Code written into contracts**: Wakeham reported that the code was gradually being incorporated into editor's contracts of employment and those of some journalists. This was welcomed by the government but they awaited further evidence of disciplinary sanctions. 'Sanctions are a crucial issue. . . . Should not proprietors consider dismissal in appropriate cases, and the commission make recommendations to that effect?' (Ibid.: 33).

**Compensation fund**: The government wishes to see compensation paid to those whose privacy is unjustifiably infringed by the press. Wakeham did not mention this in his letter to the Secretary of State, Virginia Bottomley. Her letter says: ' The government is also attracted to the idea of a compensation fund. . . . It would represent a form of insurance – there are no doubt ways in which contributions of the different papers could be equitably assessed' (ibid.). Newspapers disagreed. How, argue many proprietors, could a system be set up to build a compensation fund with contributions from papers as diverse as the *Stornaway Gazette* and the *News of the World*? How could you compare the extent of the invasion, the intent of the paper, and the damage done?

**Contents of the Code of Practice**: Whilst accepting that Lord Wakeham was attempting to develop the Code, the government made it clear that a number of specific improvements were still needed. There was also a need to involve the public and the PCC in the framing of a code that at that time was wholly the preserve of the Code Committee – a body set up by Pressbof under the chairmanship of Sir David English of Associated News. This could have caused the PCC some problems. They made considerable play of the fact that the Code is drawn up by the industry. Although the Code Committee is, to all intents and purpose, self-selecting from amongst editors and therefore can be considered flawed, it does give the PCC a chance to stand away from the Code and say that it is not the PCC Code, but the Editors' Code. The PCC believes this ties the editors into the system much more closely.

In his introduction to the PCC's Annual Report of 1995 Lord Wakeham talks about what he sees as a momentous year for the PCC: '. . . We were finally taken off probation and given the green light to get on with working to provide a first-class complaints handling service to the public' (PCC, 1995: 2). He explains that three things happened to convince him that self-regulation is the way forward:

1 The Commission renewed its independence from the industry that pays for it.
2 The PCC became far more consistent in its application of the Code of Practice.
3 There has been growing confidence in the system by the public. (PCC, 1995: 2)

Lord Wakeham pointed to an increase in complaints as evidence of rising public confidence. The number of complaints rose in 1995 by nearly 30 per cent on 1994 to a high of 2,508. 'Ordinary people won't waste time complaining to a toothless body' (PCC, 1995: 2). The Press Council in 1995 received a record number of 1,588 complaints. Lord Wakeham was convinced the new high figure was entirely down to confidence in the PCC rather than falling standards sparking more complaints.

Although Lord Wakeham had made sweeping changes to the PCC, he was still fine-tuning the organisation. Mark Bolland, the youthful director who took over from Ken Morgan in 1992, had joined the Prince of Wales's press team and with a new director in place, Wakeham had virtually a completely fresh team. Rumours continue about tensions between Wakeham and Sir David English, then chair of Pressbof's Code of Practice Committee. This committee of editors draws up the Code of Practice used by the Commission. Lord Wakeham had expressed his determination to review the Code of Conduct and the way that it was drawn up. In his letter to the Secretary of State Wakeham made it clear he was unhappy about a Code Committee composed solely of editors: 'It is arguable that the committee responsible for the initial framing of the Code should not be composed only of editors and convened under the aegis of Pressbof' (Department of National Heritage, 1995: 28). Wakeham had been encouraging outside organisations to express their views on the Code of Conduct and was firm in his expressed determination only to accept a new Code that was completely satisfactory to the Commission. Sir David, on the other hand, whilst accepting that the Commission must ratify the Code, made much of the fact that it was a committee of editors who drew up the Code: 'The Code is, crucially, the industry's own Code. Although it must be ratified by the independent PCC to take effect, it is the fact that the Code is drafted *by* industry practitioners *for* the industry that ensures the unswerving commitment of all sectors of the newspaper and magazine publishing sector to self-regulation' (PCC, 1995: 11). Sir David used the rest of his 1995 report to clarify the range and number of changes the Committee had made to the Code in the previous few years. His intention was to praise the Code Committee's flexibility although he also succeeded in laying bare the inadequacies of the PCC's Code and its constant need to change in an effort to catch up with the latest breach.

## Broadcasting

Broadcasting regulation also underwent a major change during the early 1990s, following the signing of the Broadcasting Act 1990. This introduced a more flexible approach to broadcast regulation. The BBC continued under the control of the Board of Governors, but the Independent Broadcasting Authority

(IBA) was replaced by the Independent Television Commission, the Welsh Authority, S4C, and the Radio Authority. These came into operation on 1 January 1993. The Broadcasting Complaints Commission was also retained, as was the Broadcasting Standards Council, now with statutory authority. Their responsibilities remained largely unchanged. They were charged with investigating complaints but could punish only by insisting on the transmission of findings.

One of the main changes of the Broadcast Act was to remove from the ITC the control of programming that the old IBA had had. The ITC is not able to vet programmes before they are shown; it can only deal with complaints made after they are broadcast. The Broadcasting Act 1996 (first published on 15 December 1995 and receiving Royal Assent on 25 July 1996) brought in three main changes that need concern us. One was to introduce changes in the way licences for existing broadcasting stations are granted. The requirement remained for licence holders to be fit and proper persons who have to follow a set of regulations, while the rules on cross-media ownership were significantly loosened, allowing big media groups to own far more. These rules came into effect on 1 November 1996 and allowed independent radio stations to own one AM, one FM and one other (AM or FM) service instead of a maximum of one FM and one AM service in overlapping areas. It allowed local newspapers to own local radio services in overlapping areas for the first time. Local newspapers with a circulation under 20 per cent were allowed to own one AM, one FM and one other service, like any other company. Papers with 20 to 50 per cent circulation in an area were allowed to own one AM and one FM service in that area, and those with more than 50 per cent were allowed to own one service in that area (provided there was more than one independent local radio service in the area). The Act also removed ownership controls on cable operators.

The second big change was to introduce digital TV and to offer the large number of digital multiplex channels to broadcasters. A multiplex is a frequency band on which several programme services and sometimes additional data services can be combined. The Department of National Heritage said six television and seven radio multiplexes were to be available initially and, with the exception of the BBC's television and national radio multiplexes, were to be licensed to multiplex providers by the Independent Television Commission and the Radio Authority. These multiplex operators in turn offered a range of programme services on each multiplex. Existing broadcasters were being offered half a multiplex for each existing channel. This gave the BBC full control of a multiplex. Channel 3 and Channel 4 share a multiplex, on which capacity is also reserved for the public teletext service. Channel 5 have half of the third multiplex and S4C were offered the other half of this multiplex in Wales. Terrestrial television broadcasters had to declare their intention to take up their guaranteed places on terrestrial digital multiplexes by 15 October 1996. Most did and digital services were launched in late 1997 and 1998. No fee is payable for the first of the twelve-year multiplex licences which will be awarded to the applicants whose proposals are 'most likely to promote the development of digital terrestrial broadcasting. Companies must demonstrate a commitment to the "roll-out" of transmission and to promoting the take-up of receiving equipment. They must also be able to demonstrate that they intend to supply a variety of programming, that their plans are commercially viable and sustainable and that they will deal fairly with broadcasters' (Deptartment of National Heritage, Press Release, July 1996).

The third change made by the Broadcasting Act was to alter the regulations and to order the amalgamation of the BSC and the BCC into a new Broadcasting Standards Commission with a wider remit but similar powers. The amalgamation came into effect on 1 April 1997.

National Heritage Secretary Virginia Bottomley announced in July 1996 that Lady Howe of Aberavon would be the Chairman of the new Broadcasting Standards Commission with Lord Dubs as one Deputy Chairman and Jane Leighton as the other. Lady Howe had been appointed Chairman of the old BSC from 1993 and so had continuity of experience.

Regulations on the requirement for regional programming were tightened up by the new Act, whilst provision was made for a list of major sporting events that could not become exclusive to pay-per-view or subscription television to be drawn up. The news service for Channel 3 would be provided by a company selected by the ITV companies from a field which met the ITC's quality threshold.

The Act also empowers the Independent Television Commission to regulate the BBC and S4C's commercial activities and privatises the BBC's transmission network. From 13 August 1996, the Independent Television Commission and the Radio Authority were allowed to give decisions on the public interest test they intended to use on the common ownership and control of newspapers and broadcasters.

## More changes on the way

At the end of October 1996, Lord Mackay of Clashfern, then the Lord Chancellor, announced, in reply to a question in the House of Lords, that the government intended publishing a consultation paper about a new law preventing the payment or offer of payment to a witness in a trial which is pending or imminent. Announcing the proposals and inviting comments, he condemned what he called 'widespread and flagrant breaches' of the PCC's Code. The consultation document released by the Lord Chancellor's department explained that as many as nineteen witnesses were believed to have accepted payments from the media in the Rosemary West trial. 'The existence or possibility of payment by the media does increase the danger of a witness's evidence being distorted. . . . The Government therefore considers that legislation is needed to deal with the threat which payments to witnesses pose to the proper administration of justice. Press self-regulation did not prevent the payments in the West case or others' (Lord Chancellor's Department, 1996: 6). The consultation paper asked for comments on whether payments, offers of payment and requests for payment should be prohibited, and on specific questions relating to:

- Whether the prohibition should take the form of a contempt of court or a criminal offence.
- Whether a risk of prejudice to the proceedings needs to be proved.
- Whether an intention to interfere with the course of justice needs to be proved.
- At what stage the prohibition should begin.
- Whether the prohibition should cease at the end of the trial.
- Whether there should be any defences. (Ibid.)

Lord Mackay was concerned that witnesses might omit something from their evidence in court to leave something exclusive for a story in the media, or that witnesses might exaggerate evidence in order to make their stories more newsworthy. Witnesses might also become so committed to their particular accounts that they would be unwilling to examine points put to them in court.

Even where witnesses are not swayed by contracts, Lord Mackay believed it was likely that cross-examination would raise the existence of contracts, suggesting that their evidence might be flawed, sowing doubts in juries' minds. The Lord Chancellor said payments to witnesses risked damaging the integrity of the administration of justice. The government also noted that the PCC's Code of Practice did not apply to broadcasting journalists (Department of National Heritage, Press Release, 30 October 1996).

The NUJ National Executive Council, which discussed the consultative paper at its meeting in December 1996, agreed that there should be a strengthening of the law and that the contempt of court restrictions should be extended to cover this issue. The National Heritage Select Committee also agreed that there should be an extension, although they believed there should be a new law. The Bar Council also supported an extension of legislation on the payment of witnesses.

Several editors and the Press Complaints Commission itself opposed changes, saying that the Code was able to deal with the problem – despite the Rosemary West case – suggesting that this was not the case. The bill was not to be, as the Labour Party came to government in June 1997 before the bill could be made law.

## A change of government

The Labour government has made it clear that it is happy with self-regulation and does not intend to introduce statutory control or privacy legislation. One of its election pledges was a Freedom of Information Bill and a draft was presented to parliament in June 1999 to general condemnation.

Lord Wakeham agreed at the end of 1996 to a further period as chairman of the Press Complaints Commission and as his steadying hand on the tiller has continued to win general praise, press regulation in the UK seems set for more of the same. The Broadcasting Standards Commission has hardly had a chance to show its mettle, so changes here are also unlikely.

The death of the Princess of Wales and the subsequent anger of the public over what was, at the time, believed to be the involvement of the paparazzi gave a wobble to self-regulation, with many people calling for a new law on privacy. The full report on the crash, which blamed chauffeur Henri Paul for driving too fast whilst under the influence of alcohol, came two years later – too late to prevent the attacks on the media. Although the government had called for a period of 'calm reflection', both Media Secretary, Chris Smith, and Prime Minister Tony Blair made it clear they did not favour a privacy law. Earl Spencer, the Princess's brother, delivered a stinging attack on the tabloid press, accusing them of trying to bring down the Princess. Several newspapers responded by vowing not to use intrusive pictures of the Princes William and Harry and several agreed not to use paparazzo pictures at all. Her death produced a new Code of Practice for the PCC but the other resolutions did not last long and papers were soon printing paparazzo pictures again. The introduction of the Human Rights Act 1998 was one of the new government's major pieces of legislation in terms of its effects on the media.

The PCC came to a new deal with the Prince of Wales in early 1999 about coverage of his sons, the Princes William and Harry, following the publication of a series of intrusive pictures of them. The deal saw new guidelines issued to the press in return for the Royal Family being more open with the media.

## Summary

- This chapter looked at history of self-regulation in the UK.
- It considered the development of press regulation, culminating in the Press Complaints Commission.

- It presented some of the approaches to media regulation suggested by different authorities in the UK over the past fifty years.

- It looked at the changes in broadcast legislation that led to regulation in the broadcasting media, and some of the differences of approach taken between broadcasting and the press.

- It explained how governments have viewed the media and its regulation and considered how the present government might change things.

## Questions

1 Why do you think the industry was so supportive of David Calcutt's idea to set up a self-regulatory body in 1990 but so condemnatory of his plans to scrap it in 1993?

2 The Broadcasting Act of 1996 made a number of important changes in the way broadcasting is regulated in the UK. Which do you think were the most significant?

3 The limit of frequencies has always been used as the reason for licensing radio and TV stations, whilst the freedom of all to set up a newspaper has been given as the reason for not licensing the press. With the advent of digital TV and radio, is this limit on broadcasting still justified and is there really freedom for all to publish a paper?

4 Several government-sponsored inquiries have called for some form of stronger media legislation. Why do you think this has not happened?

5 Have the press started behaving responsibly in the past few years or are there other reasons for the relative lack of attacks on the media?

# Chapter 11

••••••••••••••••••••••••••••••••••••••••••••••••••••••••••••••••••••••••••••

# Regulatory systems

## Chapter Outline

This chapter examines:

- The structure and methods of the Press Complaints Commission.
- The structure and methods of the Broadcasting Standards Commission.
- The structure and methods of the Radio Authority.
- The structure and methods of the ITC.
- The structure and methods of the BBC Complaints Panel.
- The structure and methods of the NUJ's Ethics Council.
- The position abroad and the different methods which can be used to regulate the media.
- Some of the ethical topics which are current abroad but are not problems in the UK.

There are several regulatory councils in the UK charged with guarding media standards. All but two have statutory powers. The exceptions are the voluntary Press Complaints Commission, set up by the print media to police a Code of Practice, and the NUJ's Ethics Council, set up by the union to educate journalists in ethics and to police its Code of Conduct.

## The Press Complaints Commission

The PCC was set up following the first Calcutt report solely to resolve complaints. Calcutt's recommendation that the Commission should not become involved in press freedom issues was regretted by the old Press Council. It felt that to seek to adjudicate on complaints that were not measured against the need for press freedom was to leave the media vulnerable to censorship. Despite these regrets, the old Press Council shut its doors in December 1990 and the PCC took up the reins in January 1991 under the leadership of Lord McGregor of Durris who had chaired the 1974–77 Royal Commission on the Press and was chairman of the Advertising Standards Authority. The PCC is funded by Pressbof (the press board of finance), a body set up by newspaper publishers' organisations after the publication of the Calcutt report. It raises finance from publishers to pay for the PCC. The PCC chairman is appointed by Pressbof. The members of the Press Complaints Commission are selected by the Appointments Commission. The Appointments Commission has five members: the PCC chairman, three members nominated by the PCC chairman and the chairman of Pressbof. The nominated members each serve for four years.

There are sixteen members of the Commission, including the chairman. Seven of the sixteen are the press members, who should be working editors or senior journalists in executive positions. The independent members cannot be involved with, or interested in, the business of publishing newspapers, periodicals or magazines. 1998 saw some big changes on the Commission with seven of the members leaving and the death of Sir David English, then chairman of the Code of Practice Committee. Eight new members (six of them editors) have been appointed.

The PCC does not normally initiate enquiries and does not require a legal waiver from complainants. Under the old Press Council, a legal waiver had prevented complainants going on to sue the newspaper through the courts, using a council judgement in their favour as evidence.

The PCC judges complaints by a Code of Practice drawn up by a committee of editors nominated by Pressbof.

## How the PCC works

The PCC is a lay committee, with a small professional secretariat to service it. As well as dealing with complaints, the PCC also advises editors before publication. According to Lord Wakeham, who took over as chairman of the PCC in January 1995, more and more editors seek the advice of the PCC on particular stories or the approach to particular stories before publication. The hot-line to the PCC was established shortly after Wakeham took over at the PCC. McGregor had not been keen on the idea, as he feared it smacked of prior restraint.

The PCC also has an important role to play in providing material on self-regulation and the Code of Practice for trainee journalists and students. In its *Annual Report* of 1995 it says that the PCC chairman, members and staff lecture extensively to universities, colleges and in-house training schemes across the country. Much of this work was undertaken by Professor Robert Pinker, who delivered twenty-nine training lectures in 1997 (PCC, 1997: 14). Certainly the administration staff have always been very helpful in providing me with the material I have needed for teaching and researching for this book.

The PCC also offers general guidance to editors. In 1995 it warned editors about intruding on the privacy of Prince William's arrival at Eton in September 1995 and issued guidance about the naming of lottery winners. This warned editors not to seek to obtain information about winners from the operators of the National Lottery in breach of any duty of confidentiality which the operator owed to winners under the terms of its licence. The guidelines did recognise that the press might be justified in identifying a winner in the public interest. They also recognised that the press should not be turned into a scapegoat where it was the actions of the operator or of winners which had breached confidentiality (PCC, Report No. 29, 1995: 26).

The Commission also attempts to raise the awareness of the public with regional tours by the chairman; the wide distribution of its 'how to complain' leaflet; advertisements in newspapers and magazines, using space donated by the publishers; a touring exhibition; participation at conferences; and distribution of literature. A help-line is also available to the public on 0207–353 3732. An average of 120 calls a week were received in 1995.

### How to complain

The PCC issues a leaflet to help show would-be complainants how the system works. A complaint should be sent to the Commission where a decision is taken on whether the matter presents a possible breach of the Code of Conduct. It is here that the importance of the Code becomes clear. Only if the Code is potentially breached can a complaint be considered.

The editor of the publication is then sent a copy of the complaint and it is suggested that he or she deals with it direct. This can often be done with a correction, some form of right of reply or an apology. If the matter is resolved to everyone's satisfaction at this stage, the PCC would not normally pursue it further. If the situation is not resolved, the Commission would go on to adjudicate the complaint. If the complaint is upheld, the publication is obliged to print the full text of the adjudication. If the complaint is dismissed, then no further action is taken. In both cases, the complainant is sent full copies of the adjudication.

The PCC attempts to deal with complaints as quickly as possible. It will normally only deal with complaints made within one month of publication or within one month of a reply from an editor to whom a complaint had been made. It will also not normally deal with third-party complaints, that is complaints made by someone not directly involved in the complained-of story. The PCC will approach the subject of the story, if it does decide to follow-up a third-party complaint, to seek his or her co-operation and will normally drop the proceedings if that person does not wish to become involved. If the complaint is about a story that involves litigation, then the

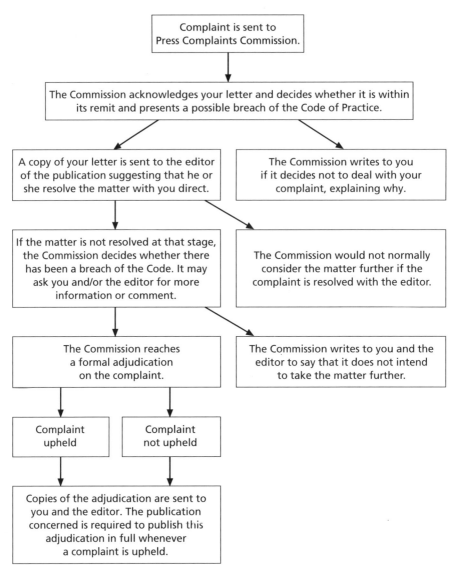

**Fig. 11.1 How your complaint is dealt with, Press Complaints Commission (adapted)**
(Reproduced by kind permission of the Press Complaints Commission)

PCC will normally wait until proceedings are over before proceeding with the complaint. Figure 11.1 shows how the PCC deals with complaints.

## Types of complaint

All figures in the following section are abstracted from the appropriate PCC *Annual Report*. The PCC received 2,508 complaints in 1995, an increase of almost 30 per cent on 1994. This leapt up again in 1996 to 3,023 (a 20 per cent increase) but stayed at about the same level in 1997 at 2,944. The number of complaints fell again the following year to 2,505. The Commission said in 1997 that it believed the increase in complaints to that date was due to increasing awareness rather than falling standards. No attempt was made by the Commission in its 1998 *Annual Report* to explain the substantial fall in complaints. Two-thirds of the 1998 complaints (1,960) were not pursued as they were either third-party complaints (outside the remit of the PCC), disallowed because of unjustified delays or not seen as prima facie breaches of the Code. The number of third-party complaints which were not pursued rose dramatically in 1997 (the year of the Princess of Wales's death) from 146 to 335, but fell again to 205 in 1998. Those complaints that fell outside the Commission's remit in 1989 (689) concerned advertising material, contractual disputes or matters of taste. A further 112 were disallowed on the grounds of unjustifiable delay.

Most of the remaining complaints in 1998 (555) were resolved within a few days, after the editors concerned published an apology, correction or, occasionally, offered the complainant an opportunity to reply. Some complaints fell, as they were not followed up by complainants. This left a total of 86 complaints for 1998 (82 in 1997) which were adjudicated on by the Commission; 45 (34 in 1997) of these complaints were upheld. (See Table 11.1 for a breakdown of these figures.)

## Table 11.1 PCC complaints

|  | 1991 | 1992 | 1993 | 1994 | 1995 | 1996 | 1997 | 1998 |
|---|---|---|---|---|---|---|---|---|
| No prima facie breach of code | 347 | 584 | 704 | 914 | 1026 | 897 | 914 | 954 |
| Disallowed as from third party | 0[‡] | 107 | 114 | 87 | 77 | 146 | 335 | 205 |
| Resolved with editor | 72 | 182 | 231 | 356 | 413 | 393 | 514 | 555 |
| Disallowed for delay | 46 | 64 | 97 | 85 | 91 | 110 | 93 | 112 |
| Outside remit | 137 | 232 | 447 | 427 | 800 | 1125* | 593 | 689 |
| Adjudicated – upheld | 32 | 31 | 40 | 34 | 28 | 27 | 34 | 45 |
| rejected | 28 | 49 | 57 | 54 | 35 | 54 | 48 | 41 |
| **Total complaints made** | **1,520** | **1,963** | **1,782** | **2,091** | **2,508** | **3,023** | **2,944** | **2,505** |

Notes:
1 The total is not a total of complaint types, but the total number of complaints made, according to the PCC. No explanation is given in the report as to why there are differences, but it could be due to some complaints being carried forward into the next year.
2 1991 sub-totals are for January–November only. There was no December 1991 report.
3 All figures are from the appropriate PCC *Annual Report*.
* Includes Euro 1996 complaints.
‡ Third-party complaints were not listed separately in 1991.

As in previous years, the majority of the complaints received in 1998 (62.7 per cent) were about accuracy, the right of reply or presenting comment as fact. It is difficult to make comparisons with the previous year as the PCC presents the statistics in line with its Code of Practice. Since the new Code now combines accuracy and comment as fact in clause 1, and since statistically the PCC combines clauses 1 and 2 (right of reply) figures in its *Annual Report*, direct comparisons are difficult (see Figure 11.2 for comparisons). However, the 1998 *Annual Report* totals accuracy, right of reply and comment at 70.3 per cent for 1997. In 1997, 3.6 per cent of complaints were about the right to reply and 12.8 per cent were about confusing comment as fact.

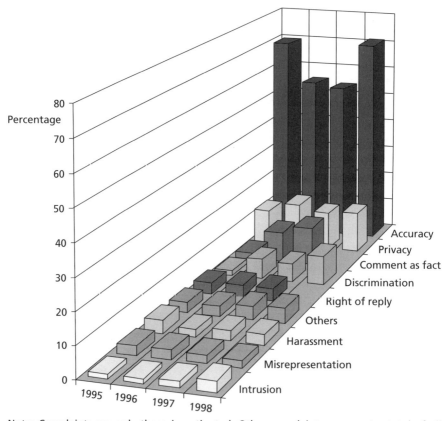

Note: Complaints are only those investigated. Other complaints represent a total of all other complaints against any particular clause of the Code of Practice and individually account for less than 1 per cent. 1998 figures for right of reply and comment as fact are now included in accuracy. All figures are from the PCC Annual Report for the year listed.

**Fig. 11.2 A comparision of PCC complaints by type**

Only 13.8 per cent of the complaints investigated in 1998 were related to privacy, a slight increase from 1997. The Commission had appointed Professor Robert Pinker as the Privacy Commissioner in 1995 to investigate these complaints. The PCC said: 'The Commission is especially vigilant in cases involving intrusion into privacy, and brings instances of severe or calculated breach of the Code to the attention of publishers in order that the need for appropriate disciplinary action may be considered' (PCC, 1995: 7). Salisbury Square reeked with the smell of smug self-righteousness in June 1995 when, in a highly publicised incident, Rupert Murdoch severely reprimanded Piers Morgan, editor of the *News of the World*, after the PCC adjudicated that the paper had invaded the privacy of Countess Spencer. The more cynical commentators felt this was more of a PR event for the PCC than the effective disciplining of an editor, especially as Morgan left soon after to take up the editorship of the *Daily Mirror*.

Misrepresentation (2.2 per cent), harassment (3.3 per cent) and intrusion into grief (3.3 per cent) are the other key areas for complaints in 1998.

The PCC is very keen to trumpet its work as a conciliator to explain why so few complaints end up in formal adjudication. 'The PCC is highly successful in its role as a conciliator. In 1997, just under 9 in 10 cases in which there was a case for the newspaper to answer were resolved. This is higher than in previous years and underlines the increasingly effective way in which self-regulation and its informal methods of conciliation work in the interests of the public. Achieving this high level of resolved disputes would be impossible in a formal legal system' (PCC, 1997: 8).

## Third-party complaints

The PCC is only obliged to consider complaints from those directly affected. However, the Commission may decide to consider a complaint from a third party. It would normally do so only when the issue was of public interest. Because of the way the PCC looks at complaints, the decision on whether it is a third-party complaint is not taken until it is decided whether there is a prima facie breach of the Code. An idea of the extent of the PCC's dealings with third-party complaints can be gained from an editorial in the PCC's report of September 1992. Of 530 complaints from third parties, only 12 made it to adjudication, with 50 per cent of those being upheld. The Commission prints copies of all its adjudications in a regular report. These used to be published monthly but in the last couple of years have been produced every two or even three months.

# Broadcasting

The situation in broadcasting is far more complicated, as we might expect in a regulatory system supported by legislation. Broadcasting regulation has undergone a number of major changes over the past decade. The Broadcasting Act 1980 set up the Broadcasting Complaints Commission to adjudicate on complaints of unfair treatment in television and radio programmes or of 'unwarranted infringement of privacy'. The Broadcasting Standards Council was launched in 1988, at the peak of one of the outcries of moral outrage which has so characterised the 1980s and 1990s, to deal with complaints from viewers and listeners about decency. Before the introduction of these two bodies, complaints had been handled either by the BBC Complaints Panel or the Independent Broadcasting Authority, as appropriate. The Broadcasting Act 1990 changed that, introducing new regulatory and complaints authorities. Control of broadcasting was lodged with the BBC (through its Charter), the Independent Television Commission and the Radio Authority, whilst complaints and conduct were dealt with by the BCC and the BSC. The BCC was never very popular with broadcasters and few tears were shed when it was amalgamated with the BSC by the Broadcasting Act 1996.

## Independent Television Commission

The Independent Television Commission was established under the Broadcasting Act 1990, taking over from the Independent Broadcasting Authority the licensing of all commercially-funded TV stations in the UK. Its powers were extended by the Secretary of State for National Heritage in March 1996 to cover all TV broadcasts from the UK no matter where they are received. The ITC has four main functions:

1 It licenses all commercially-funded television in the UK, whether delivered terrestrially or by cable or satellite, public teletext and certain other text and data services.
2 It regulates these services through its published licences, codes and guidelines, and has a range of penalties for failure to comply with them.
3 It has a duty to ensure that a wide range of television services is available throughout the UK and that, taken as a whole, they are of a high quality and appeal to a variety of tastes and interests.
4 It has a duty to ensure fair and effective competition in the provision of these services. (ITC, 1992: 1)

The chairman, deputy chairman and the eight members of the Commission are appointed by the Secretary of State for Culture, Media and Sport.

The regulation of services does not concern us as an ethical issue, although its impingement into the freedom of the media, in terms of both control and the dangers of unrestricted ownership, can be significant in terms of the effect on loyalty.

The Independent Television Commission does have a role in regulating the services it licenses. The main areas it covers are: privacy, taste and decency, violence and bad language, and impartiality. If the Independent Television Commission believes that a broadcasting company has gone too far, it can require the company to broadcast an apology or fine it. A history of such breaches could lead the Independent Television Commission to remove a company's licence to broadcast. Channel 4's *You Don't Know Me But . . .* ran into trouble when covering the issue of live animal exports. The presenter launched a public attack on the Minister for Agriculture and his wife and children. 'Channel 4 immediately acknowledged this error of judgement and themselves took the decision to broadcast an apology for the offence caused' (ITC, 1995: 30). In 1998 the Commission decided that a programme called *The Connection* was largely fabricated. 'The ITC imposed a fine of £2m on Central Television, the level of the fine indicating the ITC's view that it is imperative that the bond of trust between programme makers and viewers must be maintained' (ITC, 1998: 4).

The final penalty is used extremely rarely but is still there. Med TV, a Kurdish satellite channel, had its licence revoked by the ITC in April 1999 following four broadcasts which 'included inflammatory statements encouraging acts of violence in Turkey and elsewhere'. These were judged by the ITC as 'likely to encourage or incite to crime or lead to disorder'. This is against UK law, as set out in the 1990 and 1996 Broadcasting Acts.

Such extreme penalties put into perspective the PCC's claims that self-regulation is sufficient. Cable and satellite TV are also regulated by the Independent Television Commission but do not need to conform to the same standards as terrestrial TV. There is no quality threshold but there is an obligation to be impartial and fair.

The Independent Television Commission does not issue figures about complaints upheld in its *Annual Report* although it does publish reports about them. The Independent Television Commission also has a regulatory role over ITN, the nominated news provider for Channel 3. In 1998 ITN proposed moving its famous *News at Ten* main bulletin. The proposed bulletins would be at 6.30pm with a further twenty-minute bulletin at 11pm. The ITC agreed after a public consultation exercise with the provisos that there should be a headline service at about 10pm and a thirty-minute slot for high-quality, regional programmes in or just outside peak times on weekdays. The ITC also said it would review the situation after a year (ITC, 1998: 32).

In earlier years the ITC had followed up complaints about 'compassion fatigue' and images of violence or distress, but in every case the images used were found to be justified. 'Television news cannot side-step the horrors that may occur but it is important, equally, that the expectations of the viewing public as a whole are not exceeded' (ITC, 1995: 111). The Independent Television Commission also investigated whether the news was biased towards London and South-East England. ITN denied this and the Independent Television Commission found that supporting evidence was not particularly strong. They also followed up claims that ITN had tended to shift down market. Whilst the ITC found that topics were sometimes treated in less depth than by competitors, and that the ITN's agenda was adapted for different times of the day, the Independent Television Commission did not feel that the ITN was any less effective as a news source. The changes in scheduling, though, will once again make this important for the ITC (ITC, 1995: 110).

The ITC revamped its programme code in 1997 and issued a new one in January 1998 (ITC, 1998: 29). It covered the following areas:

- Offence to good taste and decency, portrayal of violence.
- Privacy, gathering of information.
- Impartiality.
- Party political and parliamentary broadcasting.
- Terrorism, crime, anti-social behaviour.
- Other legal matters.
- Images of very brief duration.
- Charitable appeals and publicity for charities.
- Religion.
- Other programme matters.
- Communication with the public. (ITC Code of Practice, 1998)

The Code is drawn up under the ITC's obligations under sections 6 and 7 of the Broadcasting Act 1990. It gives effect in the UK to a number of requirements relating to television programmes in the European Community Directive on Television Broadcasting and Council of Europe Convention on Transfrontier Television and applies to all terrestrial, cable and satellite services licensed by the ITC. The ITC says that in drawing up its Code it has 'taken into account the requirement "to reflect the general effect" of the Broadcasting Standards Commission (BSC)'s code, under Sections 107 and 108 of the Broadcasting Act 1996. However, licensees themselves should be aware of the BSC's code' (ITC Code of Practice, January 1998).

Any viewer can complain to the ITC, which may investigate and raise the concern with the relevant television company. In serious or persistent breaches of the ITC Code, it can issue a warning to the company. It can also require the company to broadcast an apology or correction, impose a fine, shorten the term of a licence or, in extreme cases, withdraw it altogether.

All complaints that are upheld are reported in the ITC's monthly *Programme Complaints and Interventions Report* and *Television Advertising Complaints Report*. The ITC does have links with the Broadcasting Standards Commission and is notified by the BSC of all complaints it receives. The ITC can also take action on complaints upheld by the BSC if it wishes, since it has much tougher powers than the BSC. Table 11.2 lists the number of complaints received by the ITC by category in 1997 and 1998.

**Table 11.2 The total number of complaints to the ITC (by category), 1997 and 1998**

| | News/factual (1997) | | | | News/Factual (1998) | | | |
|---|---|---|---|---|---|---|---|---|
| | ITV | Ch4 | C/S* | Ch5 | ITV | Ch4 | C/S* | Ch5 |
| Accuracy | 101 | 20 | 2 | 7 | 86 | 27 | 11 | 5 |
| Impartiality | 44 | 37 | 7 | 0 | 18 | 26 | 1 | – |
| Other unfairness | 313 | 192 | 3 | 3 | 145 | 215 | 19 | 10 |
| Sexual portrayal | 53 | 8 | 4 | – | 15 | 11 | 5 | 6 |
| Language | 21 | 14 | 3 | 2 | 34 | 7 | 2 | 2 |
| Violence | 13 | 13 | 3 | 7 | 32 | 4 | 12 | 2 |
| Other taste and decency | 237 | 57 | 16 | 12 | 484 | 101 | 30 | 35 |
| Racial offence | 105 | 11 | 4 | 5 | 21 | 9 | 10 | 3 |
| Religious offence | 23 | 8 | 3 | – | 4 | 3 | 1 | – |
| Scheduling | 30 | 2 | – | – | 103 | 4 | 1 | 2 |
| Regionality | 8 | – | – | – | – | – | – | – |
| Miscellaneous | 87 | 15 | 25 | 3 | 92 | 19 | 202 | 3 |
| Sub totals | 1,035 | 377 | 70 | 39 | 1,034 | 426 | 294 | 68 |
| Total Complaints (including entertainment and fiction) | 2,894 | | | | 3,257 | | | |

* Cable and Satellite

## Radio Authority

The Radio Authority was formally established on 11 December 1990. It took up the reins from the old Independent Broadcasting Authority on 1 January 1991, following the introduction of the Broadcasting Act 1990 which replaced the old Independent Broadcasting Authority (IBA) with the Independent Television Commission, Radio Authority and Welsh Authority. The chairman, deputy chairman and five other members of the Authority were appointed by the Department of Heritage (now the Department of Culture, Media and Sport) following its take-over of broadcasting from the Home Office in the early 1990s. They are supported by twenty-eight full-time and three part-time staff. The Radio Authority members serve for a maximum of five years.

The Radio Authority regulates all independent radio services and is responsible for granting the licences to 'fit and proper persons' (Broadcasting Act 1990). It covers all the independent national, local, cable, national FM subcarrier, satellite and restricted services. It also regulates all short-term services and highly localised permanent services such as hospital and student radio stations. The Authority is responsible for monitoring licence holders and ensuring that they adhere to the licence requirements under the Broadcasting Act. 'It plans frequencies, awards licences, regulates (as necessary) programmes and radio advertising and plays an active role in the discussion and formulation of policies which affect the independent radio industry and its listeners (Radio Authority, 1994: 1). It is also responsible for publishing codes to which licensees must adhere. These cover engineering, programmes, advertising and sponsorship.

There are rules on ownership, the most important being that the person holding the licence must be a fit and proper person. There are also limits on how many stations a person may own, although these were changed and enlarged by the Broadcasting Act 1996. The Authority can remove the licences of those who break the rules, although it would normally persuade the licence holder to make the appropriate changes under the threat of licence removal. Other sanctions include the broadcasting of apologies and/or corrections, fines and the shortening of licences.

Licensees pay an annual fee to the Radio Authority which is the Authority's only source of income. The Authority also collects money from the licence holders which it passes on to the Broadcasting Standards Commission.

The Authority received 689 complaints in 1995 (444 in 1994), including advertising and programme complaints. Of these 447 were programme complaints, 89 of which were upheld.

The Authority is able to impose a number of sanctions should a licence holder breach a 'Promise of Performance' of either of the two Programme Codes:

Code 1: News and current affairs, public policy, political or industrial controversy.
Code 2: Violence, sex, taste and decency, children and young people, appeals for donations, religion and other matters.

These sanctions can include fines or a reduction in the length of licence period. In 1995, the Authority imposed six fines. Two of them were for failure to provide the log tapes (stations are obliged to keep recordings of all their broadcasts for 42 days). The Codes to which the licence holders must adhere cover:

- Undue prominence and impartiality.
- Expressions of opinion by licensees.
- Party politics.

The news Code calls for all news programmes to be accurate and impartial. An appropriate range of views should be reported within a single news bulletin or a range of bulletins. Differences are perceived between national and local licence holders. National stations are obliged to be impartial, whilst other licence holders may express a particular view provided that where other views exist, these are reflected within a reasonable period of time following the broadcast. The Authority issues rules on the conduct of interviews, insisting that checks are made that interviewees are able to speak for the groups they purport to represent, and that interviewees are made aware of both the format and nature of the interview and are told of the other proposed participants and their role. Edited versions of interviews must not misrepresent the person's position. A right of reply should be offered to a relevant person. Party politicians are not allowed to appear as newscasters or interviewers during the period of an election and the licence holder has to keep a written record of all appearances by MPs and MEPs.

The Radio Authority's Code is much clearer and easier to follow than that of the old Broadcasting Standards Council. The Independent Television Commission did not introduce a code until 1997 and the BCC never introduced one.

## Broadcasting Complaints Commission

The Broadcasting Complaints Commission ceased to exist on 1 April 1997. Its powers were taken over by the Broadcasting Standards Commission. The BCC was set up to consider complaints about broadcasts that were unfair or an unwarranted infringement of privacy. Its remit was reviewed by the Broadcasting Act 1990 and it was charged with considering and adjudicating on 'complaints of unjust and unfair treatment in sound or television programmes actually broadcast or included in a licensed cable or satellite programme service or upon complaints of unwarranted infringement of privacy in, or in connection with the obtaining of material in, such programmes'. This role covered all sound and television programmes including advertisements and teletext. The Commission only accepted complaints from people with a direct interest in the programme.

**Table 11.3 Complaints to the Broadcasting Complaints Commission**

| Year | Received | Outside remit | Adjudicated | Upheld |
|------|----------|---------------|-------------|--------|
| 1982 | 90 | | | |
| 1983 | 190 | | | |
| 1984 | 180 | | | |
| 1985 | 218 | 185 | 35 | |
| 1986 | 208 | 161 | 42 | 13 |
| 1987 | 222 | 174 | 21 | 12 |
| 1988 | 152 | 93 | 26 | 10 |
| 1989 | 348 | 249 | 39 | 21 |
| 1990 | 550 | | | |
| 1991 | 930 | 803 | 44 | |
| 1992 | 1,048 | 928 | 53 | 32 |
| 1993 | 928 | 813 | 52 | 34 |
| 1994 | 1,049 | 893 | 68 | 33 |
| 1995 | 1,135 | 945 | 73 | 35 |
| 1996 | 1,093 | 926 | 61 | 39 |

The BCC was never a particularly busy body, being content on relying on the IBA (later ITC) and the BBC's duty to publicise the Commission. This it did with regular advertisements in *The Listener* and the *Radio Times*, but these were not enough to bring the Commission to the attention of the public. Consequently, complaints during the 1980s were low compared with those sent to the other broadcasting bodies. But in the 1990s, the number of complaints rose dramatically. It is difficult to see why this should be. The changes in the 1990 Act did not directly affect the BCC and there seems no reason for this sudden increase apart from a general awareness of these issues. The Calcutt Committee reported amidst much publicity and the changes from the Press Council to the PCC may have been responsible for sensitising the public to regulatory issues and sparking off more complaints. There is little or no evidence that broadcast programmes took a sudden dip for the worse. The BCC's workload was growing, however, and it complained that the changes in December 1992 meant that it now had to deal directly with all the franchise holders rather than just with the ITC and the BBC. Table 11.3 details the complaints received by the BCC for the period 1982–96.

The year 1994/95 was a difficult one for the Commission as it dipped into financial deficit. This arose solely because of legal costs incurred in defending challenges in the court by broadcasters.

## The Broadcasting Standards Council

The Broadcasting Standards Council was superseded by the Broadcasting Standards Commission in April 1997. The Broadcasting Standards Council was set up in 1988 by the Home Secretary in answer to a series of complaints about standards of television. The BSC was set up initially on a non-statutory basis pending legislation and it covered both independent broadcasting and the BBC. During this pre-statutory phase the Council's role, as outlined by the Home Secretary, was to:

- Draw up, in consultation with the broadcasting authorities and the other responsible bodies in the broadcasting, cable and video fields, a code on the portrayal of violence and sex and standards of taste and decency.
- Monitor and report on the portrayal of violence and sex, and standards of taste and decency, in television and radio programmes received in the UK and in video works.
- Receive, consider and make findings on complaints and comments from individuals and organisations on matters within its competence and ensure that such findings are effectively publicised.
- Undertake research on matters such as the nature and effects on attitudes and behaviour of the portrayal sex and violence in television and radio programmes and in video works; prepare an annual report, which the Home Secretary will lay before parliament.

In addition, the Council was consulted by the government on developments in Europe on the future regulation of trans-frontier broadcasting (undated BSC leaflet, 'The Broadcasting Standards Council and its Activities').

Lord Rees Mogg was appointed the first chairman with Jocelyn Barrow as deputy chairman. The Council met for the first time in September 1988. A director (Colin Shaw, formerly director of TV with the IBA) and deputy director (David Houghton) were appointed in November 1988. The management team was augmented by a research director and a press and programmes officer and a further ten staff were employed to administer the Council's business.

The Council immediately launched itself into the research required of it by the government. It toured the country in a series of road shows and carried out a number of surveys about people's attitudes to TV and portrayals of sex and violence. It also drew up a code of practice for broadcasters, which was published in November 1989. It must be one of the longest codes of practice in the world at 52 pages, covering sex, violence, bad language and taste and decency, but it was sympathetically received, according to Lord Rees Mogg, who said in his *Annual Report*, it 'was a source of real satisfaction to the council' (Broadcasting Standards Council, *Annual Report*, 1990: 5). The 1990 Broadcasting Act gave the BSC statutory powers.

The Council also started to take its European transnational role more seriously, getting deeply involved in European directives on television standards. The move to statutory status in 1990 saw the Council start to take complaints from the public about the standards of programmes. This was new work

**Table 11.4 Complaints (by type) to the Broadcasting Standards Council**

| Type | 1990/91 | 1991/92 | 1992/93 | 1993/94 | 1994/95 |
|---|---|---|---|---|---|
| Total | 749 | 2,662 | 2,023 | 2,390 | 2,838 |
| Within remit | 509 | 1,130 | 1,355 | 1,711 | 2,247 |
| Taste | 246 | 436 | 587 | 687 | 939 |
| Sex | 53 | 217 | 273 | 342 | 529 |
| Violence | 38 | 68 | 230 | 205 | 258 |
| Violence and sex | 29 | 32 | 13 | 23 | 34 |
| Taste, decency and sex | 27 | 100 | 33 | 109 | 172 |
| Other multiples | 9 | 45 | 56 | 107 | 100 |

for the Council, started on 1 January 1991. Far from getting off to a slow start, the Council received more than 700 letters about programmes or advertisements in the first five months. The Council upheld its first complaint in April 1991 and a summary of its findings were published in the *Radio Times* at the end of May.

In its first year, the BSC received 749 complaints of which 509 were within its remit. Of these, 402 referred to specific programmes while the rest were of a general nature. Of these, 16 were upheld and seven were partially upheld. The types of complaint received by the BSC are shown in Table 11.4. During 1991–92 responsibility for the BSC switched from the Home Office to the Department of National Heritage. The number of complaints received had risen from 749 to 2,662. This is slightly confused by the decision of the Council to alter the accounting period to give a starting date of 1 April. As the previous report had covered until 31 May 1991, the new report covered some of the same complaints. In addition, the first report had started in January 1991, so it is impossible to give a real comparison between the two figures. Almost 60 per cent of these complaints (1,525) raised matters outside the remit, including a mammoth 1,054 about the plans by the BBC to transmit the film *The Last Temptation of Christ*.

At Christmas 1992, Matthew Parris, the writer, broadcaster and former MP, joined the Council, while Lady Howe replaced Lord Rees Mogg as chairman on 16 June 1993. In the year 1992–93, the Council received 1,355 complaints. In February 1994, the BSC and the BCC presented plans for a merger to the Secretary of State for National Heritage. In the early part of 1995 approval was given for the co-location of the BSC and the BCC. The merger was brought about under the Broadcasting Act 1996 and was completed by April 1997. The rise in complaints work also meant a reorganisation in the Complaints Committees. All members now served on three committees of two members, each serving with either the chairman or the deputy chairman. This meant each member giving 50 per cent extra time to complaints. Very few of the BSC's complaints concerned journalists. Most were about entertainment and drama.

## Broadcasting Standards Commission

Until 1996, the work of regulating television and radio journalism was split between several organisations. This led to a number of problems. If the news report you were concerned about contained invasions of privacy, then you had to complain to the BCC. If it were a matter of taste or decency, however, you should complain to the BSC. Presumably, had video been shot of an incident that was both indecent and invaded privacy and was shown on TV, then two complaints would be required. The one on privacy to the BCC and the one on decency to the BSC. Of course the complainant could also have complained to the ITC.

Lady Howe was appointed chairman of the new Commission in April 1997. There are twelve other Commissioners, all appointed by the Secretary of State for Culture, Media and Sport. The Broadcasting Standards Commission investigates and adjudicates on complaints about fairness and unwarranted infringement of privacy. It will also consider the portrayal of violence and sexual conduct and other matters of taste and decency on radio and television. It is the only organisation to cover all television and radio, including the BBC and text, cable, satellite and digital services. The Commission has three main tasks according to the Broadcasting Act (1996):

- To produce codes of practice relating to standards and fairness.
- To consider and adjudicate on complaints.
- To monitor, research and report on standards and fairness in broadcasting.

The Commission has drawn up its own codes of guidance to broadcasters and it monitors and reports on the portrayal of violence and sexual conduct. It also commissions and publishes research into public attitudes.

The new Commission took over all the work of the former bodies on 1 April 1997. The BSC works in a similar way to the PCC. Any viewer or listener can complain in writing about any programme. Complaints need to be made within two months of a TV broadcast and within three weeks of a radio programme. The BSC will not handle a complaint which is the subject of legal proceedings in the UK, or if it relates to a matter which could become the subject of legal proceedings. Once the complaint is received, the BSC requires the broadcaster to provide a recording of the programme. It then decides if this breaches its code. Occasionally the BSC may call a hearing and the complainant and the programme maker may be required to attend.

If the BSC decides to uphold the complaint, a copy of the decision will be sent to the complainant and the programme maker before its publication in the BSC's monthly *Bulletin*, which is distributed to broadcasters, government and the media. In some cases the BSC will require the broadcaster to publish a summary of its decision either on-air or in a newspaper or magazine. In complaints of unfair or unjust treatment, the complainant must have a direct interest in the programme, that is that he or she is the subject of the programme. Cases of infringement of privacy can be brought within three months or six weeks for radio programmes, but only by the person whose privacy has been infringed or by someone acting on his or her behalf. The BSC invites the ITC to be involved in any complaint hearings and informs the ITC of its findings and adjudications. There is no appeal against the Commission's adjudications.

The ITC is obliged by law to send the BSC a report of any supplementary action taken in consequence of the BSC's findings, either by the ITC or its licensee or any other person responsible for making or providing the programme. It is the ITC only that has the power to fine or remove a licence.

The BSC issues regular reports of its activities. It also carries out research on broadcasting matters and its Research Director, Andrea Millwood Hargrave, is one of the leading researchers in this field. The BSC issued a draft of its new code in July 1997 and, despite some criticism, issued the finalised code with only minor changes in January 1998. In its *Annual Report 1997–98* the BSC shows that there were a total of 3,559 complaints, of which 914 (26 per cent) were outside its remit, 150 (4 per cent) were about fairness, and the remainder were about standards. The majority of complaints were about dramas and entertainment programmes rather than news and current affairs and it is impossible to separate these in the *Annual Report*.

## British Broadcasting Corporation

The BBC serves a dual role to confuse further the way broadcasting is regulated. With the renewal of its Royal Charter and Agreement, which came into effect on 1 May 1996, the BBC was required to draw up a code on a range of ethical issues. The Charter also places a duty on the BBC Board of Governors to ensure that the BBC's employees and programme makers comply with it, giving the governors similar powers to the ITC in this area. The new Charter means that the BBC remains the UK's main public service broadcaster until 31 December 2006. It also establishes and defines the BBC's existence and regulates its constitution.

The Agreement, a formal contract between the BBC and the Secretary of State for National Heritage (now Culture, Media and Sport), runs concurrently with the Royal Charter and explains how the BBC is to meet its broad objectives and duties. It formally guarantees its editorial independence in programme content, scheduling and management. It also means the licence fee will remain the primary source of finance for the BBC until at least the year 2002.

Commenting on the new Charter and Agreement, Virginia Bottomley, the then Secretary of State for National Heritage, said:

> Looking to the future, the BBC will be operating in an increasingly competitive environment. The new Charter and Agreement provide them with the tools to respond effectively to new challenges and take advantage of the opportunities created by digital technology. The BBC will remain the UK's main public service broadcaster, with the licence fee as its principal source of funding for at least the next five years. There are new arrangements for it to develop its commercial services further, alongside, and for the benefit of its licence-fee-funded services.
>
> The BBC is now formally required to maintain standards of taste and decency and impartiality. I expect them to set the benchmark in the digital future by which all UK broadcasters will be judged by viewers and listeners. (Central Office of Information Press Release, April 1996)

A new chairman of the Board of Governors, Sir Christopher Bland, took up office on 1 April 1996. The BBC produced its new code – the *Producers' Guidelines* – in November 1996. This hefty document was welcomed by the Secretary of State. It lays out guidelines for producers and is the basis for complaint arbitrations. The Governors, if necessary, take action against programme makers who have breached the guidelines. This could be done following a complaint or by the governors acting on their own.

The *Producers' Guidelines*, the BBC's ethical 'bible', contains thirty-seven different sections, but the main ones that concern us here are contained in the BBC's 'Values and Standards, Issues in Factual Programming and Politics'. They cover the following issues: impartiality and accuracy, fairness to contributors, privacy and the gathering of information, taste and decency, violence, imitative and anti-social behaviour, portrayal of children in programmes, and conflicts of interest. 'Issues in factual programming' includes interviewing, reporting crime, relations with the police, confidentiality and the release of programme material, terrorism and national security, Northern Ireland, and material from outside sources. 'Politics' covers politics, parliament and politicians, broadcasting during elections, and opinion polls. Finally, 'commercial issues in programmes' includes commercial relationships, support services, covering outside events, on-air references to products, services and publications, using free or reduced cost facilities, competitions, prizes and coverage of the National Lottery, premium-rate telephone services, charities, and charity appeals.

The BBC's Executive Committee, whose members also sit on the broader-based Board of Management, are led by the Director-General. The members of the Board of Governors are appointed by the Queen in Council to monitor the BBC's performance and standards against set objectives. The chairman is Sir Christopher Bland, Deputy Chairman of the Independent Broadcasting Authority (1972–79) and Chairman of LWT (Holdings) Plc (1983–94).

## National Union of Journalists

The NUJ was the first body in the UK to introduce a code of journalistic ethics. This was drawn up at the union's annual conference in 1936. The union introduced the code into the rule-book, making a breach of the code a disciplinary offence. A journalist who is a member of the union could be reprimanded, fined or even expelled from the union for breaching the code.

In 1986, the union set up an Ethics Council. Until 1979, the union had been a part of the Press Council but, after leaving over what it saw as the Council's failings, many members felt that the union should set up its own council. The Ethics Council was established for two seasons:

- To educate members and help promote better ethical standards.
- To hold hearings on complaints against members who were alleged to have breached the Code of Conduct. (NUJ, 1998: 16)

The second aim was always controversial. Many members argued that it was not the role of the union to discipline its own members; but others felt there was little point in having a code of conduct if it was not going to be upheld.

The anti-union stance of the government during the 1980s and 1990s led to a general weakening of union power and this played a part in reducing the role of the Ethics Council. No longer did journalists have to have an NUJ card in order to work in the more prestigious jobs in television and what used to be Fleet Street. This meant that breaching the NUJ code, with the consequent risk of discipline and possible expulsion, was no longer the risk it once might have been. The union, too, was less inclined to deal harshly with members as workers became less confident of the benefits of belonging to a union.

The rules were changed in the early 1990s after a number of attempts to remove the disciplinary role from the Ethics Council altogether. Now the Ethics Council will hear complaints about members who have allegedly breached the Code of Conduct, but only if they are made by another member. The Council no longer hears complaints lodged by members of the public. This has reduced complaints to a trickle. The Council has the power to decide that the Code of Conduct would be best promoted by resolving the complaint by educative rather than disciplinary means. But if a complaint hearing is held, and the member is found to be at fault, then the Ethics Council can reprimand that member or pass the case on to the National Executive Council with a recommendation to impose a stronger punishment, which can include fines of up to £1,000, suspension of membership or expulsion.

The Council has tended to concentrate on its educational and promotional role in the last couple of years, giving talks to students in colleges and producing guidelines for journalists on a range of issues, from reporting on mental health issues to child abuse. It has also had informal talks with the PCC on issues of mutual concern, particularly the PCC's Code of Practice.

The union's 1998 annual conference changed the Code of Conduct, the first time that had happened for a number of years. The move, in line with the reaction of other regulatory bodies to the death of the Princess of Wales, was to strengthen the code in the area of privacy. The conference also decided to back a call for a clause dealing specifically with the digital manipulation of pictures.

## The experience abroad

Methods of regulation vary widely throughout the world. The two main types of regulation revolve around those countries with constitutions and those without. But these can be sub-divided into those with strong legal protections or methods of suppression and those without. It is not possible to produce three or four groups of those with laws and those without. There is such a wide variation around the world that there is a steady gradation of control, starting with countries which allow journalists a free hand and ending with countries that have almost total state control.

### International protection

All EU countries are signatories to the European Convention on Human Rights. This is used by the European Court of Human Rights as the basis for the rights of citizens in Europe. It is now included in British law through the Human Rights Act 1998. There are two main clauses in the Convention that concern us here. One is about freedom of expression and the other involves invasion of privacy (Exhibit 11.1).

The Council of Europe has also looked at the subject of the media and drafted its own resolution. This does not have specific power on its own, though, and is merely an expression of policy (Exhibit 11.2).

## Exhibit 11.1 The European Convention on Human Rights

8 All persons have the right to respect for their private and family life, for his abode and his correspondence. . . .

10 (1) Anyone has the right to freedom of expression. This right includes freedom of opinion and freedom to receive or communicate information or ideas without interference from public authorities and regardless of borders. This article does not prevent states from subjecting radio or television broadcasting or cinema enterprises to a system of authorisations.

(2) The exercise of these freedoms with their accompanying duties and responsibilities may be subjected to certain formalities, conditions, restrictions or sanctions defined by law, which constitute measures necessary in a democratic society to national safety, territorial sovereignty or public safety, defence of order and prevention of crime, protection of health or morals, protection of the reputation of rights of others, in order to prevent the divulging of confidential information or in order to guarantee the authority and impartiality of judicial power.

## Exhibit 11.2 The Council of Europe Resolution 1003 (1993)

7 The media's work is one of 'mediation', providing an information service, and the rights which they own in connection with freedom of information depend on its addressees, that is the citizens.

8 Information is a fundamental right which has been highlighted by the case law of the European Commission and Court of Human Rights relating to Article 10 of the European Convention on Human Rights and recognised under Article 9 of the European Convention an Transfrontier Television, as well as in all democratic constitutions. The owner of the right is the citizen, who also has the related right to demand that the information supplied by journalists is conveyed truthfully, in the case of news, and honestly, in the case of opinions, without outside interference by either the public authorities or the private sector.

9 The public authorities must not consider that they own information. The representativeness of such authorities provides the legal basis for efforts to guarantee and extend pluralism in the media and to ensure that the necessary conditions are created for exercising freedom of expression and the right to information and precluding censorship. . . .

15 Neither publishers nor proprietors nor journalists should consider that they own the news. News organisations must treat information not as a commodity but as a fundamental right of the citizen.

The other international code which supports the right to freedom of expression and contains the individual rights of citizens is the UN Declaration on Human Rights. This also contains two clauses, one on privacy and one on freedom (Exhibit 11.3).

**Exhibit 11.3 The United Nations Declaration on Human Rights**

| |
|---|
| 12 No-one shall be subjected to arbitrary interference with his privacy, family, home or correspondence, nor to attacks upon his honour and reputation. Everyone has the right to the protection of the law against interference or attacks. . . . <br> 19 Everyone has the right to freedom of opinion and expression. This right includes freedom to hold opinion without interference and to seek, receive and impart information and ideas through any media regardless of frontiers. |

Although a large number of countries are signatories to the Declaration, it does not always mean that they adhere to it.

## Constitutional protection

America and some European countries have full and effective constitutions which guarantee, amongst other things, the freedom of the press or a more general freedom of expression. By and large these countries are more likely to accept the protection of some citizens' rights, in areas such as privacy, in the knowledge that press freedom is secured by the constitution.

The US constitution is one of the most obvious examples. The First Amendment to the constitution is precise and thoughtful: 'Congress shall make no law . . . abridging the freedom of speech, or of the press. . . .' This gives journalists in the US considerable support, more than enough for them to feel confident about allowing protections for ordinary citizens, and the privacy laws in the US allow far less invasion than in Britain. There are four different types of complaint that can be made about invasions of privacy in the US:

- Intrusion, phone tapping or trespassing without consent.
- False light – resembles libel in that it attempts to prevent the circulation of untrue stories.
- Misappropriation – a person's name or likeness is used without consent.
- Embarrassment – an objection to the publication of private information. (Dill, 1986: 135)

Public interest is a defence against a charge of invading privacy. Indeed, the burden is on the person claiming privacy to prove that there is no public interest in the story. This is rarely easy to do and consequently there are few successful embarrassment cases. Nevertheless, an attempt at protection does exist (ibid.: 136).

In a case cited by Barbara Dill (ibid.: 132), the first woman ever to be elected president of a student body was later found to be a transsexual. The woman had gone to great lengths to keep this secret and when it was publicised by the *Oakland Tribune* she was devastated and brought a suit against the paper. She won and was awarded $775,000 (including $525,000 punitive damages and $25,000 against the writer of the article personally). However, this was later overturned on appeal, on a technicality, and when a new trial was ordered, the college's insurance company ordered the paper to make an offer, which was accepted. There can be no doubt that if this story were translated to Britain, the *Star* or the *Sun*, uncovering a confidence of this sort, would have no hesitation about publishing it – and not in a small gossip-style column but as a major lead story.

In another case cited by Dill, a woman was taken to hospital for a pancreas problem which led to her to eating enough for ten people but still losing 25lb in a year. Her picture was taken without her consent in hospital. The subsequent story and picture were used by a paper. The court ruled that although the story may have been newsworthy, her name was not. The case was not helped by the strong-arm tactics used by the news agency that gathered the story. If this case had happened in the UK, although the PCC's Code would have been breached, in that the picture should not have been taken in the hospital without permission, the story (and name) would certainly have been used with a picture if it could have been obtained in some other way.

If the law on privacy were the same in the UK as it is in the US, it could present a major problem for the UK press. One only has to consider the number of times in recent years that photographs have been published of major celebrities showing more than they had intended while manoeuvring in and out of cars in short skirts. The laws on trespass and intrusion are also very limiting. Taping interviews without permission, trespass or using trickery are all potentially illegal. Trespass is not often a problem as it is difficult to bring a case, provided the journalist leaves when asked by a person with suitable authority.

America was one of the first countries in the world to have a code of conduct. Nelson Antrim Crawford, in *The Ethics of Journalism*, identifies the first as being the Kansas Editorial Association's Code of Ethics for the Publisher, written in 1910 (Crawford, 1969). This sets out codes of practice for advertising departments, circulation and news. Many of the early codes varied from being mission statements for the paper to being disciplinary codes. They covered everything from drinking on duty to dealing with customers to truth and objectivity. A large number of early US codes are published in Crawford's *The Ethics of Journalism* and they are well worth reading, if only to enjoy their diversity. Many newspapers in the US still have codes, although most of them are more like mission statements.

The Society of Professional Journalists in the US, which has a membership of about 13,500, has a code of conduct which it borrowed from the American Society of Newspaper Editors in 1926. It wrote its own code in 1973 (the SPJ was still known as Sigma Delta Chi in those days) and revised it in 1984 and 1987. Its present version was adopted in September 1996 after a lengthy debate amongst its membership, part of which was conducted on the Internet. The Code is substantially different from UK codes in its presentation but is not all that different in content. The Code does underline some of the differences I have mentioned before: presumption of innocence in criminal law is covered in this Code, for instance. The Code also recognises that the people the media come into contact with have rights. 'Minimise harm' is one of the duties expressed in the Code. The Code says: 'Journalists should recognise that private people have a greater right to control information about themselves than do public officials and others who seek power, influence or attention. Only an overriding public need can justify intrusion into anyone's privacy.' The Code also calls on journalists to 'Show good taste. Avoid pandering to lurid curiosity' (http://spj.org/ethics/code.htm).

In many ways the Code is much more high-minded than those on offer in the UK, yet in other ways it is more practical: 'Journalists should always question sources' motives before promising anonymity' (http://spj.org/ethics/code.htm), it says, like an old and wise news editor warning an enthusiastic trainee journalist. It's good advice, but is it ethics? There is more excellent advice about accepting gifts or bribes, but there is little in the Code that a UK journalist would disagree with in principle. This is not the only code in existence. In the Associated Press (AP) Managing Editors' Code we find another theme that crops up in US codes time and time again. They are much more concerned about lobbying government to ensure they maintain free access to information than in the UK. It is ironic that it was Margaret Thatcher who pushed a private members' bill to give the media access to public meetings, yet as Prime Minister she privatised all of these institutions, thus ensuring their meetings were once again held in secret.

The managing editors say in their code: 'The newspaper should fight vigorously for public access to news of government through open meetings and records' (http://www.apme.com/html/ethics.html). This of course is in a country which has a Freedom of Information Act, allowing journalists free access to all public documents.

The Radio–Television News Directors' Association also has a code of conduct (http://web.missouri.edu/~jourvs/rtcodes.html). Again it includes the right to a fair trial but, interestingly, this code talks about the need to be impartial. None of the print codes felt this was necessary. With no laws limiting broadcasters' right to say what they like (because of the first amendment), it was felt necessary to put this in a code of ethics. In the UK of course, the law has already included this. But why did broadcasters in the US feel obliged to make it an ethical issue when the print journalists did not, especially in a country where television is seen as having many of the qualities of the tabloids in the UK? American journalists seem, from the outside at least, to take ethics more seriously than their UK counterparts. There are a number of books, codes have been around since the 1920s and the subject is taught seriously in journalism schools. Yet their laws are a lot more straightforward. The freedom of the press is protected by the constitution and freedom of information is guaranteed. There are few restrictive laws, with the exception of privacy and defamation. There is no Press Council, however, or other body to police the codes of conduct on a federal basis. News councils do exist though. The Minnesota News Council, for instance, has been in existence since 1971. It attempts to promote media fairness by encouraging the public to 'insist upon responsible reporting and editing'. It holds public hearings on ethical complaints and has the support of the local media. The complaints hearing has local media representatives sitting on it with a high court judge presiding. According to its Internet web site, the News Council offers the following services:

- Public hearings on complaints brought by individuals or organisations named in a story who feel damaged by it (selected third-party complaints are also accepted if they are of compelling public interest and raise a significant ethical question).
- Public forums on topics of media ethics.
- Private forums to facilitate communication between the media and organisations and communities experiencing trouble in working with the media.
- Mediation assistance between the public and media.
- Public speaking to civic and educational groups.
- It publishes a quarterly newsletter, *NEWSWORTHY*.
- It transmits a cable television programme, *NEWSWORTHY*, premièred in August 1996 and broadcast on the Twin Cities regional cable channel (http://www.mtn.org/~newscncl/).

Other news councils have come and gone, so these voluntary, self-styled organisations depend entirely on the enthusiasm of the small group determined to run them and the support, or lack of it, of the local media.

## Countries with no constitutional protection of freedom

Let us now move on to countries which, although they do not have constitutional freedom of expression, seem in many respects to be very similar to America. Sweden was the first European country to become involved in regulating journalism ethics. It set up its first press council in 1874. Sweden's Code of Conduct is not enormously different from that of the PCC. It is a much more straightforward, though, spelling out of the issues with little of the fine rhetoric of the US codes. The approach of the Swedish journalist is very different from that of the UK journalist. With few laws to consider, the Swedes take their code of ethics very seriously. It is difficult to tell why this might be. Perhaps they are more responsive to social pressures? Perhaps they are less concerned with gossip? Perhaps there is less competition? Certainly the press compensation funds which allow for state support of newspapers may remove some of the market pressure faced by UK journalists.

Sweden has a media council supported by all sectors of the industry. It deals with complaints from the public and measures them against a code of conduct. It is slightly unusual in that it has a media council and not just a press council. It also has an ombudsman who can take up complaints on behalf of a reader or viewer.

Dutch journalists also seem to take ethics very seriously. They too have very few laws limiting the media, and think hard about their ethics. Interestingly, although Sweden has a strong code of ethics, which journalists support strongly, journalists in the Netherlands have opposed having such a code. There is a general acceptance of the 'Bordeaux' Code of the International Federation of Journalists (http://www.uta.fi/ethicnet/ifjindex.html). Their collective view, according to Huub Evers, an author and lecturer in journalistic ethics at one of the journalism schools in the Netherlands, is that codes are too restrictive. A detailed code, covering all the issues a journalist needs to know, is too inflexible to work in everyday practice (see Chapter 6 on working with codes). The editors in chief of a number of Dutch papers did try to formulate a code in the mid-1990s, but this was rejected by most journalism groups within the Netherlands and the Press Council continues to discuss complaints case by case and make a declaration of principle. According to Mr Evers, the Council's reputation is growing. Adjudications of the Dutch Press Council are printed in the union's journal, *The Journalist*.

## Legal controls

Some countries, of course, go further and require legal controls of some areas of media work. Italy takes a different approach to regulation from most other European countries. It has a code of conduct and, like America, there is strong constitutional protection for the rights of the citizen and personal honour, including the right of ownership of a person's own image. This means that in certain circumstances a person needs to give permission before his or her photograph may be used in the media. There is also a limited amount of freedom of information. This is mainly at a local level. In addition, the law enforces the journalist's right to protect sources. The journalist is obliged 'to respect professional secrecy with regard to sources of information, when this is required by its confidential nature . . .' (Ordine dei Giornalisti, 1993: 7).

There is strong legal protection for the code of conduct through professional registration. A journalist may only work in Italy if he or she is a member of the Ordine dei Giornalisti and is listed on the Professional Register. This professional body ensures that only properly trained people, who have passed their professional exams, taken before a committee of five journalists and two magistrates appointed by the court of appeal in Rome, may be listed on the register and hold a press card. No one under the age of twenty-one can become a journalist. Breaching the code of ethics may mean a member being expelled and their livelihood removed: 'A member can be removed from the professional register if his [sic] conduct has seriously compromised professional decorum in such a way that his continuation in the professional register or lists is incompatible with the dignity of the profession' (Ordine dei Giornaliste, 1993: 14). Journalists may only reapply for membership after five years. A warning, reprimand or suspension is a more usual punishment.

Professional registration for journalists is an uncommon approach around the world because of the damaging effect having only professional journalists writing for publication can have on press freedom. Such limiting of access to the media must also limit its ability to provide a range of ideas and opinions. 'Journalism is not a profession. It is the exercise by occupation of the right of free expression available to every citizen. That right, being freely available to all, cannot in principle be withdrawn from a few by any system of licensing or professional registration' (Robertson, 1983: 3). This concern has not escaped the Italians and a referendum was held in June 1997 to decide whether professional registration should stay. The Radical party in Italy opposes registration because it say it limits press freedom. A number of journalists, many of them influential in the Italian unions, oppose change. They say that more pressure could be put on journalists by proprietors and editors to write biased copy. It would be easier to buy in political viewpoints. A limit on entry into the profession gives Italian journalists more freedom to write what they want than journalists in the rest of Europe. 'Journalists have the unsuppressible right of freedom of information and criticism, limited by compliance with legislation designed to safeguard the privacy of others, the irrevocable obligation to respect the substantial truth of the facts, and respect for the obligations imposed by honesty and good faith' (Ordine dei Giornaliste, 1993: 7).

There are other countries which pick up specific laws to control areas of journalistic work. All of these areas tend to appear in codes of conduct, but individual countries consider them important enough to single out. They cover the following subjects:

- Privacy.
- Presumption of innocence.

- Children.
- Protection of personal honour.
- Media silence.
- Reality TV.

**Privacy**. Privacy is one of the areas of difference in journalistic practice around the world. Italy and France, for instance, both have privacy legislation whilst Britain, Sweden and the Netherlands do not. Generally this is protection from invasion of privacy but some countries also protect from publication.

Laws preventing phone tapping, bugging and other forms of invasion of privacy are common throughout Europe. Less common are laws allowing complainants to take action about a published invasion of their privacy. France enforces the right to a private life through article 9 of its civil code: 'Each has a right to respect for his private life' (http://www.uta.fi/ethicnet/).

**Presumption of innocence**. One of the areas of ethics which varies widely across Europe is coverage of court cases and in particular the rights of defendants to protect their reputations. A Swedish journalist, for instance, would be very cautious about naming a person accused of a crime and facing trial. Whilst this can be partly ascribed to the different legal system, which means that the case can be heard in full before a lower and a higher court, leading to possible prejudice of the case at the higher court, the main thrust of ethical argument in Sweden seems to be the protection of civil rights. Only after the trial and a finding of guilt might a Swedish journalist consider using the convict's name. In Britain, of course, the name is used without a second thought. It is assumed to be the right thing to do. Naming the person is not seen as an invasion of privacy, a secondary punishment, but an assurance that justice is done. In April 1996, the then Lord Chief Justice, the Rt Hon Lord Taylor of Gosforth, spoke to a Commonwealth Judges and Magistrates' Association Symposium which was considering allowing TV cameras into courts. He said: 'It is crucial in a democracy that justice is administered in public: "Justice must not only be done, but must be seen to be done."' Although he opposed the idea of cameras in courts as putting too much pressure on witnesses and defendants, he said: 'It is healthy that the media, and through them the ordinary citizen, should observe closely and critically how public institutions and services are run.'

The Lord Chancellor, Lord Mackay of Clashfern, agreed, although with reservations. In a letter to all judges in 1997 he expressed his concern at the standard of some press reporting of judicial decisions, whilst re-stating his belief that the criminal justice system is, and should be, the subject of public scrutiny. Recommending that before passing sentence in cases which might attract media attention judges should produce a written note of their sentencing remarks for distribution, he said: 'It is unfair to the individual judge concerned, as well as to the public's perception of the judiciary as a whole, if criticism by the media is based not on the facts as laid before the judge but on a markedly different account of the situation.' The Press Complaints Commission described the Lord Chancellor's initiative as a 'useful recommendation'.

The Netherlands follows the same route as the Swedes. Court cases are covered, but reporters talk about a '28-year-old man from Amsterdam' or maybe '28-year-old A.B. from Amsterdam'. The Dutch also believe that defendants' chances of rehabilitation should not be harmed by identifying them.

Yet things are changing. In line with the move away from 1960s' liberalism into the more authoritarian approach of the 1990s, both the Swedes and the Dutch are reconsidering their views. Already, some cases in both countries have led to people being named and there are moves to allow TV cameras into courts in the Netherlands. Cameras are not actually banned at the moment, but it requires the judge's approval in each case and this is rarely granted. The new law, if passed, would allow cameras in unless the judge refused. Since that would presumably require the judge to have a specific reason for refusal, this is a complete change about for the Netherlands. It seems that as society becomes more concerned with punishing the guilty than rehabilitating them, the journalistic ethic will change. This change is slow, but will almost certainly happen. Already, reporters from those countries which a few years ago would not have considered naming suspects or convicts and would have been horrified at the suggestion that they should, are prepared to consider the principle case by case. If TV cameras are introduced into the Dutch courts on a regular basis, then it is extremely unlikely that anonymity will continue for long, although editors generally would prefer to continue that tradition.

**Children**. Children are protected in two main ways: by taste and decency and by confidentiality. Germany, for instance, has strong laws to protect the young from corruption. 'Gesetz über die Verbreitung Jugendfahrender Schriften 1961' (Law on the dissemination of publications endangering the young) established an examining board of twelve members who may list a publication which is considered to be of a violent, pornographic or racist nature. Although daily newspapers and political periodicals are not covered, if a publication appears on the list twice in the same year, it may be removed from circulation for up to a year.

**Protection of personal honour**. Several European countries offer protection of personal honour under their constitutions and this spills through into their codes of ethics. The International Federation of Journalists' Code of

Conduct, for instance, says: 'The journalist shall regard as grave professional offences the following: plagiarism, malicious misrepresentation, calumny, slander, libel, unfounded accusations' (International Federation of Journalists' Declaration of Principles on the Conduct of Journalists, http://www.uta.fi/ethicnet/). This is picked up in quite a few European codes as a quick look through http://www.uta.fi/Ethicnet/ will confirm. In the UK there are no codes of ethics which pick up this point and the issue tends to be left entirely in the domain of defamation. If someone's personal honour is called into question, their only recourse is to sue.

*Media silence*. Another debate that has cropped up in Europe concerns voluntary 'media silences'. A spate of incidents in the Netherlands sparked off this debate. Nine divorced fathers, in completely separate incidents over a space of a year, killed their children and then in most cases killed themselves. Academic research in the Netherlands by a child psychologist suggested that the media coverage was sparking other such incidents. In other words, reading about the events of an earlier case was likely to provoke another. The US psychologist David Philips has done similar work which also claims to prove this link. As a result, there were calls for a media silence on these cases. Editors ignored these calls but did alter the way they used the stories, putting them inside the paper rather than on the front page and not using photographs. Apart from not being entirely convinced by the argument, the editors also thought that it was their duty to inform people. The cases would still have been heard of locally, and indeed several of the cases happened only streets from each other, suggesting that any copycat effect did not require the newspapers.

*Reality TV*. This is another ethical dilemma that is yet to hit Britain in a big way. Although we do have some programmes which contain footage from surveillance cameras or police car cameras, and there are a few programmes, such as the Roger Cook show, which have unplanned interviews which can involve invasion of offices or homes, there are not many such programmes. But in other parts of Europe, such as the Netherlands, Reality TV is becoming a problem. In the Netherlands, freelance camera teams roam around filming road accidents and similar incidents as they happen. As only the more exciting footage is screened on TV, there are suggestions that such footage is sometimes elaborated. It is also important that victims are recognisable. This involves some close-ups of road accident victims which viewers found too much. Some protests followed.

## Countries with considerable media controls

There are, of course, some countries which are very heavily controlled by law or the government. Whilst there are certainly some authorities which merely use military power to suppress journalism, some use the law to restrict the media and to allow censorship. One of the most difficult countries in the world in which to work at the moment is Algeria. Of the forty-nine journalists killed throughout the world in 1995, twenty-two were working in Algeria. In total, fifty-seven journalists were murdered in the three years leading up to 1996. Fifty-five publications were suspended and twenty-three journalists were detained for longer than forty-eight hours, whilst a total of thirty-nine were arrested (Reporters San Frontieres, http:www.calvancom.fr/rsf/).

One such incident, according to Reporters San Frontieres, was the arrest of Chawki Amari, a cartoonist and columnist with the privately-owned Algerian daily, *La Tribune*. He was accused of producing a cartoon poking fun at the Algerian ruling classes. The courts used Article 160 of the Penal Code, which condemns 'anyone who deliberately and publicly tears up, defaces or defiles the national symbol', to prosecute him. Chawki Amari was given a three-year suspended prison sentence in July 1996. On 3 September 1996, *La Tribune*, a French-language newspaper, was suspended for six months by an Algiers court, on the orders of the Interior Ministry, on the basis that it should have an Arabic edition. It was the first time such an argument had been used, says Reporters San Frontieres, pointing out that hardly any French papers have Arabic editions.

Iran has similar problems. A law there prohibits ownership of satellite dishes, making it impossible to receive foreign national stations. Iraqi nationals are not allowed to own dish aerials either. The two internal TV stations and two radio stations are state-owned and the journalists are classed as civil servants and are answerable to the Information Ministry.

Egypt is another country with a poor record on press freedom. The law ensures that only the government and the political parties can own newspapers. Reporters San Frontieres explains:

> Launching an independent newspaper – in other words one that is not controlled by the government or affiliated to a political party – is theoretically possible. But the legal conditions that would have to be fulfilled are such that it would be almost impossible in practice. The first obstacle is that the newspaper would have to obtain a publication licence from the Higher Press Council. In addition, the law imposes financial conditions that are difficult to fulfil. Anyone wanting to start a daily, for instance, has to have 250,000 Egyptian pounds (70,000 dollars) in capital available, and shareholdings are not allowed to exceed 500 pounds (140 dollars). These conditions effectively prevent the emergence of an independent press in Egypt. At the moment no truly independent newspaper exists. (http://www.rsf.fr)

Radio and television are also state monopolies, making dissent extremely difficult. In May 1995, the government passed a law which toughened the penalties for authors of articles deemed 'libellous' or 'liable to damage state institutions or the national economy'. The country's journalists opposed this vigorously, claiming that the law was overly vague. Since its introduction, no fewer than ninety-three journalists have been charged and six have been given prison sentences.

Journalists in Egypt campaigned vigorously for the law to be repealed. They won some concessions, but the day after the vote on the law, President Mubarak spoke out in support of the new law, stressing that no journalist would be imprisoned because of his opinions; only because of accusations against third parties. 'I am 100 per cent in favour of press freedom, but not freedom to libel', the president said. 'No writer will be prevented from making criticism, even if it is harsh, as long as he avoids defamation' (http://www.rsf.fr, as at May 1999). The president claimed that the new law was needed as the journalists' own code of conduct was not applied strongly enough. Once again the link between press freedom, ethics and the law is thrown into stark relief.

## Global code of ethics

A global code of ethics was suggested at a World Association of Press Councils meeting in Istanbul in 1998 and the European Commission has suggested a pan-European code. This has not received any support within the industry in the UK and the chairman of the PCC, Lord Wakeham, is strongly opposed. Speaking at a meeting of the Commonwealth Press Union in 1998 he said a code could 'end up doing much mischief and be misused by those who seek to bring in often draconian controls against the press through the back door, under the guise of a respectable international body' (PCC, 1998: 3). He pointed out that it would be impossible to produce a global code of conduct that would be acceptable to all societies without curtailing the freedom to report in many of them.

## Summary

- This chapter examined the structure and methods of the Press Complaints Commission.
- It considered how the new Broadcasting Standards Commission is structured.
- It examined the wider role of the new BSC.
- It explained the working of other bodies with an ethical viewpoint in the UK.
- It examined the position abroad and looked at the different regulatory methods which can be used.

- It considered some of the ethical topics which are current abroad but are not problems in the UK.

## Questions

1 Describe the structure and complaints procedure of the PCC. Describe the structure and complaints procedure of the BSC. Compare the two systems. What are the advantages and disadvantages each system offers?

2 How else can those complaining against broadcasters get their complaints heard?

3 Consider the efficacy of Italy's system of regulating journalists by licensing by comparing it with the UK's self-regulatory system.

4 Are there disadvantages to licensing journalists?

# Chapter 12

## The future

### Chapter outline

- **This chapter examines the problems that the weakening of national borders throughout Europe might bring.**
- **It considers how the Internet is altering the way journalists work.**
- **It touches on the problems that multi-media brings.**
- **It discusses the problems that will arise when attempts are made to introduce a pan-European code of ethics.**

A number of issues will concern the media in the future. It is probable that none of these will change the basic moral problems that face journalists in their daily work, but it is possible that they will make decision-making more difficult. Working across international borders will emphasise the differences in moral approach between cultures and the use of the Internet will add other problems. Interactivity is an important new element of the Internet. The consumer changes from the passive reader or viewer of what is offered to someone who can actively track down the information he or she requires and respond instantaneously by e-mail. The consumer can supply his or her own slant on the news directly to the supplier. Journalists at BBC on-line are often alerted to stories by readers e-mailing for information on a breaking story. This unique element is what many commentators see as the most important facet of the Internet. It should allow more input from a vast range of sources, most of which are more likely to be pushing their own viewpoint. With this wider range of available material, the filtering process, if only in terms of time available to read all this information, will become more difficult.

Many people see the present grip on the media by a small number of moguls as being broken by the Internet and this growing interactivity. I am sceptical enough to believe that where big money and control are involved, the reverse is more likely to be true. We may well fall into the hands of an even smaller, more powerful group of moguls. Already there is evidence that consumers find the sheer quantity of information that is available overwhelming, and turn to portal sites to assist. Portal sites are Internet sites whose sole purpose is to direct the consumer to sites of specific interest. If you are interested in media ethics (and you may not be by now) then there are several portal sites which would guide you on to other sites about media ethics. Many portal sites are now growing up. They usually have their own material and then direct the consumer on to specialist sites for in-depth information.

Many of these have been developed by existing mainstream news providers. The BBC, Electronic Telegraph, and the Guardian on-line are such sites. Some have developed out of the new technology industries, but aim to do the same thing: Yahoo and MSN are two such portals. They provide information content of their own, filtered and tailored in a traditional way, and provide access to an indexed range of additional sites.

## Cross-border working

As the journalist becomes more international, so working across borders will seem less and less unusual. At the moment the journalist's forays abroad tend to be for spells as a foreign correspondent or to cover a war or election in a particular spot for a short period before returning home. Technology is making it much easier for the journalist to research in a foreign country from their desk, as well as making it more likely for them to be working for a multinational employer on a multinational publication. Moving news on to the World Wide Web ensures that journalists will be working for a multinational audience.

Although it is unlikely this will bring new moral problems, it does make the regulatory system more difficult. Something illegal in one country may be legal in another but highly unethical in a third. Covering courts, for instance, is an important part of the media's business in Britain. Naming the accused, their alleged crime and defence is seen as an important part of ensuring that justice is seen to be done. Whilst some people might argue that some of the more unsavoury details of court cases should not appear in the media (much of the detail of the Rosemary West trial was voluntarily suppressed by many papers as being unsuitable for a family newspaper), hardly anyone in this country opposes the view that the media should publish details of major trials to ensure that public justice is done. Yet in Sweden, journalists are horrified at the idea of naming the accused during trials. Even in important trials, the normal practice is not to name the accused until after a finding of guilt, and often not even then. Journalists will need to be even more aware of the systems in other countries if they are working globally.

## The Internet

The Internet throws up a number of ethical problems that have yet to be seriously addressed by journalists. Concerns over copyright have already led some commercial operators to start withdrawing their intellectual property from the Internet. Pictures of film stars or of scenes from cult favourites, which had been spread liberally on the Net for the enjoyment of fans, are now being withdrawn as they start to appear in publications both on and off the Net. *The X-Files* TV show, for instance, had built up a large Internet-based following, possibly because its fans are young, moneyed and technologically literate. So damaging did the copyright infringements become, with pictures and scripts being passed around the Net, that Fox Television issued a cease and desist order in the US against an unofficial site which Fox claimed had been using copyright material.

Much material is being placed on the Net by organisations in the hope of attracting journalists. The UK government, for instance, now puts out all its press releases this way and charges freelance journalists for sending out hard copy of press releases. Many commercial organisations, such as film and video distributors and fashion houses, also distribute press information this way. Details on major film releases, along with pictures and star interviews, might be just the ticket for a local paper hoping to flesh out its review pages. Whilst this sort of PR work is only a technological update of the old press handout, there is a greater temptation to use the already keyed-in copy rather than write a new piece from scratch using the handout as notes.

Internet material is much easier to access than traditional methods, but it is also much more difficult to be certain that one is getting the most up-to-date information. The use of the Internet as a research tool is becoming more important in many news rooms, although journalists, in the UK at least, lag well behind other researchers in this area. The burden of proof for any source is more difficult on the Internet as the element of trust and credibility is not there. Even if a site carries the name of a large company, there is no guarantee it is an authorised site. Many sites are now being set up to attack the credibility of a company. A disgruntled ex-employee or former customer can easily set up a site with a credible name to give damaging hoax information about the company. All Internet information needs to be treated with caution unless one is confident about the site.

We also need to remember that Internet information only gives one side of the story. Information on the Net is only there because copyright owners want to put it there. Whether it is information they have painstakingly gathered to expose government corruption, or a multi-colour presentation on the latest model of car put out by its manufacturer, it all must be treated with the same scepticism that should be used about any source.

Sad 'anoraks' no longer scribble their pet obsessions in green ink on jagged-torn pages of lined exercise books. Their reports are now as superbly presented on the Net as any corporate presentation. This slickness appears to add veracity where none exists. Much material on the Net comes from unofficial or commercial sources and needs to be treated with suspicion.

### Case study 12.1 Small fish in a big pond

Because Internet material is self-generated but widely available, a small organisation can put out masses of material and make itself appear to be a big player with more influence than its real power base. A number of organisations have now seen that this is an ideal way to contact young, literate, moderately wealthy individuals. Cult religions, political and religious extremists, as well as small but financially strong pressure groups, are starting to use the Internet to attract this key audience which is growing by the thousands every day. For instance, creation–evolution theory has attracted support amongst fundamentalist Christians in the US southern states before and since the Scopes monkey trial. A law proposing equal time for creation-science as evolution-science in Arkansas schools was opposed by individual plaintiffs who included the resident Arkansas Bishops of the United Methodist, Episcopal, Roman Catholic and African Methodist Episcopal Churches, the principal official of the Presbyterian Churches in Arkansas, other United Methodist, Southern Baptist and Presbyterian clergy, as well as several persons who sued as parents and friends of minor children attending Arkansas public schools. Organisations included the American Jewish Congress, the Union of American Hebrew Congregations, the American Jewish Committee, the Arkansas Education Association, the National Association of Biology Teachers and the National Coalition for Public Education and Religious Liberty. The plaintiffs won their case to have evolution taught as the main theory of human development in those schools. Yet a quick search on the Internet using the word 'creation' produced more than thirty web sites in favour of creation-biology compared with only fifteen for evolution. A small but vocal and determined minority had been able to build up their pet theories to appear far more widely believed than they really are.

The issue of credibility of information and trust on the Internet is an important one for the Public Relations industry. Practitioners want to be able to find a way to assure journalists and customers that the information is accurate. The question of credibility is also important for journalists. Many traditional newspaper and broadcast organisations now have very sophisticated web sites. The importance of the validation of information being put out under the banner of, say, the BBC, *Guardian* or *Daily Telegraph* cannot be underestimated. This is one of the main reasons why the big players will eventually dominate on the Net as far as news services are concerned. Why get your news from Joe Bloggs's web site when you can go direct to the

BBC or the *Daily Telegraph* and get a validated service from a provider you already trust?

Some organisations are seeking to put together a regulation body to validate web sites by ensuring they stick to a code of conduct. The anarchic background from which the World Wide Web sprang makes it very resistant to this sort of change. Most users are more concerned about the risk of censorship than they are about validating the information on the web.

One organisation pressing for ethics on-line is Better Ethics Online (http://actionsites.com/beo/index.html), but even this site is more concerned with protecting members' intellectual property and explaining how to prevent unsolicited e-mail. A news item on the Industry Standard web site (billed as the news magazine of the Internet economy) said on 10 December 1998: 'Online journalists who toil at some of the "name" sites are forming a non-profit-making group to work out ethical and credibility issues' (http://www.thestandard.net/articles/article_print/0,1454,2814,00.html). There are very few other details however.

Many governments are keen to bring in regulation, particularly over pornography on the Net. There are now several software systems designed to allow parents to prevent their children accessing sexually explicit sites. Both the PCC and the ITC believe that they have a duty to regulate at least some part of the Internet. The PCC said in its 1997 *Annual Report*: 'The PCC has extended its jurisdiction to certain publications on the Internet – making it, as far as it is possible to discern, the first press self-regulatory body anywhere in the world to do so.' It said that any newspaper or magazine that presently subscribed to the Code of Practice would have this extended to their Internet version (PCC, 1997: 6).

## Multi-media journalism

As technology develops, so the old divisions between radio, TV and press grow narrower. Journalists already work in all three fields at once on the Internet and this development is likely to continue. This will almost certainly combine with some level of interactivity with the consumer, probably linked with digital TV. At the moment digital TV is only a sophisticated way of providing us with more channels, and therefore more programmes with higher quality transmission, but the cabling of the UK, combined with the power of the Internet, opens all sorts of possibilities for digital TV which are only just being experimented with.

Interactivity means that advertisers, publishers and broadcasters will be able to build up complex databases on our likes and dislikes and feed us information, advertising and programming, both passive and active, that are tightly targeted at our individual needs and desires. This already happens to a limited extent through the post. Junk mail is becoming much more tightly focused to our needs and wants. Digital TV and the Internet can take this a stage further. This may well mean that the present regulatory councils will need to be adjusted and it will become important to have a multi-media ethics council that is able to consider the problems of broadcasters, advertisers and publishers. With statutory regulation largely in place for broadcast, but desperately avoided by publishing, this will cause some friction. Will the government of the day be prepared to give up statutory regulation? Will the publishers be prepared to take on statutory regulation? Will TV broadcast on the Internet be regulated by the Broadcasting Act or will it be unregulated? With the growth of cable, satellite and digital broadcasting, the old argument for regulated, impartial TV and radio will become less compelling and many of the present conglomerate owners, who are also the driving forces behind the new communication methods, will be pressing for more open forms of regulation or even total deregulation. Adult, subscription-only channels will become available, giving the Broadcasting Standards Commission problems. Combining the Broadcast Standards Commission and Press Complaints Commission as a voluntary, self-regulatory council on the Swedish model, with no remit for impartiality, may well seem the ideal way forward for many.

## Pan-European codes of ethics

Europe is even now looking at the possibility of a pan-European code of media ethics. With the problems over open borders and the Ecu, this has not been very high on the agenda but some discussions have taken place alongside talks on media pluralism and concentration of ownership. With the different views on media ethics across Europe it is difficult to see a quick solution on a pan-European code unless it is so bland and general as to be almost pointless.

There has also been talk about the possibility of a global code of ethics although this has been opposed by Lord Wakeham (see Chapter 11). It is difficult to see how a global code of ethics could work across so many different cultures. The risk is that it, too, would be so bland as to be virtually meaningless.

## Summary

- **This chapter considered the problems that the weakening of national borders might bring.**

- **It examined some of the problems the Internet brings for consumers.**

- It considered how the Internet will alter the way journalists work.

- It touched on the problems that multi-media will bring.

- It discussed briefly the problems that will arise when attempts are made to introduce a pan-European code of ethics.

## Questions

1 Is it ethical to use pictures or text copied from the Internet in a publication?

2 The Internet raises special problems about guaranteeing information. How can you be sure that what you read on the Internet is accurate and truthful?

3 What additional ethical problems would there be for the journalist working in multi-media or on the Internet?

4 What areas of a pan-European code of conduct would be the most controversial in the UK?

# Appendix 1: PCC Code of Conduct (January 1998)

This is the full text of the Code of Practice. Items marked* are covered by the exceptions relating to the public interest.

All members of the press have a duty to maintain the highest professional and ethical standards. This code sets the benchmarks for those standards. It both protects the rights of the individual and upholds the public's right to know.

The code is the cornerstone of the system of self-regulation to which the industry has made a binding commitment. Editors and publishers must ensure that the code is observed rigorously not only by staff but also by anyone who contributes to their publications.

It is essential to the workings of an agreed code that it be honoured not only to the letter but in the full spirit. The code should not be interpreted so narrowly as to compromise its commitment to respect the rights of the individual, nor so broadly that it prevents publication in the public interest.

It is the responsibility of editors to co-operate with the PCC as swiftly as possible in the resolution of complaints. Any publication which is criticised by the PCC under one of the following clauses must print the adjudication which follows in full and with due prominence.

## PCC Code of practice

### 1 Accuracy

(i)   Newspapers and periodicals should take care not to publish inaccurate, misleading or distorted material, including pictures.

(ii)  Whenever it is recognised that a significant inaccuracy, misleading statement or distorted report has been published, it should be corrected promptly and with due prominence.

(iii) An apology must be published whenever appropriate.

(iv)  Newspapers, whilst free to be partisan, must distinguish clearly between comment, conjecture and fact.

(v)   A newspaper or periodical must report fairly and accurately the outcome of an action for defamation to which it has been a party.

### 2 Opportunity to reply

A fair opportunity to reply to inaccuracies must be given to individuals and organisations when reasonably called for.

### 3 Privacy*

(i) Everyone is entitled to respect for his or her private and family life, home, health and correspondence. A publication will be expected to justify intrusions into any individual's private life without consent.

(ii) The use of long-lens photography to take pictures of people in private places without their consent is unacceptable.

Note – Private places are public or private property where there is a reasonable expectation of privacy.

### 4 Harassment*

(i) Journalists and photographers must neither obtain nor seek to obtain information or pictures through intimidation, harassment or persistent pursuit.

(ii) They must not photograph individuals in private places (as defined in the note to Clause 3) without their consent; must not persist in telephoning, questioning, pursuing or photographing individuals after having been asked to desist; must not remain on their property after having been asked to leave and must not follow them.

(iii) Editors must ensure that those working for them comply with these requirements and must not publish material from other sources which does not meet these requirements.

### 5 Intrusion into grief or shock

In cases involving grief or shock, inquiries must be carried out and approaches made with sympathy and discretion. Publication must be handled sensitively at such times, but this should not be interpreted as restricting the right to report judicial proceedings.

### 6 Children*

(i) Young people should be free to complete their time at school without unnecessary intrusion.

(ii) Journalists must not interview or photograph a child under the age of 16 on subjects involving the welfare of the child or of any other child, in the absence of or without the consent of a parent or other adult who is responsible for the children.

(iii) Pupils must not be approached or photographed while at school without the permission of the school authorities.

(iv) There must be no payment to minors for material involving the welfare of children nor payment to parents or guardians for material about their children or wards unless it is demonstrably in the child's interest.

(v) Where material about the private life of a child is published, there must be justification for publication other than the fame, notoriety or position of his or her parents or guardian.

## 7 Children in sex cases

1 The press must not, even where the law does not prohibit it, identify children under the age of 16 who are involved in cases concerning sexual offences, whether as victims or as witnesses.

2 In any press report of a case involving a sexual offence against a child:

(i)   The child must not be identified.

(ii)  The adult may be identified.

(iii) The word 'incest' must not be used where a child victim might be identified.

(iv)  Care must be taken that nothing in the report implies the relationship between the accused and the child.

## 8 Listening devices*

Journalists must not obtain or publish material obtained by clandestine listening devices or by intercepting private phone conversations.

## 9 Hospitals*

(i)   Journalists or photographers making inquiries at hospitals or similar institutions must identify themselves to a responsible executive and obtain permission before entering non-public areas.

(ii)  The restrictions on intruding into privacy are particularly relevant to inquiries about individuals in hospitals or similar institutions.

## 10 Reporting of crime*

The press must avoid identifying relatives or friends of persons convicted or accused of crime without consent.

## 11 Misrepresentation*

(i)   Journalists must not generally obtain or seek to obtain information or pictures through misrepresentation or subterfuge.

(ii)  Documents or photographs should be removed only with owners' consent.

(iii) Subterfuge can be justified only in the public interest and only when material cannot be obtained by any other means.

## 12 Victims of sexual assault

The press must not identify victims of sexual assault or publish material likely to contribute to such identification unless there is adequate justification and, by law, they are free to do so.

## 13 Discrimination

(i)   The press must avoid prejudicial or pejorative reference to a person's race, colour, religion, sex or sexual orientation or to any physical or mental illness or disability.

(ii)  It must avoid publishing details of a person's race, colour, religion, sexual orientation, physical or mental illness or disability unless these are directly relevant to the story.

## 14 Financial journalism*

(i)  Even where the law does not prohibit it, journalists must not use for their own profit financial information they receive in advance of its general publication, nor should they pass such information to others.

(ii) They must not write about shares or securities in whose performance they know that they or their close families have a significant financial interest, without disclosing the interest to the editor or financial editor.

(iii) They must not buy or sell, either directly or through nominees or agents, shares or securities about which they have written recently or about which they intend to write in the near future.

## 15 Confidential sources

Journalists have a moral obligation to protect confidential sources of information.

## 16 Payment for articles*

(i)  Payment or offers of payment for stories or information must not be made directly or through agents to witnesses or potential witnesses in current criminal proceedings except where the material concerned ought to be published in the public interest and there is an overriding need to make or promise to make a payment for this to be done. Journalists must take every possible step to ensure that no financial dealings have influence on the evidence that those witnesses may give. (An editor authorising such a payment must be prepared to demonstrate that there is a legitimate public interest at stake involving matters that the public has a right to know. The payment or, where accepted, the offer of payment to any witness who is actually cited to give evidence must be disclosed to the prosecution and the defence and the witness should be advised of this.)

(ii) Payment or offers of payment for stories, pictures or information, must not be made directly or through agents to convicted or confessed criminals or to their associates – who may include family, friends and colleagues – except where the material concerned ought to be published in the public interest and payment is necessary for this to be done.

## The public interest

There may be exceptions to the clauses marked* where they can be demonstrated to be in the public interest.

1 The public interest includes:
  (i)   Detecting or exposing crime or a serious misdemeanour.
  (ii)  Protecting public health and safety.
  (iii) Preventing the public from being misled by some statement or action of an individual or organisation.

2 In any case where the public interest is invoked, the Press Complaints Commission will require a full explanation by the editor demonstrating how the public interest was served.

3 In cases involving children, editors must demonstrate an exceptional public interest to override the normally paramount interests of the child.

# Appendix 2: NUJ Code of Conduct

1 A journalist has a duty to maintain the highest professional and ethical standards.

2 A journalist shall at all times defend the principle of the freedom of the press and other media in relation to the collection of information and the expression of comment and criticism. He/she shall strive to eliminate distortion, news suppression and censorship.

3 A journalist shall strive to ensure that the information he/she disseminates is fair and accurate, avoid the expression of comment and conjecture as established fact and falsification by distortion, selection or misrepresentation.

4 A journalist shall rectify promptly any harmful inaccuracies, ensure that correction and apologies receive due prominence and afford the right of reply to persons criticised when the issue is of sufficient importance.

5 A journalist shall obtain information, photographs and illustrations only by straightforward means. The use of other means can be justified only by overriding considerations of the public interest. The journalist is entitled to exercise a personal conscientious objection to the use of such means.

6 A journalist shall do nothing which entails intrusion into anybody's private life, grief or distress subject to justification by overriding considerations of the public interest.

7 A journalist shall protect confidential sources of information.

8 A journalist shall not accept bribes nor shall he/she allow other inducements to influence the performance of his/her professional duties.

9 A journalist shall not lend himself/herself to the distortion or suppression of the truth because of advertising or other considerations.

10 A journalist shall mention a person's age, sex, race, colour, creed, illegitimacy, disability, marital status or sexual orientation only if this information is strictly relevant. A journalist shall neither originate nor process material which encourages discrimination, ridicule, prejudice or hatred on any of the above-mentioned grounds.

11 No journalist shall knowingly cause or allow the publication or broadcast of a photograph that has been manipulated unless that photograph is clearly labelled as such. Manipulation does not include normal dodging, burning, colour balancing, spotting, contrast adjustment, cropping and obvious masking for legal or safety reasons.

12 A journalist shall not take private advantage of information gained in the course of his/her duties before the information is public knowledge.

13 A journalist shall not by way of statement, voice or appearance endorse by advertisement any commercial product or service save for the promotion of his/her own work or of the medium by which he/she is employed.

# Appendix 3: NUJ Working Practices

1  A member shall study and obey the rules of the union and the code of conduct.
2  A member shall not act, by commission or omission, against the interests of the union or of the trade union movement.
3  A member who is terminating his/her employment shall give notice according to individual or collective agreement or custom and practice unless the employer consents to a variation.
4  A member shall not, by unfair methods, seek promotion to or obtain the position of another journalist.
5  A member shall not exploit the labour of another journalist by plagiarism or the unauthorised use of his/her work for any purpose.
6  A member who does lineage work shall surrender part or whole of that work to conform with any pooling scheme approved by the NEC to provide a member with a livelihood.
7  A member who is a staff reporter shall not normally take photographs and a member who is a staff photographer shall not normally report. Freelance reporters shall not take photographs or freelance photographers report, if by so doing they deprive another freelance of income.
8  Members shall ensure, by support of union organisation and of their colleagues, that participation in union activity does not damage a member's employment, advancement or employment prospects.
9  A member shall not directly or indirectly attempt to obtain for himself/herself or anyone else any regular or occasional lineage work, connection or commission which is rightfully undertaken by another member.
10 A member in staff employment shall first serve the organisation which employs him/her. In his/her own time, a member is free to engage in journalistic work, provided that in so doing he/she is neither depriving a freelance or unemployed member of work nor occupying a job which would normally be a full-time staff position; and provided that he/she has contacted the chapel in the office in which the work is to be done and established that he/she is not taking work which can be undertaken by a freelance or unemployed member.
11 A member in a position to commission freelance work shall always attempt to offer it first to a freelance or unemployed member of the union. No member with authority to commission work shall attempt to induce any freelance or casual to perform work for a lower rate of pay or under less favourable conditions than those laid down by any union agreement covering the work in question, or to allocate work to any non-member unless he/she can prove to his/her branch that no suitable member is available and willing to do the work in question. A member who commissions work shall do all in his or her power to ensure payments are made on time.

12 A member shall treat other journalists with consideration.

13 A member shall not accept employment on terms and conditions inferior to those provided for in collective agreements which apply to his/her place of work.

14 It shall be the duty of any member to inform his/her F/MoC of his/her terms and conditions of employment, on request.

15 Freelance members of the union employing salaried assistants shall do so in all respects in accordance with union agreements, the policies of the union and the recognised customs and practices of journalism.

# Appendix 4: Radio Authority Code

## News

A news programme in whatever form must be accurate and impartial. An appropriate range of views on controversial subjects should be reported either within a single news bulletin or in a series of news bulletins which are as adjacent as is reasonably possible.

# Appendix 5: BBC Code of Ethics

The BBC has one of the most comprehensive codes of ethics for journalists and broadcasters in the world. It is too long to publish here but is available on the Web at http://www.bbc.co.uk/info/editorial/prodgl/contents.htm.

The guidelines explain the BBC's values and standards regarding impartiality, accuracy, fairness, privacy, taste and decency, violence, minors and conflicts of interest. Aspects of reporting, including interviewing and confidentiality, are also covered, as are elements of the law such as defamation and copyright.

# Appendix 6: International Federation of Journalists

## Declaration of Principles on the Conduct of Journalists

Adopted by the Second World Congress of the International Federation of Journalists at Bordeaux on 25–28 April 1954 and amended by the 18th IFJ World Congress in Helsingör on 2–6 June 1986.

This international Declaration is proclaimed as a standard of professional conduct for journalists engaged in gathering, transmitting, disseminating and commenting on news and information and in describing events.

1 Respect for truth and for the right of the public to truth is the first duty of the journalist.
2 In pursuance of this duty, the journalist shall at all times defend the principles of freedom in the honest collection and publication of news, and of the right of fair comment and criticism.
3 The journalist shall report only in accordance with facts of which he/she knows the origin. The journalist shall not suppress essential information or falsify documents.
4 The journalist shall use only fair methods to obtain news, photographs and documents.
5 The journalist shall do the utmost to rectify any published information which is found to be harmfully inaccurate.
6 The journalist shall observe professional secrecy regarding the source of information obtained in confidence.
7 The journalist shall be aware of the danger of discrimination being furthered by the media, and shall do the utmost to avoid facilitating such discrimination based on, among other things, race, sex, sexual orientation, language, religion, political or other opinions, and national or social origins.
8 The journalist shall regard as grave professional offences the following: plagiarism – malicious misrepresentation – calumny, slander, libel, unfounded accusations – the acceptance of a bribe in any form in consideration of either publication or suppression.
9 Journalists worthy of that name shall deem it their duty to observe faithfully the principles stated above. Within the general law of each country the journalist shall recognise in professional matters the jurisdiction of colleagues only, to the exclusion of every kind of interference by governments or others.

# Appendix 7: BSC Code of Conduct

Available at: http://www.bsc.org.uk

# Appendix 8: ITC Code of Practice

January 1998 (index only: for full code, see http://www.itc.org.uk)

# Appendix 9: NUJ Guidelines

The NUJ have, over the years, produced a number of guidelines for journalists. These cover the following topics and are available on application to the NUJ: race, women, HIV/AIDS, lesbians and gays and mental and physical handicap.

# Appendix 10: Addresses for regulatory bodies

### British Broadcasting Corporation

Broadcasting House, London, W12 7RJ
Tel: +44 (0)208 743 8000
URL: http://www.BBC.co.uk

### Broadcasting Standards Commission

7 The Sanctuary, London, SW1P 3JS
Tel: +44 (0)207 233 0544   Fax: +44 (0)207 233 0397
URL: http://www.bsc.org.uk

### Independent Television Commission

70 Foley Street, London, W1P 7LB
Tel: +44 (0)207 255 3000   Fax: +44 (0)207 306 7800
e-mail: 100731.3515@compuserve.com
URL: http://www.itc.org.uk

### National Union of Journalists

Acorn House, 314 Gray's Inn Road, London, WC1X 8DP
Tel: +44 (0)207 278 7916   Fax: +44 (0)207 837 8143
e-mail: Acorn.house@nuj.org.uk
URL: http://www.nuj.org.uk

### Press Complaints Commission

1 Salisbury Square, London, EC4Y 8AE
Tel: +44 (0)207 353 1248   Fax: +44 (0)207 353 8355
URL: http://www.pcc.org.uk

### Press Standards Board of Finance

Merchants House Buildings, 30 George Square, Glasgow, G2 1EG

### Radio Authority

Holbrook House, 14 Great Queen Street, London, WC2B 5DG
Tel: +44 (0)207 430 2724   Fax: +44 (0)207 405 7062
URL: http://www.radioauthority.org.uk

# Glossary of terms

**Broadcasters**  Television and radio equivalent of newspaper proprietors.

**Consumers**  A collective term used to refer to readers of publications, viewers of TV, listeners to radio, Internet surfers, teletext viewers and other information receivers. By this term I mean they are consuming the information provided by a journalist, not that they are necessarily buying the product, whether it is a publication or a broadcast.

**Hard news**  A term used by journalists to mean stories that have immediate impact and drama. They must be topical. Plane crashes, deaths, political decisions, stock market crashes, murder, court verdicts and anything which involves shouting 'stop the press' is hard news.

**Soft news**  This is a term used by journalists to define stories that do not have immediate impact. Often such stories have more of a manufactured feel to them as a PR agency or a journalist has tried to build them up into a hard news story – known as giving the story a harder edge. Soft news stories are likely to be about people, possibly showbiz, certainly gossipy, or about events which do not have immediate impact. Often soft news stories are used as features, and many features are soft news stories.

**Information**  Used in its widest sense to mean anything that is printed by magazines or newspapers or transmitted in news and current affairs programmes by radio and television or over electronic systems as part of the editorial content. In this context it can mean 'hard news', 'soft news', analysis, comment, opinion, conjecture, and so on.

**Publish**  Includes broadcast as well as publication in the traditional senses.

**Reader**  Used as a general term to mean receivers of the message when this is transmitted by print.

# Bibliography

Andre, Judith (1992) 'Censorship: Some Distinctions', in Elliott D. Cohen (ed.), *Philosophical Issues in Journalism*. Oxford University Press, Oxford.

Aristotle (1976) *The Ethics of Aristotle* (translated by J.A.K. Thompson). Penguin Classics, London.

Aristotle (1980) *The Nicomachean Ethics* (translated by W.D. Ross). Oxford University Press, Oxford.

BBC (1996) *BBC Producers' Guidelines*. BBC, London. World Wide Web URL: http://www.bbc.co.uk/info/editorial/prodgl/contents/html

BBC (1999) *The Changing UK*. BBC, London.

BCC (1981–96) *BCC Report*. HMSO, London.

Bell, M. (1998) 'The Journalism of Attachment', in M. Kierans (ed.), *Media Ethics*. Routledge, London.

Belsey, Andrew and Chadwick, Ruth (1992) *Ethical Issues in Journalism and the Media*. Routledge, London.

Benn, P. (1998) *Ethics*. University College London Press, London.

Broadcasting Act (1981) HMSO, London.

Broadcasting Act (1996) HMSO, London.

Broadcasting Standards Commission (1998) *Annual Review*. BSC, London.

Broadcasting Standards Commission (1998) *Codes of Guidance*. BSC, London.

Broadcasting Standards Council (1994) *A Code of Practice* (2nd edn). BSC, London.

Broder, David (1983) 'Newsmen Work for the Reader', *International Herald Tribune*, 21 July 1983.

Bundock, A. (1957) *A History of the NUJ*. Oxford University Press, Oxford.

Calcutt, QC, Sir David (1993) *Review of Press Self Regulation*. HMSO, London.

Carey, P. (1996) *Media Law*. Sweet and Maxwell, London.

Christians, Clifford G., Rotzoll, Kim B. and Fackler, Mark (1998) *Media Ethics: Cases and Moral Reasoning* (5th edn). Longman, New York.

Cohen, Elliott D. (ed.) (1992) *Philosophical Issues in Journalism*. Oxford University Press, Oxford.

Cohen, Stanley and Young, Jock (eds.) (1973) *The Manufacture of News: Deviance, Social Problems and the Mass Media*. Constable, London.

Committee on Privacy (1972) *The Report of the Committee on Privacy*. London, HMSO.

Committee on Privacy and Related Matters (1990) *Report of the Committee on Privacy and Related Matters*. HMSO, London.

*Concise Oxford English Dictionary* (1964). Oxford University Press, Oxford.

Cooley, Thomas (1888) *Torts* (2nd edn).

Crawford, Nelson Antrim (1969) *The Ethics of Journalism*. Greenwood, New York. (Originally published 1924.)

Crone, T. (1995) *Law and the Media*. Focal Press, London.

Curtis, Liz and Jempson, Mike (1993) *Interference on the Airwaves*. Campaign for Press and Broadcasting Freedom, London.

Department of National Heritage (1995) *Privacy and Media Intrusion – The Government's Response*. HMSO, London.

Dhavan, Rajeev and Davies, Christie (1978) *Censorship and Obscenity*. Martin Robertson, London.

Dill, Barbara (1986) *Journalist's Handbook on Libel and Privacy*. Free Press, New York.

Fuller, Jack (1996) *News Values*. University of Chicago Press, Chicago.

Galtung, Johan and Ruge, Mari (1973) 'Structuring and Selecting News', in Stanley Cohen and Jock Young (eds.), *The Manufacture of News: Deviance, Social Problems and the Mass Media*. Constable, London.

Garneau, George (ed.) (1993) *Free Press Threat in Europe*. Garneau, Paris.

General Council of the Press (1954–63) *The Press and the People*. GCP, London.

Gilbert, Harman (1977) *The Nature of Morality: An Introduction to Ethics*. Oxford University Press, Oxford.

Glasser, Theodore L. (1992) 'Objectivity and News Bias', in Elliott D. Cohen (ed.), *Philosophical Issues in Journalism*. Oxford University Press, Oxford.

Gordon, David A. et al. (1998) *Controversies in Media Ethics*. Longman, New York.

Halberstam, Joshua (1992) 'A Prolegomenon for a Theory of News', in Elliott D. Cohen (ed.), *Philosophical Issues in Journalism*. Oxford University Press, Oxford.

Hare, R.M. (1995) *The Language of Morals*. Clarendon Press, Oxford.

Hargrave, Andrea Millwood (1991) *Taste and Decency in Broadcasting*. BSC, London.

Harris, Nigel G.E. (1992) 'Codes of Conduct for Journalists', in *Ethical Issues in Journalism and the Media*. Routledge, London.

Hartley, John (1982) *Understanding News*. Routledge, London.

Hausmann, Carl (1987) *The Decision-making Process in Journalism*. Nelson-Hall, Chicago.

Inness, Julie C. (1991) *Privacy, Intimacy and Isolation*. Oxford University Press, Oxford.

ITC (1992) *Annual Report and Accounts*. ITC, London.

ITC (1993) *Annual Report and Accounts*. ITC, London.

ITC (1994) *Annual Report and Accounts*. ITC, London.

ITC (1995) *Annual Report and Accounts*. ITC, London.

ITC (1996) *Annual Report and Accounts*. ITC, London.

ITC (1997) *Annual Report and Accounts*. ITC, London.

ITC (1998) *Annual Report and Accounts*. ITC, London.

Kant, Immanuel (1948) *Groundwork of the Metaphysics of Morals* (translated by H.J. Paton). Routledge, London.

Kant, Immanuel (1990) *Foundations of the Metaphysics of Morals* (translated by Lewis White Beck). Prentice-Hall, Englewood Cliffs, NJ.

Kant, Immanuel (1993) *Grounding for the Metaphysics of Morals* (3rd edn) (translated by James W. Ellington). Hackett Publishing Company Inc., Indianapolis, Indiana.

Kierans, M. (1998) *Media Ethics*. Routledge, London.

Klaidman, Stephen and Beauchamp, Tom L. (1987) *The Virtuous Journalist*. Oxford University Press, Oxford.

Koch, T. (1990) *News as Myth*. Greenwood Press, New York.

Lambeth, E. (1992) *Committed Journalism*. Indiana University Press, Bloomington, IN.

Leapman, Michael (1986) *The Last Days of the Beeb*. Allen and Unwin, London.

Lewis and Short (1900) *Latin Dictionary*. Clarendon Press, Oxford.

Lord Chancellor's Department (1996) *Payment to Witnesses*. HMSO, London.

Lord Chancellor's Department (1993) *Consultation Paper on the Infringement of Privacy*. HMSO, London.

Matelsk, Marilyn J. (1991) *TV News Ethics*. Focal Press, London.

McKay, J. (1999) *Manuals For Courtesans*. The Association for Journalism Educators Conference, London.

Meyer, Philip (1987) *Ethical Journalism*. University Press of America, Lanham, MD.

Mill, John Stuart (1991) 'What Utilitarianism is', in *On Liberty and Other Essays*. Oxford University Press, Oxford.

Mill, John Stuart (1998) *Utilitarianism* (edited by Roger Crisp). Oxford University Press, Oxford.

National Heritage Committee (1993) *Report on Privacy and Media Intrusion*. HMSO, London.

Nietzsche, F. (1973) *Beyond Good and Evil* (translated by R.J. Hollingdale). Penguin Books, Harmondsworth.

Nordlund, Stig (1991) An address to the Stockholm Symposium on Press Councils and Press Ethics, June 1991.

Norman, R. (1983) *The Moral Philosophers: An Introduction to Ethics*. Clarendon Press, Oxford.

NUJ (1998) *Rule Book*. NUJ, London.

Ordine dei Giornaliste (1993) Regulation Governing the Profession of Journalism (Law No. 69 of 3 February 1963).

PCC (1991) *Annual Report*. Press Complaints Commission, London.

PCC (1992) *Annual Report*. Press Complaints Commission, London.

PCC (1993) *Annual Report*. Press Complaints Commission, London.

PCC (1994) *Annual Report*. Press Complaints Commission, London.

PCC (1995) *Annual Report*. Press Complaints Commission, London.

PCC (1996) *Annual Report*. Press Complaints Commission, London.

PCC (1997) *Annual Report*. Press Complaints Commission, London.

PCC (1998) *Annual Report*. Press Complaints Commission, London.

PCC (published regularly since 1991) *Report Nos 1–39*. Press Complaints Commission, London.

Philo, G. (ed.) (1996) *Media and Mental Distress*. Glasgow Media Group, Glasgow.

Potter, Jeremy (1989) *Independent Television in Britain. Vol. 3 Politics and Control*. Macmillan, London.

Press Council (1953–90) *The Press and the People. Annual Report of the Press Council*. Press Council, London.

Press Council (1991) *Press at the Prison Gates. Press Council Booklet No. 8*. Press Council, London.

Prichard, H.A. (1949) *Moral Obligation*. Oxford University Press, Oxford.

Prichard, H.A. (1968) *Moral Obligation and 'Duty and Interest'*. Oxford University Press, Oxford.

Radio Authority (1991–98) *Annual Report and Financial Statement*. Radio Authority, London.

Randall, David (1996) *The Universal Journalist*. Pluto Press, London.

Robertson, Geoffrey (1983) *People against the Press*. Quartet, London.

Rosnow, Ralph L. and Fine, Gary (1976) *Rumor and Gossip: The Social Psychology of Hearsay*. Elsevier, London.

Ross W.D. (1930) *The Right and the Good*. Oxford University Press, Oxford.

Royal Commission on the Press (1949) HMSO, London.

Royal Commission on the Press (1962) HMSO, London.

Royal Commission on the Press (1977) HMSO, London.

Schlesinger, Philip (1978) *Putting Reality Together: BBC News*. Constable, London.

Shakespeare, W. (1993) *Othello*. Addison Wesley Longman, Harlow.

Shibutani, Tamotsu (1966) *Improvised News*. Bobbs-Merrill, Indianapolis.

Singer, P. (1994) *Ethics*. Oxford University Press, Oxford.

Snoddy, Raymond (1993) *The Good, the Bad and the Unacceptable*. Faber and Faber, London.

Stephenson, H. and Bromley, M. (1998) *Sex, Lies and Videotape*. Addison Wesley Longman, London.

Taylor, John (1999) *Body Horror*. Manchester University Press, Manchester.

Times/Mirror Center for the People and the Press (1994) *Eight Nations, People and The Press Survey*. Washington DC (published 16 March 1994).

Venables, John (1993) *What Is News?* ELM Publications, Huntingdon.

Wacks, Raymond (1995) *Privacy and Press Freedom*. Blackstone Press, London.

Warburton, N. (1998) *Philosophy: The Classics*. Routledge, London.

Ward, Gary (1997) *Mental Health and the National Press*. Health Education Authority, London.

Wellings, Kaye and Field, Becky (1996) *Stopping Aids: Aids/HIV Public Education and the Mass Media in Europe*. Longman, Harlow.

Welsh, T. and Greenwood, W. (1995) *Essential Law for Journalists*. Butterworths, London.

Whitaker, Brian (1981) *News Limited: Why You Can't Read All About It*. Minority Press Group, London.

Wilson, John (1996) *Understanding Journalism*. Routledge. London.

X, George (1997) 'Leave My Child Alone', in Mike Jempson (ed.) *Child Exploitation and the Media*. Smallwood Publishing, London.

## Internet sites of interest

UK Parliament: http://www.parliament.uk

European codes of conduct can be found at: http://www.uta.fi/ethicnet/

The Department of National Heritage: http://www.heritage.gov.uk

The BBC: http://www.bbc.co.uk

*BBC Producers' Guidelines*: http://www.bbc.co.uk/info/editorial/prodgl/index.htm

Open Media Research Institute: http://www.omri.cz/index.html

Journalism UK: http://www.octopod.demon.co.uk/journ_UK.htm
Journalism news: http://bcn.boulder.co.us/campuspress/sjmc/journnews.html
European journalism: http://www.demon.co.uk/eurojournalism/
Broadcasting Standards Commission: http://www.bsc.org.uk
Press Complaints Commission: http://www.pcc.org.uk
National Union of Journalists: http://www.nuj.org.uk
Reporters San Frontieres: http://www.calvancom.fr/rsf/

# Index